JONATHAN CLEMENTS is the author of many books about China, including a history of Beijing and biographies of Chairman Mao, Marco Polo, Khubilai Khan and the diplomat Wellington Koo. The Chinese translation of his life of the First Emperor was published in the People's Republic in 2007. He was a consultant and interviewee on the National Geographic documentary *Koxinga: A Hero's Legacy*, which drew heavily on his book *Pirate King*. His biography of a famous Silk Road traveller, *Mannerheim: President, Soldier, Spy* was released in 2009. He wrote the 'Asia & the World' chapters for the Oxford University Press *Big Ideas* history series, which won an Australian Publishing Association award for Excellence in Educational Publishing. His recent works include *The Art of War: A New Translation* (2012), which revisits Sun Tzu's military classic for the twenty-first century, and *All That Matters: Modern China* (2013), an introduction to contemporary issues in the People's Republic.

The Silk Road: A Biography

FROM PREHISTORY TO THE PRESENT DAY

Jonathan Clements

SPEAKING
TIGER

SPEAKING TIGER PUBLISHING PVT. LTD
4381/4 Ansari Road, Daryaganj,
New Delhi–110002, India

First published in Great Britain as *An Armchair Traveller's History of The Silk Road* by the Armchair Traveller at the bookHaus, 2013
First published in India as *The Silk Road: A Biography* in paperback by Speaking Tiger, 2016

ISBN: 978-93-85755-04-0

10 9 8 7 6 5 4 3 2 1

Printed at Thomson Press India Ltd.

For Ilse Schwepcke
who wanted to come with me

Acknowledgements

MY THANKS TO THOSE CHINESE who have been so welcoming to me in my travels, particularly professors Li Qi and Wang Ye of Xi'an Jiaotong University, their families, and their many friendly graduate students, especially Li Pei, Zhang Yu and *their* families, my sometime driver Andrew Li Jiang and whatever anonymous replacements he periodically rustled up to drive us to the middle of nowhere. My wife Kati and son Alexander have been enthusiastic travelling companions and occasional guinea pigs, uncomplaining about experiments in dining or trips to distant, dusty temples. In Finland, the Mäki-Kuutti family, particularly Matias, Raija and Seija, and Ritva Parkkonen kindly helped out with housework and childminding, in order to help me find the time to finish this book.

Back in Britain, the staff of Haus Publishing has been flexible and accommodating. Ilse and Barbara Schwepcke commissioned this book, Harry Hall looked the other way when I wanted two more months to write, and Ellie Shillito kept things on track from manuscript delivery to the finished article. Andrew Deacon commented on an early draft of the manuscript and hunted for errors, although any that remain are sure to be mine.

Acknowledgements

Contents

PART TWO: BEING THERE

Part One

THE VIEW FROM THE ARMCHAIR

I

The Invention of the Silk Road

THE 'SILK ROAD' is a modern idea, dating only from 1877 when Ferdinand von Richthofen, uncle of the more famous Red Baron, published a multi-part atlas of China. His first volume included a map of '*Die Seidenstrasse*', Richthofen's term for the route that, he assumed, Chinese silk had taken towards the Greco-Roman world in antiquity. Key points included the trading centres of Samarkand and Xi'an (formerly known as Chang'an), from which branches would shoot off in multiple directions. Between those two towns the route was simpler, and limited to only a couple of branches that traversed the west Chinese region known today as Xinjiang.

Richthofen's term had a romance to it, a sense of mystery and wonder that proved infectious. The term 'Silk Road' is now in widespread use, even in the regions through which the trade passed. In Chinese, it is translated as *Sichou zhi Lu*, an oddly classical construction that makes it sound like some ancient term, and not something knocked up by a German geographer only 150 years ago. In Uyghur, a Turkic language spoken by many natives of the region, it's *Yipek Yoli*, connoting, as in other languages, a solid, physical *road* to the exotic west.

Just to confuse matters, there *is* a concrete, identifiable Silk Road today. It is the name of a motorway that curves along the northern reaches of the Taklamakan Desert, with signage helpfully written in English so that tourists can feel that they are getting somewhere. But none of the travellers on the historical Silk Road ever used that term. Only a handful of men and women ever travelled its entire length. For most of the participants in the trade route, the 'road', if there was even a real road, was only to the next town or oasis. Artefacts and articles might meander along the route from China to the Mediterranean, but only in stops and starts, traded back and forth, buffeted by changing conditions and markets, until they suddenly tumbled out at the far end to the bafflement of their final buyers.

In fact, there was never a single line, even in Richthofen's original atlas – he spoke of a single Silk Road, but also referred to the route in the plural as Silk *Roads.* Many writers prefer the term 'Silk Routes' in order to point out that there is no single identifiable road, but a number of well-travelled paths and tracks, worn by camel caravans over the years. Towns, of course, were places where caravans of camel-drovers could grab new supplies, rest a little and graze their animals. But the pathways between them fluctuated on the basis of weather, war and local politics – even the towns of the Silk Road could fall in and out of favour, left high and dry by the ebb and flow of trade and by drastic changes in water tables or river courses.

Richthofen's classical education had exposed him to the writings of the Roman author Pliny the Elder, who complained about all the coins being sent east to pay for silk, and it seems that this was what led Richthofen to draw his line joining China to the Mediterranean. Nor was the traffic all in a single direction. Much of the silk that headed west from China was intended for the Ferghana Valley in what is now Uzbekistan, where it was traded for the region's highly prized horses. No coins of the Roman republic or early empire have ever been found in China. Those few Byzantine coins that made it all the way along the Silk Road were of little use at its terminus, except as odd souvenirs. Far more Roman coins, in fact, made their way to India, and in such quantities that they were sometimes repurposed as local currency. In fact, much of the material that Richthofen assumed to have reached Rome down his Silk Road may have instead trickled south from Xinjiang, through what is now India and Pakistan, and then by sea to Roman Egypt.

The same trade routes carried glass and gemstones, musical instruments and slaves, medicinal herbs and strange spices. As early as AD 331, princes of Ferghana were sending gifts of cotton east to the rulers of north China. In the distant past, the same routes had carried the ancestor of the modern apple westward from central Asia, and the bulbs of a flower that the Persians called *dulband* ('turban'), and which entered medieval Latin as *tulipa*. However, silk seems to have been the commodity most likely to travel the entire length from east to west. This was partly because of its value at the western end, but also because of its portability and durability. Silk, in both woven and raw form, was a major form of currency for certain early Chinese dynasties, far more convenient than mere coins. It was transported, usually on camels, west from China to the forbidding deserts and steppes as bribes, gifts or soldiers' salaries, depending on the political situation among the border tribes. Those groups, in turn, would pass the silk on, with much of it continuing further west as payment for livestock or luxuries. Valerie Hansen, in *The Silk Road: A New History*, comments that trade in the region was more often than not 'a byproduct of Chinese spending', as great quantities of silk arrived in lieu of cash money, obliging the locals to get rid of it somehow by bartering it elsewhere.

Meanwhile, other commodities travelled *east* on the same routes, back towards China. Jade, from Khotan at the southern edge of the Taklamakan Desert, has been found in Manchuria, in sites dated as early as 3000 BC. Coral, from the Red Sea and Eastern Mediterranean, was highly prized in Buddhist cultures for its use in statuary and decoration.

But few other European commodities were hardy enough to be reliably traded over the entire length of the routes. Drop a bolt of silk and it is not necessarily damaged, whereas intricate Roman glassware or similarly fragile items were less likely to survive the journey. As a result, European items were most often traded midway, in exchange for something more durable.

Beginnings and endings

Where does the Silk Road begin? There is a reasonable case to be made for Xi'an, which was called Chang'an and was the capital of China for much of the time that trade flowed across the desert. From Xi'an, all goods could head down the Wei River into the mighty Yellow River and all the canals and tributaries that spidered away from it. However, for a substantial proportion of the Silk Road's medieval peak in the Tang Dynasty, the Chinese capital was moved several hundred kilometres east, to Luoyang. The two cities have had a sly rivalry ever since, today fought in tourist brochures that proclaim each place's prominence on the Silk Road. Furthermore, not content with having the Terracotta Army on its outskirts, the city of Xi'an has carved its claim literally in stone with the sculpture *The Start of the Silk Road*, a massive edifice in the middle of a city junction, depicting a camel train heading west. Notably, the statue is called the *Start* – it is rare that the Chinese public recognise that any artefacts travelled east towards China.

Where does the Silk Road end? Does it end in Colchester, the old Roman town of Camulodunum, where a tiny fragment of silk, no bigger than a postage stamp, has been unearthed and is displayed in the local museum? Or Marseilles, the old Roman town of Massilia, where ships from the eastern Mediterranean would unload their wares for the wealthy of Gaul? I would argue that its real end is in Samarkand in what was then Sogdiana and is now Uzbekistan, the city from which eastern goods would scatter north, south and west to reach their final destinations.

Silk itself is a commodity that can exist in a number of different states, from gunge exuded out of a worm's mouth, to cocoons, to raw silk, to thread, and beyond into many forms of material, each of which might have its own specialist area. Chengdu, capital of Sichuan province, is not normally regarded as integral to the Silk Road, but those are fighting words in Chengdu itself, which prides itself as being the home of brocades. If we treat the Silk Road as everywhere that silk ends up, we are forced to write a history of the entire world – books on the Silk Road in Japanese, for example, often continue the line eastward from Xi'an, all the way to Japan's medieval capital of Kyoto. Paul Wilson's *The Silk Roads: A Route and Planning Guide* (3rd edition, 2010), attempts the broadest possible compass, including diverse sites as far afield as Turkey and Pakistan. But for the purposes of this book the Silk Road spans a much smaller area, from Xi'an or Luoyang, through the sand-blasted Gansu Corridor that plots a trail around the edge of the mountains of Tibet, and across the fabled deserts of Xinjiang to the nexus of Kashgar, from which it leads through mountain passes, out of the Chinese world and into Central Asia.

None of the people involved in trade on the Silk Road regarded themselves as part of a long route stretching between China and Europe. Nomads of the steppes only knew that the Chinese would bribe them to stay away by sending them gifts – of trinkets, women or cloth.

People in Khotan, who sifted jade pebbles from the nearby riverbeds, only knew that mounted traders would buy their stones to take east. The horse-breeders of Ferghana only knew that their steeds were highly prized in distant China, and that the Chinese would pay for them with silk. If the people of Ferghana had too much silk, they could always offload it on the Bactrians, who would flog it on to Parthians or Romans, and so on.

Geography and topography

The region now known as Xinjiang takes up a sixth of the territory of the People's Republic of China, an area larger than the UK, France and Germany combined. A folksong of Xinjiang asks '*Why are the winters so cold? / Why are the summers so hot?*' The answer is 'continentality', a geographical condition where the absence of large bodies of water causes inland regions to heat and cool to greater extremes. Xinjiang is enclosed by a wall of mountains on the north, west and south, with only a few hazardous mountain passes linking it to the world beyond. Its eastern side is also mountainous, but with substantially larger gaps affording access to north China and Mongolia. This 'rain shadow' on all sides means that clouds dump their precipitation on the mountains, leaving no water for the area in the middle. Ask the modern Chinese about Xinjiang, and they are liable to evoke desert sunsets and camel-trains on the sands. Some will speak of grasslands and steppes, since parts of northern Xinjiang do indeed border on the Mongolian plains, and share several ethnic groups and traditions with the nomads of the steppes. The less geographically-minded or unforgivably thick are apt to confuse *Xinjiang* (the 'New Frontier') with *Xizang* (Tibet), and end up spinning a bunch of complete fictions about yaks and yetis. On several occasions, pushy Chinese shopkeepers have tried to sell me Tibetan music when their Xinjiang stock proves lacking, as it is 'almost the same thing.'

'*Our Xinjiang is a good place*,' begins the most famous regional propaganda song of the 20th century, '*with good pastures south and north of the Tianshan*.' Despite the high temperatures and the legendary desert, it can be shocking to the visitor to discover just how green parts of it can be. Tourist advertisements, aimed at the internal Chinese market, present great vistas of pine forests and meadows, snowy peaks and clear mountain streams like something out of *The Sound of Music*. The images seem, quite deliberately, to evoke distant Europe, and then hit the onlooker with the twist in the small print... this is Xinjiang! Come and see!

Despite the lush imagery, those parts of Xinjiang can only be found in a relatively narrow strip around the edges of its better-known desert. At the end of his two-year spying mission in Central Asia, the cavalry officer Gustaf Mannerheim filed a secret report to the Russian Tsar in 1908, outlining Xinjiang's value in a putative war with China. It was all but worthless, he thought. But even 'barren' ground has modern values that he did not really consider – oil, gas and precious metals delivering larger returns on China's investment in the region. Xinjiang remains a remote region of China, but its value to modern China as a whole is indisputable. In the distant past, however, many evaluated Xinjiang in terms that foreshadowed Mannerheim's; as an unpleasant interlude to be endured on the way to somewhere else.

The desert was a natural deterrent to travellers. Early in the Tang Dynasty, one of Empress Wu's advisers suggested that she draw the borders of China at the *eastern* edge of the desert in Dunhuang, all the better to sap the strength of any enemies who had to cross the Taklamakan wastes to raid China. But Wu, and other rulers of the Tang Dynasty, remained interested in what lay beyond the sands, and in trade and possible alliances with rulers in what are now Uzbekistan and Afghanistan. However, while the Taklamakan region was incorporated within Chinese territory, it remained a peripheral area.

The very inhospitability of the Silk Road has often made it a dumping ground for refugees, prisoners and exiles. Entire tribes, fleeing the steppe conquests of the Kyrgyz or the incursions of Arab invaders, have been uprooted and settled among the oases. Entire armies of rebels have been given a last chance out on the frontier, shoved into no-man's-land on parcels of meagre, parched earth, and told that it is theirs as long as they can hold it against the elements and the enemy. This wildly mixed heritage has given the survivors on the Silk

Road an incredible, vibrant vitality, unparalleled elsewhere in China.

And the Chinese *like* it that way. Go to the evening dance show at the Tang Paradise theme park in Xi'an, and the musical numbers start with mundane ballets and callisthenics – soldiers banging drums and concubines emerging from symbolic baths, celebrating the famous events of the Tang Dynasty. But the show only comes alive when it hits the dances of *Xi Cheng*, coyly untranslated in the theatre supertitles, but referring to the 'Western Regions', which is to say the deserts and mountains that we call the Silk Road. These 'Western Regions' retain a fascination for the Chinese majority, an exotic frisson of belly dancers and slave girls, romantic desert settings and rapacious bandits, lost cities and buried treasure. In other words, it retains many of the stereotypes and narrative traditions associated in Europe with the 'orient', that admixture of the Turkic and Chinese worlds that give us those staple stories of our own culture, *Aladdin* and *Turandot*.

For those who really experienced it, the Silk Road often proved anything but romantic. Aurel Stein, the great explorer, wrote of moving from 'one wretched roadside station to another, each established with its refuse-filled mud hovels and a tiny post of soldiers at a point where some shallow depression offers a scanty supply of water in a spring or a well.... the utterly barren wastes of gravel, crumbling rock or drift sand which extend between these miserable halting places could certainly have changed but little since ancient times.' A thousand years after the time of the Silk Road, Stein's travel along the route in 1907 served as a reminder to him of the harsh logistics of the region.

For medieval travellers who required animal fodder, the desert offered little opportunity to replenish stores. Caravans would need to carry much of their supplies with them. Horses and oxen, the default means of transport in China, could be more trouble than they were worth, causing the locals to rely heavily on camels. The sparse nature of habitation made it absolutely imperative that travellers would be able to lurch from oasis to oasis. One wrong turn on the sands and travellers would find themselves on a one-way trip, like one of the region's dead rivers, wandering ever further into the sands until supplies ran out and death took hold.

Even today, it is difficult to draw a map of the region. The mountains stay in the same place, of course, but the areas between them are literally formed from shifting sands, which can in turn block and reroute rivers. Sometimes the rivers just die in the middle of the desert. Sometimes they flow into a depression in the ground and form new lakes, for a season, or for a generation, before vanishing, only to reappear a few miles away. It is for this reason that the Swedish explorer Sven Hedin called his book on the search for the fabled Lop Nur *The Wandering Lake*. In an environment low on lumber, traditional buildings are often built from mud bricks. This makes them swift to erect but also swift to erode. One of the greatest dangers to the old town of Kashgar is the simple likelihood that a single earthquake might turn it back into dust.

Territory is similarly hard to define. Even those who professed to be 'kings' of parts of the region were only the rulers of dots on the map – fortress towns in the more hospitable foothills of the mountains, or clinging to oases on the periphery. But these dots can still be substantial, for example Turfan is 1,000 square miles of lush greenery, surrounded by desert and sustained by man-made underground channels, bearing water from the upper slopes of the Flaming Mountains.

In northern Xinjiang, where the Tianshan ('Heaven Mountains') cut across the middle, rivers of snowmelt cascade into remarkably green and unexpectedly lush valleys, with ample space for grazing livestock, and areas suitable for growing crops. In southern Xinjiang, similar rivers tumble down from the mountains, only to land in a vast desert – the oddest of sights on a map, familiar riverine blue lines that simply end in the middle of nowhere, evaporating in the desert sands.

'There is not a bird to be seen in the air above,' wrote the Buddhist pilgrim Faxian, 'nor an animal on the ground below. Though you look around most earnestly to find where you can cross, you know not where to make your choice, the only mark and indication being the dry bones of the dead.'

Not for nothing is Xinjiang often called the 'Crossroads of Asia'. For much of its history, it has been situated between four powerful cultures. To its east, there is China, the ancient culture of the Yellow River basin that expanded to incorporate it, and has made use of its jades since prehistoric times. To the south, the Buddhist realms of India and Tibet, which often extended religious (and hence, considering Tibet's theocracy, political) influence over the faithful in the desert oases. To the west, through the mountain passes of the Pamirs, Central Asia, which adopted a distinct and powerful new identity in the Middle Ages to form an Islamic influence that superseded the Buddhists. To the north, the nomad empires of the steppes, that long, wide strand of grassland that stretches from the outskirts of Beijing all the way to Hungary. For millennia, the migrating tribes of Mongolia have dawdled, usually in a generally westward direction, and often through the part of Xinjiang north of the Tianshan Mountains, where the millions of square miles of grassland have their narrowest bottleneck. Some inevitably turned southward instead, creating periods of Xinjiang's history when it has paid tribute or protection money to nomads.

Xinjiang was buffeted by its neighbours for centuries, until the early 1700s, when a single group achieved prominence. Those who say it was the Chinese are only half right. It was the Manchus – a nomad group that first conquered China in 1644 as the Qing Dynasty, and then launched a series of campaigns westwards in China's name. By expanding outward to incorporate those regions that had once created trouble on the borders, they ended many of their historical border problems. Tibet and Mongolia were both incorporated within the Manchus' empire, and this new multi-ethnic polity also established control over Xinjiang. When the Last Emperor gave way to the Republic of China in 1912, the old Qing borders largely stayed in place, but for the loss of Outer Mongolia. The Republic was proud of its ethnic diversity, with the stripes of five united races on its rainbow flag.

One such stripe represented China's Muslims, although they remained a group with inconveniently international connections. Occasionally, the Islamic world would offer succour and support to disaffected groups within Xinjiang. Inevitably, these disputes have been accorded some sort of religious significance, but all too often religion is the excuse, not the cause. When there is a rival state over the mountains prepared to offer support to exiles, outlaws and outcasts, there will always be trouble. By the 19th century, it was Britain and Russia who were meddling in a similar fashion, attempting to involve Xinjiang in their infamous Great Game of geopolitical rivalry.

All these influences have created in Xinjiang a hybridity of cultures and races that is without precedent. When so many Chinese cities look like all the others, Xinjiang can offer a welcome break from the monotony of Louis Vuitton concessions and concreted parks. As early as Xi'an on the journey from east to west, the sights and smells of a town's Muslim quarter can owe more to India and Arabia than China (see Chapter 9: Eating and Drinking). The marketplace no longer sells pork, but favours mutton. Rice fades from view in favour of wheat-based noodles, and nan bread (*nang*, in Chinese). In Khotan, the women wear head-scarves; by Kashgar, many are wearing veils. Words change, too, reflecting the relatively recent local adoption of Mandarin Chinese in daily life, which was only taken up within the last couple of hundred years. By the time you reach Turfan, the locals no longer use the term *shichang* for marketplace – instead they say *baza'er* ('bazaar'), reflecting the slow accretion of Middle Eastern language. By Urumqi, it is simply *baza*, a feature of which the locals are so proud that they have even written a song about it. It's not a very good song, though. The chorus translates as: '*Big bazaar, big bazaar, international grand bazaar / Big bazaar, big bazaar, Urumqi international big bazaar.*' It's at times like this that you realise why they need composers like Wang Luobin (see Chapter 7: Autonomy and Hegemony).

Historians of the Silk Road often divide its past into three main periods: the era of early contacts until AD 500, the peak of trade and culture from AD 500 to 800, and the decline from AD 800 to 1006 – the date when the Song Dynasty lost control of northern China to nomad enemies, the *Khitai* who lent their name to the word 'Cathay'. Thereafter, the route through Central Asia was largely shut off by the Mongol and Muslim upheavals, and also by a decline in the foreign demand for silk itself, much of which could now be sourced more locally. By the time trading contacts were re-established in the 1500s, they were largely maritime. Moreover, silk had become a less important commodity than tea, which was far bulkier, and more easily packed into ships by the hold-full. A wary handshake in the 1600s between Russian explorers and Chinese border guards was the first stirring of another trade route to the north, which would become fixed in the late 1800s with the inauguration of the mighty Trans-Siberian railway. But by then, it was not about silk.

We might consider that in drawing a line that linked east and west, Richthofen was displaying a certain bilateral bias. To him, there was the interesting east, and the interesting west, and between them a desolate, miserable region best glossed over. The life of the people and the story of the places along the Silk Road did not stop simply because the western world stopped buying silk. While tourists and travellers might be lured to Central Asia by the romance of the Silk Road, they are surely also interested in what has happened in the 1,000 years since.

Marco Polo, one of the most famous chroniclers of the

Silk Road, and indeed one of the few people who claimed to have travelled its entire length, did so in the late 13th century, in the dying days of its influence. Although communications flourished briefly in the reign of Khubilai Khan, squabbles among the Mongols and subsequent redrawing of boundaries by their Islamic successor states essentially shut off the old routes.

If you travel along the old Silk Road today, you will not only see 'ruins of desert Cathay'. There are geological and geographical features, and the sites of rebellions and revolutions and short-lived republics. The story of the Silk Road by the 19th century turns in upon itself, and becomes the story of the *rediscovery* of the Silk Road as explorers like Hedin and Stein, Pelliot and Mannerheim set off to investigate one of the few regions of the world as yet unmapped. Their adventures in the Taklamakan and Gobi Deserts are just as much a part of the story of the Silk Road, and form the closing chapters of this book, along with details of the Silk Road in modern times.

Names and naming

Historical accounts have an inevitable bias towards civilisations that leave a footprint. The Silk Road, therefore, is a slippery historical object. Entire civilisations have risen and fallen on the Silk Road leaving perilously little evidence of themselves. We often have only the accounts of outsiders to describe the local cultures that flourished and died in the distant past. Furthermore, many places in Xinjiang have at least two names – a Turkic one and a Chinese one, reflecting the territorial to-and-fro between Middle and Far East. These, in turn, overwrite earlier names used by the Indian cultures that dominated the region until the Dark Ages. When Xinjiang was fully incorporated within China proper in the 18th century, the Chinese replaced the existing names with ones drawn from centuries-old manuscripts, as if Italy were to reconquer Britain and decide the provincial capital was now to be called Londinium once more. As a result, simply naming somewhere in a text is often a political decision, assigning a form of textual authority to one of several masters. In the case of Loulan, the fabled city of the drifting sands, the name by which it is most commonly known was assigned to it by the Chinese. The locals called it Kroran. After the Chinese conquered it, it was renamed Shan-Shan – a name applied to both the town and the region over which it ruled.

Meanwhile, further to the west, differing accents muddle the names of towns, so that Hotan to the Turks is Khotan to the Russians and Hetian to the Chinese, although 19th-century explorers called it Ilchi. There are places on the map of the Silk Road that have had ten different names across the years, reflecting multiple rulers and influences. There are archaeologists' guesses at what a place *may* have been called by its first inhabitants. There are references in ancient chronicles that appear to be garbled foreign words. There are the names bestowed by Chinese travellers on a community of forgotten Tocharians. There is the name bestowed by Indian settlers, and its mispronunciation by the locals. There is the new name brought by Turkic conquerors, changed once more by their Chinese neighbours, then again by several jostling tribes, then again in recognition of some Islamic holy site. Then, I open a Chinese guidebook and find that the place isn't in the index at all, because it has been filed not as a town in its own right, but as a subsection of a modern county division, which itself has three different names.

This is not merely a problem for map-makers. It is a problem for writers and readers. I look up at the modern map of Xinjiang on my wall, and see that the city of Ruoqiang has four different names, in three different scripts and two languages, and that is before we try to remember what the Chinese called the old-town ruins to the north, or how Marco Polo recorded them, or what Turkic settlers decided to rename them. In this book, for the general reader, I have risked censure by often picking a single name for a particular place; inevitably this will be an anachronism to someone. This includes my use of the term Xinjiang itself, which was not applied to the region until the 19th century. When it comes to the scattered oases of the Tarim River basin, known in ancient times to the Chinese as 'The Western Regions', in the Dark Ages to the Tibetans as 'The Upper Region', and to late-medieval Islamic authors as 'The Six Cities' of the desert, I have found it much more productive, for the sake of everyone's sanity, if I pick a single name and stick to it.

This also applies in the case of individuals. Histories, signs and tour guides in modern Kashgar all speak of Afaq Khoja (d.1694), one of the region's most famous rulers, occupant of its most majestic tomb, and famous proclaimer of Sharia law, which came to overshadow Mongol culture with a new, Islamic basis for daily life (see Gazetteer: Kashgar). This is how he is most likely to be mentioned in most English-language sources, although it is not actually his name. A *khoja* is a master, often used as a term of respect for Sufi mystics, and common among the religious rulers of Xinjiang in the early modern period. Using the term *khoja* as if it were a family surname is helpful in showing the many connections between such figures, and often a victimless crime, since *khoja*-hood was usually hereditary. Afaq Khoja, however, is actually a title: 'Master of the Horizon.' The man himself was called Hidayet Allah, which itself exists in several rival romanisations. Chinese sources, however, merely repeat his title as if it is his name, until it comes out as Apake Huojia. I choose to call him Afaq Khoja, even though this is a gross simplification.

Barbarians, minorities and the historical record

If there are ruins and documents, ancient inscriptions and dynastic annals, we have an archive that we can study and analyse. But a substantial part of the history of Central Asia belongs to nomads, whose reliance on the sparse but renewable resource of grass as fodder for their herds caused them to move in seasonal rotations. Nomad tribes were less likely to have permanent town bases than general orbits of residence.

The foreign reader is apt to imagine battered tents on windswept steppes, but reportage of many nomads offers descriptions of something substantially more lavish. Entire nations were on the move on the plains. There are reports of mobile *palaces*, from the opulent Golden Orda (the 'throne-room' of Empress Toregene recalled by Friar John of Carpini), to the legendary 'pleasure dome' of Khubilai Khan, but by their very nature such artefacts are harder to pin down or point to, except in occasional grave goods.

There are gaps in the historical record. Bronze coins can be found in large quantities, but there is no silver – mainly because any silver artefacts were sure to be melted down and recycled by grave robbers. Religious documents are most likely to survive, in part because it was taboo to destroy them, but also because old or damaged scriptures were likely to be locked away or buried in a *geniza*, a graveyard of holy books. Some Chinese dynasties kept meticulous records, but also often refused to retain paperwork after a three-year cut-off, in order to avoid drowning in bureaucracy. Hence, many surviving documents come to us not in their original form, but as scrap paper, often recycled into grave goods, paper clothes and paper furniture buried as spirit-possessions for the dead. Piece by tantalising piece, these fragile, fragmentary items can be reassembled, turning lanterns and paper horses back into their original states as dockets, licences and accounting entries of forgotten clerks.

As a place of exile and limited resources, the Silk Road's history also suffers from an epidemic of forgetting. There are several asides in history books that gloss over the massacre of entire communities: the Tanguts who wiped out the Uyghurs of Gansu in the 11th century, and the Mongols and Tamerlane, the 'Sword of Islam', who killed millions more.

This is not merely a case of the collateral damage of many wars, which might be said to be common all over the world; these were cases of sanctioned genocide.

In the 14th century, Uyghurs and Mongols fell upon the Tangut kingdom of the Xixia and killed a million people, leaving the land deserted. To this day, it is called the province of Ningxia, 'the Tanguts Quelled'. In the 18th century, an army of Manchus and Chinese, with the support of local rebels, declared the end of the Zunghar Mongols, killing hundreds of thousands of men, women and children north of the Tianshan Mountains. Smallpox did for most of the survivors, wiping any sense of Zunghar identity off the map. The Kazakhs and Uyghurs who live in the region today are late arrivals; their understanding of the traditions and stories of their adopted homeland is liable to be nothing but hearsay.

In recent memory we have the destruction of the Buddhist statues in Bamiyan by the Taliban in Afghanistan, determined to wipe out idolatry in the name of God. The vandalism of these ancient Buddhist monuments is only the latest and most memorable incident in the slow attrition of all Buddhist culture from the Silk Road – many of today's Han 'colonists' in Xinjiang are bringing a religion with them that was already there before Islam took hold. Although signage and guides may rail against tomb raiders like Aurel Stein and Paul Pelliot, they often avoid mentioning the damage done to Xinjiang's heritage by the people of Xinjiang themselves. Among many Muslim residents in the 19th century, it was considered devout and noble to destroy any 'idolatrous' texts, statues and carvings, thanks in part to a local old wives' tale that held any Muslim cursed who was 'gazed upon' by a pagan image. Only scratching out the image's eyes would lift the curse, sentencing untold thousands of statues and wall paintings to destruction. For centuries, Buddhist icons in Xinjiang have been similarly defaced and destroyed by local Muslims. Not for nothing did the European archaeologists of the 19th century prefer to carry off their treasures; in part it was to preserve them from destruction at the hands of the locals. In an age where the value of such heritage in situ is finally recognised by the Chinese themselves, it is the Europeans who are now accused of vandalism. But it is not all about religion; sometimes it's just about money, and then everybody seems to share the blame.

For many decades, at least since the foundation of the Republic of China in 1912, Chinese politicians have recognised that while the Han ethnic group outnumbers all the other ethnicities in China, 'Chinese-ness' is the product of the interactions of many dozens of groups throughout history. The old Republican Chinese flag had five stripes, one each for the Han Chinese, the Mongols, the Muslims, the Manchus and the Tibetans, but several dozen minor groups are also officially recognised, some of them still with populations in the millions. With the founding of the *People's* Republic in 1949, Mao and his successors reiterated this attitude, pointing out that many supposedly peripheral or minority groups were the remnants of old aristocracies and ruling classes, whose influences had often been integrated in the distant past into what is now regarded as 'Han' culture. The legendary 'Chinese' emperors of the Shang Dynasty are argued by some to have come from a tribe cognate with the Qiang, now an obscure ethnic minority on the Tibetan periphery. The First Emperor himself was from Qin, regarded as an upstart border kingdom before it conquered the others. The Tang Dynasty, arguably the peak of Chinese imperial civilisation, was founded by a family of outlanders who married into the Chinese aristocracy. The Chinese habit of conferring Chinese names on foreign visitors, and of retroactively doing the same for their grandparents in the event of acclaim or meritorious service, often obscures their true nature, and euphemises the many historical occasions when it was the Han Chinese who were the conquered people.

It was a bold, discursive view of Chinese history, embracing all communities and all tribes, but it often sat uneasily with certain Chinese media that relegated modern minorities to the sidelines. Look hard, though, and you can see the Han majority trying very hard in modern times to give the minorities their dues. Communist Party rhetoric has long stressed that there is more to Chinese-ness than the Han majority. In recent years, a post-modern, post-colonial attitude seems to have taken hold, in which such claims are taken significantly more seriously. Some in the Han majority seem more aware of their privilege, and more welcoming of the idea of China as a diverse land of many nationalities. When the 2008 Beijing Olympics chose its mascots, it plumped for five creatures instead of one, deliberately incorporating emblems of several disparate regions, instead of a single Sichuanese panda or a mythical Han dragon. Nonetheless, non-Han Chinese will always be a minority in modern China; they currently form 10 per cent of the overall population, and face similar issues to any other minority worldwide, such as the integrity of local languages or the right to native belief. This is particularly problematic in Xinjiang, where so much of the non-Han population's modern ethnic identity is *religiously* defined, as an Islamic community in a Communist state where religion itself is only tolerated as an outmoded superstition.

In ancient times, the edge of the Chinese world was the Jade Gate, *Jiayuguan*, a fortress at the western end of the Great Wall, at the eastern edge of Xinjiang. Chinese outposts continued into the desert as a sparse line of isolated watchtowers, as if a ghost wall continued to connect them. There was occasional contact with the peoples beyond the wall, but their allegiance and relationship to the emperor was tenuous. The emperor ruled 'all under heaven', but his expectations of his subjects often ran in direct relation to their proximity to the throne.

Chinese under his direct rule were expected to pay homage to him every day. States and colonies established by the empire had to send a monthly tribute or report, or some form of acknowledgement that he was still the boss. States conquered by the empire, allowed to persist as vassals, needed to account for themselves four times a year. But beyond those realms were the 'barbarian' regions – most definitely under heaven, but of questionable relationship to the imperial centre. They might, perhaps, know of the existence of the emperor, but not fully appreciate that he was the semi-divine ruler of the world. Barbarians in the 'controlled zone', within the reach of punitive expeditions, were expected to send annual tribute. This was often little more than lip-service to the emperor's authority, and best not tested by actual demands. During the Han Dynasty, this was sometimes called a 'loose rein', as if to imply that the outlying tribes were horses firmly in their traces, but that the emperor had benignly decided to let them have some element of self-determination. The tributes themselves often took the form of goods that the empire actually needed (such as horses), and would be met with 'gifts' from the emperor to match their value – bolts of silks, luxuries, tools and metal goods, or, in times of trouble, even simple food aid.

The very idea of 'colouring in a map', and indeed of a definite border drawn on such a map, are relatively new concepts from the imperialist west. It was foreign explorers and colonists who were truly keen on establishing where Asian possessions began and ended. The Chinese worldview, and those of the races within the Chinese sphere, was somewhat different, and bore far greater resemblance to one of the Buddhist *mandalas* still to be found in many temples. The centre has the largest image and the greatest detail – a single figure representing the most powerful and the most familiar. Successive levels of lesser creatures ripple outwards, declining in size, potency and detail, until the outermost regions are populated by indistinct figures and a faded focus.

Beyond the 'controlled zone' was the 'wild zone', of tribes so hopelessly ignorant, distant or primitive that they barely knew what the emperor was. Their 'tribute' was only expected once, and usually amounted to a breathless spin from dynastic chroniclers, turning a single encounter with an envoy into a carefully-worded acknowledgement of the emperor's 'authority'. Somewhere out towards the western horizon, the subjects of the ancient emperors stopped being subjects, and turned into people with only the vaguest interest in their supposed ruler. As the old proverb ran: 'Heaven is high, and the emperor is far away.' But Chinese history, in the eyes of the Chinese since the time of legend, has often been a march of cultural progress. As the philosopher Confucius argued, true civilisation had a habit of luring the border peoples in. They are tempted by its benefits, to the extent that they cannot live without them, and soon buy, or beg, or barter them for themselves. Sometimes they steal, but eventually they are subsumed within the civilisation itself. Today, we would call it 'soft power'.

These *mandalas* of influence were also repeated in miniature form at any pro-Chinese township along the Silk Road, and if merchants were lucky, the influence and protective capabilities of each oasis would not fade into inconsequentiality before their travels brought them within the influence of the next. Banditry on the Silk Road, outlaws and 'invaders' only occurred where the power of the *mandala* diminished, and the noise of its presence faded in the desert.

Anyone studying Chinese history does not take long to stumble across dozens of assimilated groups throughout the centuries. In all cases, the wording in the imperial dynastic record is similar: 'barbarians' discover the wonder of China, often by conquering it, but soon they are bewitched by Chinese traditions and culture. Their families marry into the aristocracy, their grandchildren grow up speaking Chinese and before long, they are thoroughly absorbed. However, this long-term view of Chinese hegemony obscures many alternative readings. Christopher Beckwith, in *Empires of the Silk Road*, argues that the history of Central Asian nomads has been largely written, and read, by foreign observers on the periphery – the Europeans, Chinese and Muslims, many with little direct experience of the steppes, and often drawing on similarly ill-informed claims by earlier authors.

Beckwith points to clichés that are themselves thousands of years old – claims that nomads were naturally predisposed to warfare because of their skills in riding and archery; or claims that they were resource-poor and hence covetous of the delights of sedentary civilisations. Far from it, Beckwith notes, there is no greater likelihood of a steppe herder becoming a great warrior than there is of a farmer; it is just as easy to argue that agricultural civilisations had more time to practise and a greater supply of manpower. He argues instead that nomad society, like any other, had its rich and poor, its good times and bad times, but that in the medieval society of the steppes, life for a low-ranking herder was generally and measurably better than that of a serf in an agricultural society. Resources were certainly thin on the steppes, but that is why the nomads were *nomadic*, regularly shifting their homes in order to take advantage of renewable resources and seasonal variations. There is plenty of historical evidence of barbarian wealth, to the extent that for many periods on the Silk Road, the nomadic cultures of Central Asia were the primary customers for most of the silk! The few bolts of silk that made it to the Mediterranean world, inspiration for so much poetry and discussion, pale in comparison with the mountainous cartfuls of the stuff sent annually to the nomads by successive Chinese rulers. And while the nomads certainly traded some of it on to merchants or in barter, they also ended up wearing a great deal of it. By the late Yuan Dynasty, even the 'barbarian' Mongols favoured silk undershirts, which were capable of snagging an arrow that somehow made it through their armour.

'Barbarians' enter the history books whenever there is a border dispute or a conflict, inevitably dragging up the old clichés. But as Nicola di Cosmo argues in *Ancient China and its Enemies*, it is often the 'civilised' power that has encroached on the 'barbarian' territories. 'Central Eurasian' nomadic culture has been eternally squashed and pushed back; we might associate it today with the arid deserts of the Silk Road, but that is because much of the grasslands and pastures of ancient times have been seized and turned into farmland by the same nations that write off the nomads as 'barbarians'. Perhaps the most notable indicator of the twisted historical record is, as di Cosmo describes, the famous Great Wall of China, which was constructed not as a defensive fortification but as an *offensive* one, built on 'barbarian' territory as a staging post for Chinese expansion.

Of course, there were bad barbarians, too. There were criminals and raiders, rapists and thieves. But modern scholars plead that there is no evidence that there were any more bad barbarians than bad Chinese, and that when it comes to written accounts of century after century of interaction between these cultures, the extant documents are overwhelmingly written by the Chinese.

Furthermore, there are long hiatuses in the chronicles when nomads might be better described as *markets* for Chinese goods; trading partners and providers of vital products, such as horses and ginseng. An anti-nomad bias also ignores the many ruling 'Chinese' dynasties that were unquestionably of foreign origin, not only the famous Mongols and Manchus, but the many minor dynasties that ruled north China for 1,000 years.

2

From the Tarim Mummies to the early Han Dynasty (Prehistory to AD 6)

THERE IS A CHAMBER in the Xinjiang Regional Museum in Urumqi, the 'furthest city from the sea', where many of the ancient mummies have ended up. The casual visitor is apt to assume that they are *from* Urumqi, whereas most of them are actually from scattered sites far to the south, on the other side of the Taklamakan Desert. They are in Urumqi now because Urumqi is the capital of Xinjiang, and speaks for all its scattered oases.

This tiny group of the ancient dead has survived all the trials that nature and man could muster. These long-dead locals were interred in dry, salty ground that was never flooded, and any moisture in their corpses was swiftly baked away by the ambient heat of the desert. They were somehow rediscovered beneath the shifting sands that have engulfed whole towns, and by the *right* people, who chose to preserve them rather than burning them or scattering their remains. Furthermore, they were preserved after exhumation by the right methods, rather than the disastrous techniques that have all but ruined some of their brethren.

Now they lie beneath high-tech, Perspex variants of the wooden coverings that once obscured them, nestled in sealed atmospheres of poisoned, insect-killing air. Some of them are plainly Chinese. Some are Mongol. But the ones that the foreign tourists want to see are Caucasian.

It is unfair to call them European. Although they look like Europeans, at the time they were buried, the people who would become 'Europeans' lived somewhere between India and the Black Sea. These red-haired, long-limbed explorers were the easternmost outliers of the ancient Tocharian culture – shepherds and horsemen who once lived at the edge of a great lake.

It might as well have been a sea, as it covered 10,000 square kilometres. Far to the north and far to the south, there were mountains that the locals called Heaven – the meaning lingers today in two languages, as the Tianshan and the Kunlun mountain ranges. As the glacial ice finally melted, the water poured in torrents down the steep hillsides and filled much of the eastern end of the great valley. The cold mountain waters warmed up in the hot air and created a mist that shimmered in the distance.

The region was one of the last places on Earth to find human habitation. Perhaps they wandered in from the north, from the great grasslands and through the windswept valley where Urumqi now stands. Perhaps they struggled through the passes from the southwest. But when they reached the great water, they settled at its edge.

The lakeside was thick with trees. They used them to build their houses and to make the canoes they paddled on the fast river waters, and the upright henges – circular constructions with an internal ditch – that surrounded their graveyards. When they died, they used the wood to make the canoe-like cowlings that covered their graves. Their horses grazed on the grassland, and their children picked through the reeds at the water's edge, looking for fish. They raised sheep on the hillsides, mixing pigments with dark wool to make purple cloth. Their women wove garish, bright tartans and wore double-pointed conical headgear, like fork-topped witches' hats. The men wore trousers, all the better to allow them to sit astride their horses. Some, in the fashion of the tribes of the northern plains, let the patterns of their clothes carry over onto their flesh, as tattoos in whorls and dots.

The waters from the mountains gradually dwindled. It would not have been obvious on the ground. Old men would grumble that the rivers were higher in their day, that the forests stretched further. Women would mutter that when they were girls, it didn't seem so far to draw water from the lake. Who notices increments in inches, building up over years rather than days? Maybe it was a hot summer. Maybe the rain god was busy. Life went on, and the streams dwindled.

In geological time it was the merest blink. The great inland sea came and went in barely 1,000 years. But its lingering death took many human lifetimes. The day came when more of the lake evaporated into the mists than was replenished by the streams. Some of the streams even gave up before they reached it. The water began to taste bad. Fish became harder to catch. One day, the lakeside village was nowhere near the side of the lake, but an inconvenient walk away from it, across mud, then a thick crust of salt. The lake became little more than an ankle-deep puddle, seasonally augmented by the barest trickle of water from the hills.

They clung on. They sank wells. They stopped growing quite so much fruit. They learnt to live with less. Their grandchildren learnt to live with less still, unaware of how much had already been lost.

They buried a woman sometime around 1800 BC, in a shallow grave. The salt in the ground preserved her as if she were merely asleep. She did not come to light until 1980, when shocked archaeologists unearthed this earliest confirmed resident of the Xinjiang region, and discovered an ethereal beauty with light auburn hair, and a looming, lissom figure – she would have towered above the Chinese who come to see her in the modern museum.

Another grave survives from 800 years later, also uncovered in modern times in the salt-ridden ground. Its occupant was a towering figure, two metres tall, his ginger hair flecked with grey, with high cheekbones and an aquiline nose. He had a beard. Around his right wrist there was a cord of many colours, five plaited strands of wool – possibly a falcon tether or a fly swat, possibly a tribal ID. His feet were clad in stripy felt buskins. His robe was a dark, regal purple.

The Classic of Mountains and Seas, a Chinese gazetteer begun in the 4th century BC and much annotated for several centuries afterwards, contains tantalising references to the 'Western Regions', partly born of travellers' tales, and partly of superstition. There is talk of quicksands and a great marsh, where many migratory birds return to nest. There are areas where no crops will grow, said to be polluted by the corpse of a murdered god. There is the Wilderness of Ousi, where 'a woman kneels on a tree and spins silk from her mouth' and a place where a hundred fruits grow. And there is Mount Kunlun, which gives its name to the range, home to a hundred gods, 'wonder birds' who hang snakes from their chests, 'many wizards and witches', six-headed alligators, long-tailed apes and leopards. The only tall tale that the legends don't include is 'here be dragons', presumably because China already had a lot of those.

The lake has gone. The rivers that fed it have dried up. Even the Tarim River, the biggest waterway in the area, has radically changed direction, swept into a new course by a dam of drifted sand. Those tartan-clad herders would not recognise the arid saltpan that now stretches across the lands where they once carved proto-Celtic knotted designs in the wood from local trees. Their descendants scattered back to the north and west, or were incorporated in the polities of new nomad empires. Circumstantial evidence, in the dating of available finds, even suggests that they carried the secret of iron to China. Their language is forgotten, although perhaps a tiny handful of its Indo-European words survive in the Chinese terms for 'wheel', 'honey' and perhaps 'magic'. There is another word that has outlived them, and that is *Lop*, which may have been the name they gave to the great lake. Its sense is lost, and it means nothing to any of the contemporary ethnic groups in the region, who quarrel among themselves about what to call the lake. To the modern Uyghurs, the searing glare of the white salt pan is *Lop Nur* ('Bright Lop'); to the Mongols, it is *Lop Nor* ('Lop Lake').

The Turkic peoples who supplanted the Tocharians sometimes noticed the abandoned wrecks of their villages poking momentarily through the dust storms. In their own language, they called this forbidding waste of sand *Taklar Makan*, the Place of Ruins.

Sometimes, in the museum, among the Chinese visitors who stare blankly at the Tocharians' sleeping bodies, one sees red hair poking out from beneath a skullcap, or a flash of green eyes above a veil. The lakeside people still live on, as part of China and the Chinese.

The discovery of silk

A road, even one that is only imaginary, requires 'vehicles'. The origins of trade in Central Asia can be dated to roughly 5,000 years ago, when the domestication of the horse, and soon afterwards, the camel, made it possible for merchants to travel with more than the merest essentials for survival, and without expensive human porters. In particular, the two-humped Bactrian camel (*Camelus bactrianus*), with its invulnerability to both heat and cold, and its ability to survive for prolonged periods without access to fresh water, opened up the desert routes.

Archaeological evidence points to small, local routes that gradually expanded. The unearthly blue semi-precious stone lapis lazuli, from what is now north-east Afghanistan, appeared in India, then Persia, then ancient Egypt, travelling far from its home. East across the Pamir Mountains from Afghanistan, where the slopes levelled out into the desert, were the remote settlements of Khotan and Yarkand

– unlikely places for human habitation, rendered more appealing by the discovery of nephrite jade in the nearby hills.

Such contacts brought a trickle of items to the edges of the Persian Empire, and thence along its 'Royal Road' to the edge of the Mediterranean. In the most pronounced of many east-west oscillations along the road, Mediterranean culture washed as far east as what is now the Punjab, when Alexander the Great conquered the Persian Empire in the 4th century BC. His men returned to the west with tales of the edge of the world, but also with physical products of the Silk Road – such as walnuts, from what is now Kyrgyzstan, still called 'Greek nuts' in some languages.

Greek culture flourished longest in Bactria (in what is now Afghanistan and Tajikistan), where Alexander met his wife, the red-haired, fiery Roxana. Alexander established dozens of new cities on his travels, many bearing his name. *Alexandria Eschate*, the 'Furthest Alexandria', sat at the edge of the known (Greek) world, in the warm, dry Ferghana Valley between several imposing mountain ranges. It became home to a detachment of wounded and recuperating soldiers and their local wives, and eventually one of several 'Greek' cities in Central Asia. From there, according to the historian Strabo, 'they extended their empire even as far as the Seres and the Phryni.' There was no 'empire' to extend, but the Greeks and their descendants may have at least explored a little further to the east, into the mountain passes that led towards Kashgar and the Taklamakan Desert. In an unnamed, unremembered event, a traveller of Greek ancestry found himself somewhere in the lands where silk came from (Seres), presumably in Kashgar, or in one of the oases to its west, among the locals that Strabo calls the Phryni – maybe even as far as Khotan. Statues and depictions of men who appear to be Greek can be found in the museum in modern-day Urumqi.

It is often assumed that all silk came *from* China, and the mythical Silk Road must therefore have existed centuries before the first recorded contacts between east and west. In fact, there were several sources of silk and types of textile, from several points of origin. There are also various naturally occurring species of moth whose cocoons can be used to make silk threads, in Bangladesh, for example, and on the ancient Adriatic and Aegean coasts, stretching across the Middle East to Persia. A kind of silk was found across Eurasia as early as the Iron Age, from Europe to Siberia, long before the fabled arrival of the first caravans from China. There is some limited evidence of it in archaeological sites, either as fragments in grave goods, or as the impression left by it on other materials – what archaeologists call a 'textile pseudomorph', a pattern impressed into clay or impressed into centuries-old cheese.

We also have writings about silk from many classical authors. Aristotle wrote that the women of Cos would wind silk on bobbins to turn it into thread, and noted that their raw materials were brought from 'Asia' – modern Turkey and the Middle East. Silk's most infamous appearance in the west was not draped on the body of a Roman lady, but at the Battle of Carrhae in 53 BC, when the legions of Marcus Crassus faced the horsemen of Parthia, and were dumbfounded when the Parthians unfurled giant, shimmering flags in the desert sun. Where Roman banners hung heavily from poles, the Parthian flags whipped in the wind, impossibly far from their flagpoles, as if held aloft by some divine hand, ineffably buoyant, translucent and shining – magical.

By the early days of the Roman Empire, silk (or *sericum*) from the Greek islands, sometimes embroidered in Egypt and woven with gold thread for extra bling, was a powerful and popular fashion statement among Roman ladies and often noted by admiring poets, although a mystery remained as to what it actually was. Pliny the Elder, in his *Natural History*, noted that certain moths 'weave webs, like spiders, that become luxurious clothing for women, called *bombycina*.' But Pliny himself wasn't sure, and seemed to mix up accounts of silk and cotton, while admitting that Europeans still did not really know precisely where silk came from. He knew, however, where it went, and was neither the first nor the last Roman man to fulminate about the amount of money wasted on mere garments.

The writer Seneca grew extremely agitated about the scandalous 'glass togas' on sale:

> I see silken 'clothes', if one can call them clothes at all, that in no degree afford protection either to the body or to the modesty of the wearer, and clad in which, no woman could honestly swear she is not naked.

The more prudent Roman girls would wear a flash of silk that didn't break the bank or boggle their uncles – a ribbon or hair-band, easily acquired from the sellers of racier incense and perfumes on a street near the Forum. But a high-status Roman woman stepping into a silk robe was donning the culmination of multiple labours – harvested beyond the edge of the world through unknown means, brought to the Empire by Syrians, spun into thread on one Greek island, woven into cloth on another, transported to Egypt to be embroidered, transported yet again to Rome itself, into the hands of merchants, who sold it to tailors, who produced the final article. No wonder, then, that by the 3rd century AD, silk in Rome was literally worth its weight in gold.

Partly out of irritation that their sometime enemies were hawking luxury goods to their womenfolk, and partly through genuine concern about the price, Roman men tried to proscribe it. Real men, it was argued in the time of Tiberius, wouldn't wear silk, a claim bolstered in later generations when the more infamous 'bad' emperors were reported sporting it. Christian authors also sternly warned against it, and the more prudent penny-pinchers – including Marcus Aurelius and Plutarch – both hectored wives who squandered their husband's finances on such fripperies.

Moths and worms

Silk moths are odd creatures. Centuries of human interference have bred practically flightless creatures with decorative but impotent wings. They are notoriously fragile, and the jumpiest of farmers fret that their wriggly darlings will be disturbed by bad smells, loud noises, even the sound of a barking dog. Any worms that appear to be deviating far from the norm, in terms of size or life cycle or simply appetite, are swiftly plucked off the trays and fed to the fish in order to maintain a homogenous gene pool. Centuries of superstitions and old wives' tales have created a number of weird practices, including tickling newborn maggots with a chicken's feather, and dietary restrictions that forbid their human wranglers from eating chicory or garlic. The worms don't like the smell, apparently.

They cannot even breed without human agency. Chinese children rear them from the merest dots on mulberry paper until they grow into fat worms, whose cocoons can be prodded and pulled into flat card-shapes or the more traditional oblong. Some worms can even spit out coloured thread, although this is usually the result of a protein called sericin, which will be boiled away by silk-makers later on. Inside each full-grown silkworm lie two glands that would stretch to 15 inches if uncoiled. They secrete liquid silk, a single protein molecule that hardens into thread on exposure to air, and can stretch, unbroken, for up to a mile.

When Homer's *Odyssey* speaks of Odysseus and his shimmering shirt, 'gleaming like the skin of a dried onion', the famous hero is probably wearing a kind of silk, but silk woven from the cocoon of the *Lasiocampidae Pachypasa otus*, a moth found both in his native Ithaca and at the site of Troy. When the medieval Byzantine emperors intrigued to seize the 'secret of silk' from the Far East, they already knew many of the basics of silk production. They knew that the cocoons of certain moths could be collected, boiled and unravelled, before being spun into a fine thread, famously light, shimmery and perhaps most importantly, resistant to lice. What they did *not* know was why silk from China was so much better than silk from anywhere else.

Chinese 'true' silk, so wondrous as to lend its name to the Latin word for China itself (*Seres*), had many qualities that European 'raw' silk did not. The Chinese had the most suitable moth, *Bombyx mori*, which was only native to a crescent of territory in northern China. Whereas ancient Europeans collected wild moth cocoons in the forest, the Chinese reared domesticated caterpillars in dedicated farms, feeding them a specialised diet of mulberry leaves.

But genus, location and diet were only the beginning. The Chinese also had two crucial innovations in the way they processed their silk. Everyone boiled the cocoons to unravel them – that was common all across Eurasia. But European silk threads retained the gummy sericin protein which caused silk fibres to clump and snag, and required the fibres to be re-spun into thread. The Chinese, however, boiled their cocoons in a slightly alkaline solution, which leeched off the sericin and made it possible to unravel the thinnest possible thread. Such 'degummed' thread also took far more readily to dyes, creating deeper hues and more lasting colours.

The Europeans waited for the moths to emerge from the cocoons, not realising the implications of the moth-shaped hole that it left behind. European cocoons hence comprised many broken threads, soaked in a corrosive brown exit secretion. The silk was damaged, and even if the fibres were spun back into whole thread, they would never be as strong as the unbroken variety. The Chinese, however, threw their cocoons, worm and all, into the boiling water. This killed the larvae, but also preserved the integrity of the cocoon, allowing for much longer, thinner threads, and more diaphanous material.

As the native origin of silk worms should already imply, silk did not *come* from the oases of the Silk Road. It was first brought there 2,000 years ago by the Chinese, not in single strands but in vast quantities measured by the tonne. Before Chinese silk enchanted Persians and scandalised Romans, it swamped communities of herders in what is now Uzbekistan and Tajikistan, as payment for horses. Before it was embroidered or tailored, before it was used as stuffing in coverlets and coats, it was packed into the saddle bags of soldiers, and handed out by the bolt as payment for lodgings and food, for wine and whores.

Horse-riders and horse-traders

From 1000 BC onwards, major changes had come over the borderlands of what is now China. From the most ancient Chinese chronicles, and the archaeological record, it is clear that large areas that are now windswept steppes and farmland were once lush, green forests. Monsoon rains used to fall significantly further north than they do now, and their retreat southwards came accompanied by a rapid expansion of Chinese civilisation. Ancient woodlands in the great north bend of the Yellow River were hacked down and did not regrow. Tree coverage declined from prehistoric levels of 85 per cent to only 50 per cent by the time of the Han Dynasty, and a meagre 5 per cent by the present day. Inevitably, this deforestation created a border zone that *could* be used for farming, but also for grazing. It set the agricultural realm of the Chinese against the realm of horse-riding nomads.

There was little space in China for the flat, wide-ranging grassland required to raise horses, but the demand for horses was immense, not only for riding, but to pull chariots and carts. This need for literal horsepower forced the Chinese to constantly return to their western borders in search of deals – an addiction that only faded in the 17th century, when China's borders finally and decisively expanded to incorporate those grasslands within its own territory; and diminished again in the 20th century, when horses themselves were replaced by the internal combustion engine.

In what is now Mongolia, the most prominent nomadic people during the Han Dynasty were known to the Chinese as the Xiongnu. Since most information about them has come from Chinese sources, they are usually presented as 'barbarians'. Under a variety of names, they form the bogeymen and bugbears of several dynasties. This rather ignores the strong cross-cultural contacts between the Xiongnu (in classical Chinese 'Slaves Sick at Heart', or 'Repulsive Scoundrels') and the Chinese themselves, in which many peripheral clans became so drawn into the Chinese cultural world that they effectively became part of it. This has made it very difficult to disentangle propaganda from the truth. When Chinese soldiers get into a fight with nomad horsemen, then it is a raid by 'The Horrible Xiongnu', even if the fight was provoked by the Chinese themselves, and the 'Chinese' ranks were actually heavily staffed by soldiers of Xiongnu descent.

As in many disastrous cross-cultural encounters throughout human history, we see the interplay of an unstoppable force and an immovable object. The object is a sedentary, agricultural civilisation, its people attached to a single piece of territory, from which they often do not stray for their whole lives. The force is a mobile, drifting group of nomads, whose particular lifestyle requires them to move on with the herds. The nomads' orbit might seasonally bring them into contact with the Chinese, where there might even be friendly exchanges at a local level – of cheese and leather goods for metalwork and silk, perhaps. But with the slightest shift of climate – a warm summer or a rainy autumn, there is a shift everywhere in surpluses and deficits. Maybe the herders come further south than usual; maybe the farmers have had a bad harvest. There is a misunderstanding over a change in prices and values; someone shoves someone else's cousin. There are a million ways things can turn bad quickly, particularly in the borderlands, which are suitable for *either* grazing *or* agriculture, depending on who can hang onto them.

The Chinese didn't like the Xiongnu. Dynastic histories

are suitably cutting about their barbarian ways, claiming that they ate raw meat, drank fermented horse's milk (*koumiss*), wore animal skins and had no respect for the elderly. However, the *Book of Han* paid the long-term enemy the ultimate compliment of an entire chapter devoted to century after century of the tribe's history, observing that the very strength of the Xiongnu was their lack of access to Chinese luxuries, particularly silk clothing and fine foods.

The Chinese were particularly shocked by the Xiongnu custom of men marrying their widowed sisters-in-law, a steppe tradition designed to keep property, which was usually held by a wife, in the hands of the patrilineal family. This custom endured for millennia on the steppes, but was greeted with intense disapproval by the Chinese, for whom it was tantamount to incest. In answer to this criticism, a Xiongnu chieftain archly observed that property stayed in his family, instead of being dispersed among strangers and causing conflict, as it was sure to do among the Chinese. Dismissing the Chinese as 'You, from the earthen houses,' he scoffed at their sedentary agricultural traditions, which offered no on-the-job training for military action, as hunting and trapping did for the Xiongnu.

By the time of the Han Dynasty, the Xiongnu were moving inexorably south and west. Some of their splinter clans settled peaceably on the Chinese frontier, but others ran into conflict with the Chinese. There are indicators that the Chinese government was in the midst of a frantic arms race with the Xiongnu, trying to secure a large supply of the only item that could ensure military superiority on the borderlands – the horse. Meanwhile, the Xiongnu's wanderings had brought them close to the Tianshan mountain range, close to the townships of the desert region, and the rich grazing land of the foothills.

At first, the Chinese tried to buy off the Xiongnu, making great gestures of friendship and alliance that saw horses sent to China, and the Chinese responding with whatever the nomads wanted. Quite often, this would include the chance to be a Chinese emperor's son-in-law, as a number of Chinese princesses (and *alleged* princesses) were packed off to marry nomad chiefs.

Sometimes, we can detect a disapproving tone in historical accounts of the Han trade with the nomads, as if the Chinese were somehow derelict in their duties by not fighting a full-scale war. But war was a costly and terrible enterprise, sure to exhaust both sides, and 'winning' was a nebulous concept when one's foe could simply canter a few hundred miles west and effectively disappear. Sun Tzu, author of the definitive text on military strategy, *The Art of War*, went to battle only as an absolute last resort, and counselled using any means possible to avoid it. If that meant espionage, and the condemnation and exile of a few hundred princesses as bride-gifts to nomads, then surely it was worth the sacrifice?

True enough, the Han contact with the nomads was a form of appeasement, and like all attempts to pay off extortion, it was vulnerable and subject to exploitation. But it also probably cost farmers and silk merchants of the Chinese empire considerably less than a full-scale war, and was less likely to result in sons conscripted to die in far-off battles. Moreover, the Chinese were careful to spin their bribes as gifts bestowed upon grateful subordinate peoples, leading many observers, even today, to simply assume that the steppes should be coloured in on a map with the same shade as the Chinese empire itself.

We only *assume* that the women packed off into nomadic marriages were unhappy, largely because that's what the Han Chinese tell us. This, in turn, is because of China's ever-present assumption that it is the literal centre of the world, and that one's happiness and culture must surely decline in direct relation to how far one strays from this bright centre. One Han Dynasty princess reputedly bemoaned her fate with a poem recorded in the dynasty's annals:

My family sent me off to a marriage at the edge of the world,
Faraway to a strange land, to the king of the Wusun,
My home is a tent, with walls of felt,
My food is raw meat, my drink is *koumiss*,
All day my heart aches with yearning for home,
If I were only a brown goose, I would fly home.

But they would say that, wouldn't they? Chinese history occasionally records dissenters who instead embraced the steppe culture as a liberating respite from stuffy, hidebound Chinese conservatism. How one wishes for archaeologists to unearth a previously unseen Han Dynasty poem, along the lines of:

Thankfully, I have escaped the bitter intrigues of the court
Here among the Wusun, where I am treated as a queen,
In a lavish, mobile palace three times the size of my Chinese quarters,
Dining well, and swimming in booze,
Occasionally I remember how miserable life was in Chang'an,
And laugh at the migrating birds overhead.

There are intimations of such feelings hidden between the lines of one of the most famous stories of such brides, the story of the palace lady Wang Zhaojun, a minor and seemingly overlooked member of the Emperor's harem, who volunteered to be sent as a gift to the ruler of the Xiongnu. Glad to swap a lowly palace lady for a genuine princess, the Emperor sent her off, where she married the khan, and on her first husband's death, his successor (her stepson). However, a few centuries later, the Chinese version of the story changed. Now, it was believed that the Emperor had sent Zhaojun away by mistake – he had not even seen her until the day he gave her to the Xiongnu envoy, and only then realised what an intelligent, beautiful girl had been hidden away in his palace. Because this new version of events required a scapegoat, it was further embellished with tales of a preoccupied Emperor, who selected his bedmates by consulting portraits, and the honest-hearted Zhaojun, who alone of all the palace women, refused to bribe the court artists to sex up her image. As a result, the Emperor was misinformed about Zhaojun's beauty, and forced to bite his lip and wave her off. It is only here, in these stories written centuries later, that there is any suggestion that Zhaojun was not happy with her exile, supposedly begging to return, and eventually committing suicide. Whatever the truth of the story, it has echoes in hundreds of women's graves as far west as Afghanistan, where corpses have been found with their hands folded demurely on the tarnished remains of a Chinese mirror – one tiny reminder of the life left behind.

The appeasement policy went on for decades, although deals made with the overlord of the Xiongnu never quite guaranteed that there would not be raids by splinter groups or outcasts. Things changed with the arrival of Chinese Emperor Wudi (156–87 BC), a man whose reign title means 'Martial Emperor', and whose accession marked a forceful new style. On the understanding that the enemy of his enemy was his friend, Wudi decided to look beyond the Xiongnu, in the hope of finding an alliance on the nomads' western flank. By this point, the authority of the Han Dynasty had extended as far as the marshes of Lop Nur, presenting the Chinese with the possibility that an expedition into the desert might produce a way of making contact with the Xiongnu's enemies.

Prophecy played a role in the drama. A consultation with the soothsaying *Book of Changes* had suggested to Wudi that 'heavenly horses would arrive from the north-west.' He originally assumed that this referred to mounts sold to him by the Wusun tribe (the ancestors of the Kazakhs), but then realised that even better steeds were on offer from the

Ferghana Valley. These 'heavenly horses' had legendary speed and endurance, and were immortalised in a famous Han Dynasty statuette of a galloping horse, one of its legs resting on a swallow in flight – to this day, one of the most popular reproductions on sale in tourist shops all over China. They were also referred to cryptically as 'blood-sweating', likely to be a reference to a parasitic worm common to the Russian steppes, one of the side-effects of which is 'summer bleeding' where certain blood vessels rupture during exertion. There is no direct description of the Ferghana horses in the Chinese dynastic chronicles, but Wudi seems to have disastrously conflated two pieces of information. (1) Ferghana had lots of horses (2) The horses he had seen from Ferghana, seemingly a very limited sample, were all superb.

Determined to have Ferghana horses for his war against the Xiongnu, Wudi sent thousands of bolts of silk west to the valley kingdom, only to have his offer apparently rebuffed. In an awful misunderstanding, the king of Ferghana did not have anywhere near the quantity of horses that Wudi required, and Wudi appeared to have mistakenly believed that a top-of-the-line, pedigree model he had seen was indicative of the quality of *all* Ferghana steeds. Faced with an order for thousands of mounts when he had barely a handful of the required quality, the ruler of Ferghana could do nothing but refuse. After 1,000 miles of Chinese whispers, the message reached the Emperor that Ferghana was supposedly sold out, inadvertently initiating the War of the Heavenly Horses.

Believing that Ferghana was deliberately withholding entire herds of super-powered beasts, Wudi sent an army westwards. Hampered by long supply lines and the inhospitable Taklamakan Desert, his luckless men got into a series of scrapes with local potentates, who reasonably interpreted their arrival as an attempt by the Chinese to assert direct control over the region. By the time the army reached Ferghana it was a fraction of its initial size, and soundly beaten by local forces.

A second mission returned to the region, accompanied by a massive supply train of donkeys and camels. Laying siege to the Ferghana capital at Khujand in what is now Tajikistan, Wudi's general secured the execution of the local leader and a promise to supply the Chinese with all the horses they wanted. However, he also got to see with his own eyes the quality of the local stock. He left Ferghana with 3,000 horses, of which only a third survived the harsh desert trip back to China. Limping back into the capital, the general presented his Emperor with all the Heavenly Horses he could rustle up – of the remaining 1,000, barely a dozen were of the quality that Wudi had demanded.

Thereafter, China received an annual gift of the best horses Ferghana could provide – a mere two mounts. And the Silk Road gained a new commodity, in the form of vast quantities of alfalfa seeds (in Chinese, 'purple-flowered clover'), ordered from Ferghana in the hope that the Chinese could somehow import a wonder-food to grow their own super-horses. Meanwhile, the passage to and fro of two massive Chinese armies had encouraged many of the region's townships to proclaim at least a nominal fealty to China, in the hope that they would never have to see another one. This was to have all sorts of knock-on effects on the townships stuck in the middle, encouraging further connections, trade and sadly, more misunderstandings and conflict.

3

The Western Regions: From Han to Tang (AD 6–618)

THERE IS A STATUE in a park in downtown Kashgar, the site of an ancient fortress now within the city limits. It depicts a towering, barrel-chested man with a full, bushy beard, wearing a chunky robe that would surely make him sweat in the Central Asian heat and dust. His head is fixed with a topknot that marks him out as a Chinese official, and tucked under his arm is a rolled-up scroll of bamboo strips, the form of 'book' used in China before the invention of paper. A semi-circular wall sweeps behind him – a bas-relief depicting great battles and iconic moments. There are 36 other statues, of fierce warriors, all slightly larger than life, flanking the long pathway that leads to the base of the monument, like those that guard the sacred roads that lead to imperial tombs. But the main figure depicts neither an emperor nor a god, nor is it one of the pious Party memorials that commemorate Chairman Mao or his successors. This is a statue of Ban Chao, a Chinese general of the Han Dynasty, who lived from AD 32–102, although the statue itself is far more recent, raised only in 1996.

Ban Chao was one of several military leaders from Han Dynasty China who sallied out into the desert regions as part of a conflict that lasted for several centuries, and came to characterise much of the Han Dynasty itself. While Han China was strong, the 'Western Regions' remained loyal, but the authority of the emperors wavered around the time of the birth of Christ. For 20 years at the beginning of the Christian era, the Han Dynasty ceased to exist, and power was seized by a usurper who managed to insult many of the border tribes, and annoyed his subjects in the west so much that the desert kingdoms gave up sending tribute at all. By the time of the tentative restoration in AD 25 that would keep the Han fires burning for another two centuries, the Western Regions had fallen under the influence of the nomad peoples. Ban Chao and several fellow generals managed to wrest control of the region back, at least for a while. As Chinese power receded and the Han Dynasty drifted towards its own final collapse (which came in AD 220), the oases of the desert region were annexed by the Kushan Empire. For a vital few decades, the region was connected more closely to India than to China. This led to a transformative tide of new visitors and ideas, particularly Buddhism, which slowly crossed the desert and changed China ever after.

Even by the time of the Han Dynasty, the exotic west had made its mark on China. Many everyday foodstuffs in China once had names that contained a tell-tale marker of an origin on the Silk Road – a *xi* for 'west', or a *hu* for 'barbarian'. Similar indicators of foreign origin are to be found in, for example, the names for certain kinds of melon, cucumbers, rhubarb, broad beans, carrots, sesame, walnuts, or pepper. Many of these terms have been elided, euphemised and garbled in modern Chinese, but ancient manuscripts preserve the original names.

The word in Chinese for honey, *mi*, was borrowed from the Tocharians of the Silk Road, who brought the substance they called *mjit* east from Persia – the Indo-European root is the same as that for our own 'mead'. Grapes, or *budawa* in ancient Persian, reached the Ferghana region with Greek settlers after Alexander the Great, and drifted along the Silk Road to China as *putao*. Coriander, the Persian *goswi*, reached Chinese recipes as *husui*.

Just as occasional commodities and crops drifted east, the Chinese drifted west, driven not by a demand for conquest, but by a desire to outflank and hold off nomad enemies in the north. The Han Dynasty saw the map of China stretch gradually westward in a thin panhandle, out beyond the end of the Great Wall in a series of watchtowers and bases. China proper stopped at Dunhuang, the 'blazing beacon' at the desert edge. But Chinese power would eventually stretch all the way to Kashgar, where the mountain passes began to wind into a different world. Kashgar was the distant edge, poetically close, as the crow flies at least, to the 'Furthest Alexandria' that marked the edge of Persia.

For anyone seeking to maintain control over these Western Regions, lines of supply and communication were the real problem. For a desert chief, it was hardly any consolation to know that he was a vassal of the Chinese Emperor, when a nomad enemy could strike out of the desert, steal his herds or other valuables, and then ride off again in mere hours. It would take weeks to notify the Chinese of the attack, and months for a military expedition to arrive. When it did, it would require food and lodging, and end up costing more money, while the original thieves would be long gone.

Sited on the edge of both China and the steppe culture of the Xiongnu, the oasis of Loulan (see Gazetteer: Ruoqiang) was often caught in the middle. One king of Loulan was obliged to send one of his sons as a hostage to each of the rival territories, and both the Huns and the Chinese regarded the motives of the Loulan people with some suspicion. In 77 BC an envoy called Fu Jiezhi arrived, on his way from China to the distant western kingdoms, laden with gold and gifts for the famed horse breeders of Ferghana. But he also had some trinkets for the King of Loulan, who welcomed him with open arms. The two hit it off and got swiftly drunk, it is implied, on some of the supplies brought by Fu from the Chinese heartland. It was only then, with the King deep in his cups, that Fu revealed his other mission. An army was on its way from China, bringing the King's younger brother, who was due to be installed as the new ruler.

Loulan was renamed and rebranded as a Chinese puppet state. The new ruler, who had been raised in the Chinese capital, soon 'requested' a garrison of Chinese soldiers to protect him from any possible revolt by his disinherited nephews. The Chinese sent troops and colonists, and filed a stern-faced report in the court records of the Han Dynasty, listing the region's most abundant products as reeds, tamarisks, balsam poplars and jade. However, the same report expressed some hope that a little application from farmers might set up some irrigated fields and green the area up a little. Such hopes, written almost 2,000 years ago, parallel many subsequent Chinese assessments of the region – arid, sandy, but possible to fix up, given a little time.

Armies reach Kashgar

Our view of the world, as seen by Europeans during the time of the Roman Empire, is largely conveyed to us by the Romans themselves, often writing far away from the actual things they describe. Occasional asides, such as the suggestion in Cassius Dio that Cleopatra planned to send her son Caesarion to safety in 'India', hint at much closer contacts on the ground. However, Egypt's trade seems to have been conducted mainly by sea.

At the other end of the Silk Road, Chinese chroniclers were just as fascinated by the mysteries of the exotic west. In particular, the author Fan Ye, in his *Book of the Later Han*, attempted to assimilate a number of earlier works, now lost, in his chapter on 'The Western Regions'. Just as Roman accounts often seemed to assume that their capital was the centre of the world, and that life got progressively more barbaric the further one strayed from it, Chinese accounts contain within them the traditional assumption that China is the centre of all things. Fan Ye writes specifically of *Xi Cheng*, the 'Western Walls/Towns', conveying the sense of a region of open territory, dotted with occasional fortified oases. His use of the Chinese term for 'kingdoms' for the west seems to encompass everything from vague references to the Roman Empire (i.e. most of Western Europe) to a hamlet of dusty huts clustered around a brackish well.

Some, however, were remarkably large. The ancient city of Turfan, and several thousand square kilometres of the land around it, sits below sea level, a geographical fact that has afforded it immense advantages in the region. From the Han Dynasty onwards, the city has been fed by *karez*, underground aqueducts that collect water from a series of wells and run-offs in the nearby Flaming Mountains. Over 1,100 of these wells and channels survive today, creating an irrigation system comprising an astounding 6,000 kilometres of hand-dug tunnels. Capitalising on Turfan's low-lying situation, these ensure that gravity alone brings the precious water to the site, in such quantities that by the Tang Dynasty Turfan was even growing thirsty cotton crops. If the channels had been open to the air, as such systems are in the Mediterranean, then much of the water would evaporate before it could reach the city. By running underground, the *karez* niftily preserve water that would otherwise be lost.

In their 1942 book *The Gobi Desert*, Mildred Cable and Francesca French summed up the striking result:

> Turfan lies like a green island in a sandy wilderness, its shores lapped by grit and gravel instead of ocean waters, for the division between arid desert and fertile land is as definite as that between shore and ocean. Its fertility is amazing, and the effect on the traveller, when he steps from the sterility and desiccation into the luxuriance of Turfan is overwhelming.

Thanks to the *karez*, Turfan has a thriving agricultural community, and still presents the incongruous sight of fields and vineyards in the desert, a green island in a sea of sand. It is known in China as a prime source of grapes, dried in the flaming sun to make raisins, and in modern times, for wine.

However, Turfan's geographical situation was unique. Most of the other protectorates were substantially smaller – isolated oases, beacon towers and trading or mining towns, whose rulers were often torn in their allegiance between the Chinese and the Xiongnu. Both contending superpowers secured the loyalty of the desert 'kingdoms' by taking their children hostage, not necessarily a bad deal for the child, since these princelings got to see something of the world. By the late Han Dynasty, many of the rulers of the Silk Road kingdoms had spent at least part of their formative years in the capital of China, Luoyang.

Their deeds, as reported in the *Book of Later Han*, are limited to letter-writing and occasional battles. Their names are written in archaic but recognisable Chinese, which inevitably makes them sound as if they *were* Chinese. Far from it – the inhabitants of the desert kingdoms during the Han Dynasty appear to have been of Indian origin, worshipping Buddha, and speaking a language related to Sanskrit. There is no mention of the colour of their skin in the *Book of Later Han*, but there is hardly any mention of any other aspect of their appearance, either.

Fan Ye's accounts of 'battles' and 'armies' also often inflate the numbers. By 123 BC, the governor of Dunhuang was complaining to the Emperor that the Xiongnu were 'processing' further to the west. In other words, their annual nomadic wanderings were taking them into territory that the Chinese liked to think was theirs, and there was nobody around to stop them. The governor offered several options, ranging from sending an army of 5,000 men on a distant campaign to kill off the Xiongnu, to simply doing nothing, which was sure to eventually result in a refugee crisis as locals fled east to China, quite possibly followed by the Xiongnu themselves in search of new plunder.

The Chinese solution was relatively low-tech and low-intensity. An 'army' did head west, but it comprised 500 freed convicts, who were settled in a prominent position so that the Xiongnu faced heavier resistance next time they turned up. The Chinese called such military colonies *tuntian* ('stationed fields') – and hoped that they would not require provisioning, and would be able to operate far closer to the source of trouble. It was the first recorded example of a paramilitary element to the colonisation of Xinjiang that would extend, in one form or another, to the present day.

This seemed to do the trick, although it did not stop the people of the Western Regions fighting among themselves. In AD 129, the ruler of Khotan, in the south-west of the desert region, killed the ruler of the nearby oasis of Keriya and put his own son in charge. The new ruler sent tribute to the Chinese Emperor, but was thwarted by the governor of Dunhuang, who pointed out that one vassal of the Emperor had killed another, and that the Emperor could not condone it. Accordingly, the Emperor ordered Keriya restored to its rightful rulers. Khotan refused.

It took three years to sort the mess out, with much of the preamble taken up with the months of communication required to simply ascertain that the Emperor's order had been countermanded. Communication was particularly difficult with Khotan because the route from Dunhuang was impassable in summer, and only possible in winter when camels were able to carry spare water in the form of blocks of ice.

When justice did arrive, it was at the hands of yet another vassal, who lived even further away from the capital. On the order of the Emperor, which must have taken yet more months to reach him, the King of Kashgar marched out with a force of 20,000 men, or so he claimed, somehow multiplying his available manpower by a factor of ten. This force, likely to have been substantially smaller, was still large enough to wipe out the tin-pot general of Khotan. Several hundred

Khotanese men were beheaded, and the victorious men of Kashgar 'were allowed to plunder freely'. The son of the murdered king of Keriya was installed in his father's place and normality was, supposedly, restored, although a cynic might argue that the suzerainty of the Chinese had led to little more than a stamp of approval on another little desert war.

Nor did this resolution seem to stamp out local rivalries. Twenty years later, when a Chinese ambassador died of a 'carbuncle' in Khotan, the ruler of Keriya was swift to suggest to his bereaved son that the man had been poisoned. And so it went, on and on.

Ban Chao was originally sent west to chase away horsemen from the north, but also to establish a Chinese presence in the region to discourage any further incursions and local conflicts. When the expense of holding the desert kingdoms began to seem wastefully high (a recurring issue among rulers of the region ever since), many of the Chinese battalions were ordered to return home. Ban Chao, however, stayed on with only a few hundred men, cut off from direct supply and either seizing food or growing his own, shoring up loyal regimes friendly to China. He maintained a Chinese presence during an austere era when his emperor had all but given up, and would eventually return home full of tales of what he called the 'thirty-six kingdoms' of the desert region.

Ban Chao was heavily outnumbered. If the local oases could ever have stopped fighting among themselves and united against him, he would have been overwhelmed. During his sojourn in the Western Regions, one such alliance did threaten to arise, as the kings of Kashgar and Kucha hatched a scheme to have him killed. Feigning ignorance, Ban Chao invited the ruler of Kashgar to a banquet, only to tie him up and behead him, before murdering the ruler's entourage.

This was the first, but by no means last, disastrous dinner party in Xinjiang's history, where 'wars' were often fought and won at an intensely personal, tactical level. Allegiances were so fragile, and resources so scarce, that there are many similar tales of 'armies' dissipating like mist as soon as their general is taken out in similar surgical strikes. When we think of wars, our minds all too often imagine long columns of marching soldiers, or whole battalions of horsemen. But Ban Chao's victories were far more economical, equivalent in modern terms to a series of drive-by shootings, assassinations and simple threats. If 20 soldiers in the right place scared off a dozen Xiongnu horsemen at the right time, the Western Regions remained 'Chinese' for another season.

Inevitably, Ban Chao wondered what there was to the west of Kashgar, through the mountain passes. He formed an alliance with the Kushan Empire in what is now Afghanistan, a nation that may have comprised the remnants (or perhaps cousins) of the Tocharians who once lived by Lop Nur. Their ruler demanded a Chinese princess as part payment for military help in the region, but was refused. This, in itself, is suggestive of the imperial Chinese concept of the limits of its authority. Princesses were to be exchanged with true vassals and allies, which is to say, communities that would or could become 'Chinese', but there were limits, which seemed to stop at Kashgar.

The *Book of Later Han* records an expedition by an emissary of Ban Chao who set out in AD 97 to assess the legendary empire in the furthest west, which the Chinese called Da Qin, 'Great Qin.' The name is odd, and has confused even Chinese commentators. It may be a garbled reference to a particular place in the Roman Empire, although it is not clear where. Fan Ye made the unlikely suggestion that the people of the exotic west were tall and honest, a bit like the people of the Chinese state of Qin. But the term may have carried a more ominous implication. In the days of the Warring States, before China was unified, Qin was the name of its westernmost territory – a martially-minded, hard-headed soldier state that eventually conquered all the others. In calling the Roman Empire 'Great Qin', Chinese chroniclers may have been alluding to a distant threat, further west even than Qin, but potentially even more powerful.

The mission was thwarted partway, probably by wily Parthians who feared that an alliance between Rome and China would crush their own state, which lay between the empires. Instead, the explorer was told that Rome lay across a great sea that would take him three months to cross if he were lucky, or two years if the winds were against him. Perhaps some Parthian merchant hoped to sell him three years of provisions for such a great undertaking, although it seems more likely that he made it to somewhere on the Indian coast, perhaps the Parthian princedoms of Sind, where he received a garbled explanation of the need to wait for the monsoon winds. Whatever the reason, he turned back, reporting that in the west there were many 'precious and marvellous things', but he had not seen them. To help out a little, Fan Ye offered his own list of Roman marvels, which included shaven heads, crystal tableware (glass) and 'kings who are not permanent' but chosen from a list of the most worthy.

If such reportage seems doubtful or outright apocryphal, we might forgive them for having no other information about particular parts of the world. Historians and novelists, for obvious reasons, are liable to get particularly animated about possible contacts between Romans and Chinese, although certain travellers claiming to have come from 'Rome' might have actually been chancers picking an unverifiable home address in their dealings with local potentates.

Fan Ye, for example, also recorded that an embassy had supposedly arrived from Rome itself in AD 166. But reading between the lines of his account of these visitors from the 'King of Great Qin', everything starts to sound very suspicious. They claimed to have come from the land ruled by a man called *Andun* – if they meant Antoninus Pius, he had already been dead for several years, and had been succeeded by his adopted son Marcus Aurelius. Let us give them the benefit of the doubt, and assume that Andun is a corrupted reference to the Antonine *family*. But these supposed ambassadors turned up far away from the Silk Road, on the coast of what is now Vietnam, and if they are the source of the *Book of Later Han*'s information on Rome, they seem to have known little more than the vaguest general facts about Syria and Egypt, and very little about Rome itself, which was apparently at the far end of a bridge that stretched for dozens of kilometres from Egypt. They presented 'tribute' of 'elephant tusks, rhinoceros horn and turtle shell.' None of these commodities sound particularly Roman, nor did they much impress the Chinese, who regarded them as singularly undistinguished. Fan Ye gives the official line, which is that the embassy from Great Qin seemed rather shabby, and perhaps rumours of the empire's splendour had been gross exaggerations. He even notes, with the faint signs of a disdainfully raised eyebrow, that this distant civilisation apparently makes cloth from the cocoons of 'wild' silkworms. He does not appear to have considered that the 'ambassadors' were not official diplomats at all, but a bunch of Indian sailors trying it on. Instead, he ends his section on Rome with a literary wave of the hand in exasperation, saying that he has heard of 'many other peculiar and bizarre things that I will not record.'

Silk reaches Khotan

Roman authors were just as imprecise. Pliny the Elder also appears to have recorded a garbled description of Xinjiang in his *Natural History*. 'We come to… desert tracts tenanted by wild beasts, until we reach a chain of mountains which runs up to the sea.' There is no sea, of course, but Pliny means the mountains of Tibet are the edge of all that is interesting, and beyond them, he assumes, there is nothing but the all-circling Ocean believed to mark the edge of the world. North of the Himalayas, however, halfway along their length, Pliny records human inhabitants, whom he calls 'the Seres, most famous for the *wool* that is found in their forests.'

The chances are that Pliny was referring to Khotan, the largest oasis in the Tarim basin, which was favourably located between two rushing rivers of snowmelt. Like most Xinjiang rivers, they eventually peter out in the middle of nowhere, but in Khotan they were full enough to provide irrigation for a substantial population. Musk deer roamed the nearby hills, where jade could be found in the mines. Some distance from the oasis, it was possible to pan for gold or scavenge for jade pebbles in the river bed, which cannot have hurt the fortunes of the local residents. Most importantly of all, Khotan had somehow obtained the necessary materials to cultivate silk, supposedly as the result of a marriage between the local ruler and a Chinese princess.

At some time in the 1st century AD, this unnamed woman had been sent to Khotan, perhaps to keep the ruler sweet for the continued provision of jade for the Chinese capital – another victim of the trade in princesses. According to legend, she was told that if she wished to continue wearing silk, she would need to bring the wherewithal to make it, which she did by smuggling silkworm eggs and mulberry seeds in her headdress. The story is unlikely – whoever this fashionable lady was, she would have needed to wait a generation for the trees to grow and for the worms to breed, but there must be a germ of truth in it, since Khotan was soon a known source not only of silk, but also of paper made from mulberry bark.

Khotan became so powerful by the mid-1st century that, according to the *Book of Later Han*, it 'became arrogant', and became the first territory on the Silk Road to strike its own coinage, with Chinese numerals on one side, and an inscription giving the name of each 'king' in (Indian) Prakrit script on the other. However, Khotan does not seem to have wanted to rock the boat – the presence of Chinese numerals suggests that the coins were intended for trade within the Chinese sphere of influence, and the King of Khotan was sufficiently keen to cultivate the Chinese Emperor that he sent him a live elephant in AD 202. The mind boggles as to how it could have reached Luoyang from the edges of the desert.

Buddhism reaches China

After the fall of the Han Dynasty, China was not properly reunited for several hundred years. North China fell under the control of nomad invaders, who were eventually Sinicised as the 'Northern Wei' Dynasty. While the new rulers did not make much effort to exercise control in the Western Regions, they certainly knew about them, and about the trails that led through them to exotic foreign realms, as recorded in their own dynastic histories.

Korla, in particular, was singled out in the *Book of Wei*, largely because of the discovery not far from the oasis of a magical substance that could be found oozing from the ground. It supposedly had the power to restore lost hair and teeth, and if taken as a potion by the sick, it cured all disease. It was most notable, however, for its flammable properties, and today is better known as *petroleum*.

But oil was not the most incredible new discovery in the Western Regions. There had been talk among travellers for centuries about a religious figure in India, whose worshippers were gradually arriving in the Western Regions. There were rumours that the aging Ban Chao, returning to China shortly before his death, had brought 'statues of golden men' from his embassies beyond Kashgar.

In a legend not set down before the time of the Northern Wei, it was said that Ming Di, the father of the emperor who had sent Ban Chao west, had received visions in a dream of a god 'whose body shone like the sun,' flying through the air in front of his palace. The story reframes Ban Chao's travels in a new fashion – implying that the Chinese movement westwards was less about military strategy and more about a quest for enlightenment, and a search for more information on Buddha, said in China to have achieved immortality

– the best that the wording of the time could do to express the concept of enlightenment.

Precise dating for the arrival of Buddhism is impossible. There were certainly encounters between Chinese and Buddhists before the first recorded missionaries and preachers, but equally, many of the accounts of the earliest contacts were written long afterwards, and may have been endowed with more religious significance than was warranted. It is also difficult to be sure how Buddhist certain people were. Right up to the medieval period, the degree to which the Chinese understood Buddhism was questionable, reliant on several waves of translation of varying degrees of reliability.

Buddhism, however, was plainly on the rise in the Western Regions, and the large influxes of believers transformed many of the oases into ever more 'Indian' cities. Buddhism impacted China at every level of life. The Buddhist reluctance to take lives, even those of animals, would influence Chinese cuisine, reducing the former popularity of horse and dog meat in the diet, and vastly increasing the popularity of tofu. Tea, favoured by Buddhist monks for keeping themselves awake during prolonged periods of meditation, began to find favour with laymen.

People from all walks of life tried to buy religious merit by making donations that funded temples, statues, grottoes and other public works. This would eventually lead to massive installations designed to show off aristocratic generosity (see Gazetteer: Luoyang), and also thousands of minor and not-so-minor works of devotion all along the Silk Road, funded not only by nobles, but also by lowly travellers.

One of the most famous locations is where China proper meets the desert, at the 'blazing beacon' of Dunhuang, where travellers were apt to donate money either in gratitude for or in hope of a safe passage. This custom supposedly began in AD 353, when Lie Zun, a weary Buddhist traveller, stumbled upon the sand-worn cliffs, and believed that he saw an effulgent light in the sky from 1,000 Buddhas. Grateful to be within sight of civilisation, he commissioned the first, hesitant wall carving, initiating over a thousand years of pious masonry, which soon spread both east and west along the Silk Road, with similar 'thousand Buddha caves' springing up as far west as Kargilik (Yecheng) close to what is now the Indian border, and as far east as Luoyang, the sometime capital of China.

Kumarajiva (344–413) was the son of a man from the kingdom of Gandhara, in what is now Afghanistan and Pakistan, who settled in Kucha and married the sister of the local king – allegedly with great reluctance, but he was effectively forced to keep his holy genes going by breeding a new generation of scholar. Although born in Kucha, he spent three pre-teen years studying back in Gandhara, and by his early twenties had become a celebrated religious leader in Turfan, the easternmost outpost of the ancient Kushan empire. He was captured by Chinese soldiers during one of the periodic shifts in power in the region, and became something of a prize among squabbling Chinese upstart dynasties. Eventually, he was forcibly wrested from the hands of his non-Buddhist captors by a pro-Buddhist Chinese pretender, and brought to Chang'an (modern Xi'an), where he was feted as a great teacher. Legend has it that when he arrived, he was leading a white horse that bore priceless copies of Indian scriptures. For this reason, several Buddhist holy sites in China are named *Baima* ('White Horse'), such as the White Horse Temple in Luoyang and the White Horse Pagoda in Dunhuang.

Kumarajiva, who had learnt Chinese in captivity, was wonderfully disparaging about earlier editions of sacred texts, commenting that reading the current translations was like eating rice that someone had already chewed. He also had a better acquaintance than most with what had *not* been translated, and revealed that there was more than one school of Buddhism. Until his arrival, the Chinese had been fed a version of Buddhism that elevated the role of holy men at the expense of commoners. Kumarajiva initiated a new phase of translation, concentrating on his own interests in the Mahayana school, which notably offered salvation to everyone, not merely those who became monks. He refused to adopt the usual Chinese practice of finding local equivalents, which had tainted earlier translations by turning them into bastardised versions of Daoist or Confucian philosophy. Instead, he oversaw new translations that more carefully rendered the meaning of the originals – to this day, many Buddhist terms in Chinese show echoes of his Gandharan accent in their pronunciation. He exerted a great influence on the local ruler Yao Xing, who had formerly proclaimed himself emperor, but had downgraded himself to a mere 'king' after hearing of grim omens and portents suggesting that Heaven disapproved of his actions. Supposedly because of Kumarajiva, Yao Xing ceased his realm's military expansion, and promoted Buddhism, to the extent that an alleged 90 per cent of his people converted; this claim is likely to reflect the Mahayana leanings of Kumarajiva, which promised enlightenment to everyone, and not merely the religious elite.

By the time Kumarajiva died in 413, he had translated many of the landmark texts of Buddhism, including the Diamond Sutra and the Lotus Sutra. For 1,000 years after him, Chinese literature was flooded with a tidal wave of other Buddhist mantras, documents and manuals, introducing hundreds of new terms from Indian languages, as well as narratives, heroes and stories derived, sometimes at an almost incomprehensible distance, from Indian originals. A statue of Kumarajiva stands today outside the Kizil caves (see Gazetteer: Kucha), although his appearance is entirely artistic licence and guesswork.

Not every emperor had Yao Xing's supposed sense of duty and piety. A hundred years later, another monk from the West would walk into Luoyang and seek an audience with one of Yao Xing's successors. The monk's name was Bodhidharma, although there are conflicting accounts of his origin, which site him either in Persia or, more likely, South India. He faced an emperor of the upstart Liang Dynasty, who claimed to be a devout Buddhist, but whose donations and activities seemed more to suggest a rich man with a desire to buy his way into paradise.

Hearing that Bodhidharma was a respected holy man, the Emperor asked him how much merit he had accumulated through his various donations to temples, payments for sutra-copying, and other good deeds. Bodhidharma answered with a shrug that the Emperor's gifts were nice, but didn't amount to much 'merit'. Taken aback by this, the emperor blustered and demanded to know what, then, was the noble truth he should be seeking. Bodhidharma didn't think there was such a thing as a 'noble truth'. Just nothing, really. Bristling, the Emperor demanded to know just who the hell he was talking to. Bodhidharma shrugged again, and said he didn't really know.

It was not the most productive of meetings. Bodhidharma was kicked out, and it was only then that one of the Emperor's advisers suggested that they had just witnessed a true incarnation of the Goddess of Mercy herself. Realising he might have missed a trick, the Emperor ordered for someone to bring Bodhidharma back, but he was told that wild horses wouldn't drag the monk back to him.

Bodhidharma took up residence in the mountains a few dozen miles away at the Shaolin Temple (see Gazetteer: Luoyang), where he continued to confound orthodox Buddhists by staring at the wall of his cave for nine years. His influence, however, was wide-ranging. He supposedly advised the local monks that they were getting a bit flabby, and came up with a training regime that would keep them fighting fit... the first stirrings of Shaolin Kung Fu. His nihilistic belief system, which cast aside much of the wealth and material acquisitions of the monasteries and priests who had flourished in silk-rich China, stripping it down to a brutal search for truth in nothingness, became the influential sect of *Chan* Buddhism. Today, it is better known internationally by its Japanese pronunciation: *Zen*.

There is another story of Bodhidharma. Late in the 6th century, Songyun, an emissary from China, ran into the old monk in the mountains outside Kashgar. His work complete, Bodhidharma was on his way home to India, carrying a sandal. Songyun reported this sighting to incredulous colleagues on his return, since Bodhidharma had died three years before. But when they opened his tomb near Luoyang, there was nothing inside it but a single sandal, the other half of the pair. It is for this reason that many representations of Bodhidharma in Chinese temples show him proffering footwear, as if he has just found something in your size.

CENTURIES AFTER BUDDHISM first took root in China, it can be difficult to remember that it was once regarded as a foreign import. Competition from rival religions, particularly Islam, has eroded part of its legacy in the cities of the Silk Road, while the purges of the Cultural Revolution in the 20th century destroyed many old sites in China itself. But even in the People's Republic of China, which classes all religions as 'superstitions', Buddhist temples are everywhere. It is hard to imagine a time when a traveller would not have found one in every oasis on the Silk Road, difficult to conceive of a distant day when there were no carvings to be found in what are now justifiably called 'Thousand Buddha' caves from Kashgar to Dunhuang. The Buddhism to be found in Xinjiang today is thoroughly Chinese, with only the occasional bit of Sanskrit on a prayer wheel or a temple document to remind the traveller that it came from far away. It is difficult to conceive of the entire religious *cities* in the desert recounted by the pilgrim Faxian (337–422), with monks numbered in the tens of thousands and grand processions of wheeled, gilded shrines, preceded by queens and princesses throwing flowers.

4

The Tang Dynasty (618–907)

THERE IS A STATUE in the middle of a road junction in western Xi'an. It sits in a park of low hedges, shielded from passers-by by multiple lanes of traffic, and is attended at all times by the hoots, beeps and roars of the surrounding traffic. It is carved in brutal, impressionistic sandstone, its figures flowing one into the other in a giant unified sculpture longer than a Greyhound bus.

It depicts a camel-train attended by outriders on horses, the beasts of burden weighed down with trade goods for the west. The sculpture itself is a yellowish hue that matches the sands of the desert ahead, although it is positioned in front of a highly stylised gate in gunmetal grey, the same colour as the real city walls a few blocks behind it. A merchant sits proudly on one of the double-humped camels, and a guardsman brings up the rear on a horse. There is a bearded, hook-nosed man who seems to have retained a few Greek genes from the far west – perhaps a Sogdian – who perches in uneasy concentration atop his camel. Beside him is a long-moustached Chinese scholar on a horse, smirking thoughtfully over his shoulder at the city he has just left behind.

At the very head of the long train, there is a large bull-camel, heavily laden with silks and carpets. At its feet, a watchdog snuffles distractedly at the ground. Leading the camel by a rope is a bearded man in trousers, wearing a skullcap, staring dreamily out towards the long road ahead, to the distant west. He is, deliberately and unmistakeably, a Muslim. If China has asserted its hegemony and authority in Kashgar with its proud statue of Ban Chao, then the Silk Road asserts its own presence here in what was once the Chinese capital, 3,000 kilometres away.

The sculpture is called *The Start of the Silk Road*, a shot fired in the ongoing rivalry between Xi'an and nearby Luoyang, both former capitals of China, and hence both with a claim to be the place where the Silk Road began. Xi'an's monumental assertion is not far from an archaeological site, the great Western Market, where traders from the Western Regions would offload their wares after the long trek from the desert. It is as good a starting place as any, and certainly represented a major site on the Silk Road during the Middle Ages.

CHINA WAS FORCED BACK into a unified entity for the first time in several centuries by the short-lived Sui Dynasty (581–618) – a family of ruthless power-mongers who were toppled in barely a generation after having worn down the populace with foreign wars, heavy tax and corvée labour. The Sui were overthrown by their own cousins and in-laws, who went on to form the longer-lived Tang Dynasty (618–907). Largely glossed over in the Chinese history books are the non-Chinese amongst the great Tang families, many of whom were, if not foreigners, then certainly tainted with hints of exotic western attitudes. Their women sometimes rode out scandalously unveiled, wearing *trousers*. Their relationships with the horse-breeding pasture regions made them accomplished horsemen, and gave them a certain sense of commonality with the Turks. One group of Tang princes legendarily took on a Turkic polo team and beat them at their own game.

The Tang Dynasty's early hero was its second emperor, Taizong, who as a young warrior won the empire at the point of a sword in the name of his father. The father was soon nudged off into exile as a Buddhist monk, while the far more pro-active Taizong consolidated what is arguably one of imperial China's pinnacles.

Taizong was hugely ambitious. He had murdered his elder brother in a dispute over the throne, and was 'offered' the crown by a father who was plainly petrified of what he might do next. But where the Sui Dynasty had merely appeased the Turks in the west with bribes and brides, Taizong launched a series of military campaigns against them. Legend has it that he once rode out into the middle of the steppe and challenged the Turkic ruler to a duel. More prosaically, it was also Taizong who took advantage of internal squabbles among the Turks, dispatching a Chinese army to intercede in a civil war, and emerging as the overall victor.

One of the reasons Taizong's empire achieved such greatness was his dual status. Chinese accounts remember him as the second Tang emperor, and occasionally admit that he was also the kingmaker who won the throne on his father's behalf. Far fewer note that as well as being the Emperor of China, he was also acclaimed as the Heavenly Qaghan, which is to say as the grand Khan of the Turkic steppe nomads. The Chinese hold over the Turks did not long outlast Taizong, but he created a brief respite in the constant struggles on the borders.

The peace ushered in new trade and new commodities on the Silk Road. Spinach arrived from Nepal as a tributary gift from the local king in 647, the native word *palinga* transmuted in Chinese into *bolengcai*. Jasmine flowers, or *mallika* in Sanskrit, arrived from the west as a hair decoration for ladies of the Tang Dynasty, who called them *molihua*. They were soon added to hot water to make jasmine tea. Lemons, or *leymun* in Persian, arrived in China as *limeng*.

The Tang Dynasty is also associated with a particular kind of ceramic that clogs many of the souvenir markets of the Silk Road – look for double-chinned dancing girls, horses, scary temple guardians and merchants leading camels, all in a distinctive, 'egg-and-spinach' colour scheme of cream, green, brown and occasional blue. This is *sancai* (tricolour) ware, a lead-glazed pottery that is fired with copper (for the greens), iron (for the browns) and cobalt (for the blues). The cream base is the naked original clay.

Green-fired pottery had been used since the Han Dynasty in China, and there is evidence that *sancai* itself slightly predated the Tang period with which it is largely associated. Fired at a lower temperature than other ceramics, *sancai* ware is a common find among Tang-period grave goods, and the metallic origin of its pigments ensure that many artefacts have retained their colour over the intervening millennium. In a triumph of minimalist branding, decorative wall panels at Xi'an's modern Bell Tower metro station are a wash of *sancai* colours, evoking the region's past with what first appears to be nothing more than a chaotic swirl of paints.

Tripitaka

The most famous Silk Road traveller of Taizong's time was the man who defied him. Xuanzang, better known as Tripitaka (602–664), was a monk who suspected that despite the efforts of generations of translators, the sacred scrolls of Buddhism, as practised in China, were still a jumble of haphazard half-translations and misremembered sutras. Unsurprisingly, the hazardous, long journey between India and China across the mountains and desert, and a reliance on translations from Sanskrit into Chinese, often via intermediary languages, left much open to misinterpretation. Encouraged by a dream, the 27-year-old Tripitaka undertook a journey to the west, despite a proclamation by Emperor Taizong that nobody should risk such a journey while Turkic insurgents occupied many key districts.

Tripitaka's quest for knowledge ended up taking 17 years. He drifted from monastery to palace to desert tent, lurching from feast to famine and back again, sometimes feted in kingly processions, sometimes sneaking around by night to avoid hostile soldiers. Asides in his book *Great Tang Records on the Western Regions*, which he dictated to one his disciples on his return, point to a thriving Buddhist culture across the desert, with some monasteries inhabited by literally thousands of monks. Tripitaka's account also points to the slippery nature of allegiance at the time. When he stopped off in Hami, a town famous for its melons, he found himself in a region loyal to the nomads. Mere months after he left, Hami appears in Chinese records as a 'Chinese' town once more. In Turfan, he was welcomed by a proud king who boasted of his vassal status to the Chinese emperor – but the same ruler was friendly enough with the Turkic khan to write a letter of transit asking for Tripitaka to be kept safe in the khan's territory. Such local pragmatism might have been a realistic way of dealing with distant potentates, but it eventually backfired. The same king supposedly died of fright in 640, at the approach of a vengeful Chinese army, who marched into his territory to assert their authority once and for all.

Not far from Turfan, the sandstone foothills of the Tianshan Mountains stand barren and pockmarked, the cliff faces a vivid red against the sands, slashed with thousands of vertical striations. Seen from the desert, through shimmering daylight heat-haze, the hills seem to be on fire, leading the Chinese to name them *huoyan shan*, or the Flaming Mountains. According to local legend, a dragon was sliced into eight pieces near the hills, its blood gouging the most distinctive of the gullies. But Tripitaka's interest in the region was more likely to have been centred at Bezeklik, at the base of the mountains, where grottoes celebrating the life of Buddha were carved into the hillsides above a dramatic river gorge. In later centuries, the grottoes would grow ever larger in number, until they became known as the Thousand Buddha Caves. Or rather, one of the Thousand Buddha Caves – sacred sites with a 'thousand' Buddhas in them are relatively common along the Silk Road, and the name recurs in several places.

Few of them at Bezeklik, however, survive today. Many were defaced by Muslim vandals. Others were carted off by German archaeologists. Only a few scattered remnants are left of the originals, in foreign museums, often a world away from modern Bezeklik itself. But in extant photographs and restorations of the murals, there are tantalising glimpses of Xinjiang's multiethnic medieval Buddhism, with images of red-haired, blue-eyed monks teaching yellow-skinned Chinese.

Such a sight was plainly not all that odd in medieval Xinjiang. Not far to the west, Tripitaka had an audience with the King of Kucha, who had similar colouring to the Indo-European monks in the wall paintings and ruled over what was then the largest and most prosperous kingdom of the desert. 'This country,' wrote Tripitaka's scribe, 'yielded millet, wheat, rice, grapes, pomegranates, and plenty of pears, plums, peaches and apricots. It produced also gold copper, iron, lead and tin: its climate was temperate and the people had honest ways; their writing was taken from that of India, with some differences...'

It is sometimes easy to forget that Kucha, like other 'desert kingdoms', was at the edge of the Taklamakan, not in its midst. More confusing is the distinctly 'Indian' nature of Kucha, when oases to the east and west of it had clearer Turkic or Chinese influences. But it seems that Kucha was 'closer' to India at the time, thanks to the phantom rivers that periodically appeared in the desert. The rivers of the Taklamakan, of course, have always been unreliable fixtures, seasonally variable and with courses subject to change without notice. But it seems that Kucha may have been noticeably 'Indian' because, despite its remote location, it was at one end of a route that had its terminus at the mountain passes to India itself. At times, the snowmelt torrents that rushed into the desert at Kucha in the north and Khotan in the south were fast and deep enough to carry boats. Even though they tailed away in the centre, a little portage and heavy lifting in the middle would allow a boat to effectively sail across the desert. It is not possible today, with so many irrigation projects diverting water before it reaches the sand. But the technique of sailing across the desert was tested and proved by Sven Hedin as recently as 1899, when he undertook an 82-day trip that took him from Yarkand in the south-west to Korla near Urumqi. On occasion, the river was nine feet deep, a boisterous, buffeting rapid that was less sailed than endured. At other times, it trickled into nothingness amid steaming mudflats, forcing Hedin's 30 men to lug their barge in the heat to the next stream. But the Yarkand River connected, in some navigable sense, with the rivers of Aqsu and Muzart that flowed down from the northern mountains into the Tarim.

Sitting at a higher altitude in the foothills of the mountains, and washed by constant streams of glacial snowmelt, sometimes bearing chunks of tumbling ice, the oasis was nowhere near as parched as one might imagine. Even today it is surrounded by vistas of green hills and pasture, although one does not have to travel far out of the inhabited area for the fields to grind down into scrubland and barren pillars of rock salt.

However, Tripitaka was far from impressed with the Kucha monarch, who he regarded as a puppet of his ministers. After Tripitaka's visit, Kucha sent a gift of horses to the Tang emperor, but also proclaimed allegiance to the Turks. There are a lot of these proclamations in Tripitaka's account, which often makes the reader wonder if, despite the protestations that he was travelling without Taizong's approval, he was really functioning as an emissary of the Tang court.

The Christians

Just off the Street of the Calligraphers in modern Xi'an, in the gardens of a Confucian temple, you will find the Forest of Steles. It is a collection of stone tablets from all around the region, including proclamations and gravestones, and great mazes made of slabs carved with the Chinese classics, once available for scholars to take rubbings of the approved texts of Confucius, Mencius and other great philosophers. Tucked down one of its avenues is a slab of stone, little different on the surface from the hundreds of others. But at its top, in clear Chinese, it reads: 'A Memorial of the Propagation in China of the Luminous Religion of Great Qin' – a direct reference to the semi-mythical land of Rome.

The 'Luminous Religion' is Christianity, brought to China sometime around AD 640 by monks from the Church of the East, a Syriac sect of Christianity often referred to (although not by its own believers) as the Nestorians. The 'Nestorian Tablet' commemorates this arrival, of a religion which certainly flourished for a time on the Silk Road, but seems to have died out. Centuries later, when emperors scoffed that Christianity could not possibly be true, as its God had waited so long to reveal himself to China, some missionaries archly noted that China had missed its first chance.

The 640s were very eventful in Chinese religious affairs. Tripitaka was back with his sacred Buddhist scrolls, and here were a bunch of strange-faced Persian and Syrians, claiming that their religion, previously unheard of, was the true faith. Emperor Taizong did not seem fussed by this, and granted them welcome residence, proclaiming in 638 that the Christians were not to be harmed, and asking their leader, Alopen, to translate several Christian scriptures for his library. These are thought to be the so-called *Jesus Sutras*, Chinese documents that reflect the long journey of Christianity itself along the oases of the Silk Road. The twin dragons at the apex of the stele, cradling a giant pearl, are symbols of imperial sanction, and were likely put there to discourage persecution.

It is hard to tell how seriously Christianity was taken by the Chinese, and how much it was regarded as a new fad, or possibly another foreign sect to be appraised like a rare curio. The *Jesus Sutras* are a case in point – even their name is a translation fudge, using a term that in Chinese is respectful and scriptural, but usually used among Buddhists for the words of Buddha, and hence implying to the inattentive worshipper that Christianity is some sort of Buddhist sect. The Chinese language is forced to decide between adopting the meaning of foreign terms, or some imitation of their sound. Hence, the Messiah becomes *Mishisuo*, which means 'The Poem That Was Lost', and the Holy Spirit somehow becomes *Liangfeng*, 'The Cool Breeze' – a welcome concept in desert oases but already drifting far from the original sense of the name.

Nestorian Christianity had many odd elements. Worship was commenced with the striking of a wooden gong, or *semantron*, and prayer was conducted seven times a day, to a God that went by the name of *Alohe*. It is, perhaps, easy to see how the later practices of Islam, for example multiple prayer-times, might seem to some Nestorians to be mere twists of interpretation. Certainly, it seems that across many parts of Asia, the rapid spread of Islam had less to do with violence and compulsion, and more to do with persuasion and familiarity. While Nestorians faced persecution from other Christians, they were welcomed as guests in Islamic communities, where doubtless, within a few generations, their children might shift to Islam for reasons of familiarity, genuine faith or just a simple desire to avoid the extra tax paid by infidels.

Taizong's pet Christians flourished under his reign, although it is unclear how much effect their religion had on the local population. There are 21 priests recorded, although all of them seem to have been Persians, rather than locals. It seems likely, as one Japanese archaeologist has suggested, that the priests of Xi'an ministered to Christian believers among foreign mercenaries *garrisoned* in Xi'an, rather than any sizeable population of local believers.

Their 'temple', the ruins of which are still to be found on the outskirts of modern Xi'an, was more of a chapel within the grounds of a much larger Daoist monastery. The Nestorian Tablet itself was seemingly carved to mark the centenary of Alopen's arrival, although it too was knocked down and buried around 845, most likely during the religious persecutions of the later Tang emperor, Wuzong. Interest in exotic foreign religions, it seems, was a feature of the lavish, multiethnic Tang pinnacle, while serving the religious needs of foreign believers was a feature of the tumult as the dynasty passed its peak and leant increasingly on mercenary cavalrymen from further to the west. As the dynasty thrashed about in its death throes, culture turned inward, bigoted and fearful, rounding on all 'foreign' religions, not only Christianity, but also Buddhism, whose monks were ordered to return to lay life, on pain of death.

The jewelled surnames

Beginning in AD 648, Tang Dynasty officials began garrisoning strategic points in the Western Regions. The 'Four Garrisons' of Kucha, Kashgar, Khotan and Karashahr functioned as the base of the Protectorate General to Pacify the West – though some sources from the period refer instead to this 'Pacified West' or *Anxi* as if it were a region in its own right. This term also suggests that the west *had* been pacified, which was somewhat economical with the truth, as for the first decade after their establishment, the garrison towns were lost to the Turks, and shortly afterwards they were taken over by the Tibetans. As in the Han Dynasty, the Western Regions showed up on Chinese maps as firm possessions, even though they were more often than not hotly contested.

'Tang' settlements in the Tarim Basin also carry within their name the implication that the settlers came from China. The truth was sometimes far stranger; many of the soldiers and settlers who brought Chinese culture back to the region were outlanders themselves. When Persia fell to the Arabs in the 7th century, thousands of refugees fled eastward through the Pamir Mountains and into Chinese territory. Among them was Prince Peroz, a young son of the last Persian emperor Yazdgerd III. Peroz arrived in Chang'an in 670 and asked for aid against the Arabs. The emperor at the time was officially Taizong's son Gaozong, although since Gaozong had suffered a debilitating stroke a decade earlier, decision-making was largely in the hands of his charismatic wife, known to posterity by her later title, the Empress Wu. Although Wu allowed many thousands of Persian refugees to settle in the Tarim Basin, she also did what she could to keep Peroz's interests focused outwards. The Persian prince was given a martial title and the nominal stewardship of a new marchland in what is now Afghanistan, which the Chinese renamed the Area Command of Persia. He spent over 20 years living on this frontier, and presumably skirmishing with his Arab enemies, before either he or his son (the Tang dynastic annals are a little foggy on the details) returned in the time of Wu's son to pronounce the task hopeless.

Peroz's son Narsieh adopted the surname Li, from that of the ruling house of the Tang Dynasty, and settled with thousands of his people among the oases of the Silk Road, adding yet more variation to the already diverse gene pool. For centuries afterwards, certain villages on the Silk Road were known as 'abodes of the western prince', and the residents were popularly said to have something exotic about them – different coloured eyes, or a more prominent nose.

Sometimes, it is possible to tell the origins of Chinese with western ancestry simply by their surnames, since many of the foreigners who took up residency in China soon adopted Chinese names to blend in. Some of these 'jewelled surnames' included:

An, for families from Bukhara
Cao, for families from Kabudhan
He, for families from Kushaniyah
Kang, for families from Samarkand

Mi, for families from Panjikent
Shi, for families from Shahrisabz
Shi (a different one), for families from Tashkent

Not for the first time, the Chinese considered whether it was in their interests to stop interfering in the Western Regions, and to leave them to fester. At the end of the 7th century Empress Wu's most fearless minister, Di Renjie (better known to posterity as the inspiration for the detective Judge Dee) strongly advised her to cut her losses on the western frontier. A Turkic khan was demanding land and tribute at the edge of China, and the adviser saw it as the thin end of the wedge. He noted that the Chinese currently had to put up with high maintenance costs, insanely long and precarious lines of communication, and all for what? A big desert with a few wells in it, and a distant border with hostile neighbours. Surely, he argued, it would be far better to just abandon the Western Regions, and trim China's borders back to Dunhuang? Then, the inhospitable desert would work to China's advantage, forcing any potential invaders to waste *their* time and energies crossing a place where 'not a hair of grass would grow.'

Empress Wu, however, refused to listen, preferring to keep the borders of China at the same maximum extent achieved centuries earlier by Ban Chao. The 8th century saw the pinnacle of the Tang Dynasty's power, and of the Silk Road's influence on China. The century began in a whirl of palace intrigues among the children of Empress Wu, before matters were settled with great and brutal finality by her grandson, who led a palace coup in 710, and was installed as Emperor Xuanzong in 712. Xuanzong's reign was the longest in the Tang period, establishing continuity of traditions and institutions for 43 prosperous years.

During this time, the Silk Road enjoyed a golden age, at least in terms of safety. This, however, had the ironic effect of potentially reducing the volume of material transported along it. In ancient times, the prospect of bandits led caravans to seek safety in large numbers, with vast trains of up to 600 camels, guarded by an entire company of cavalry, but the Tang peace gave merchants in the mid-7th century a far greater degree of confidence. Accordingly, surviving references to caravans after the conquest of the Four Garrisons of Anxi allude to groups amounting to little more than a few guys and a couple of donkeys.

In the Western Regions, the Tang Dynasty squabbled and skirmished with Tibetan and new Muslim enemies. Beyond the Pamir Mountains, dozens of Indian and Afghan princedoms established diplomatic relations with the Tang emperor, suggesting, at least to the credulous authors of the dynastic chronicles, that they had accepted a position as vassal states of the Chinese. Even the ruler of distant Samarkand, buoyed up and breathless after hearing one of Tripitaka's sermons in 631, had sent an unsuccessful petition to be accepted as a Chinese vassal, and had been fobbed off with a proclamation of friendship. The region had certainly been favourable towards China for a generation, particularly in the aftermath of the occupation of Prince Peroz, but the extent to which hill tribes and local strongmen in Central Asia saw themselves as part of a Chinese 'empire' is debatable. It is more likely that they simply blew with the political wind, finding in a strong Tang military presence a reason to pay homage to an emperor they would never see, until such time as Muslim or Tibetan forces presented a strong case to offer allegiance in another direction. Meanwhile, the selfsame military presence of the Tang forces was draining vast amounts of resources. The warning of Judge Dee to Empress Wu had not been misplaced – the Tang Dynasty's foray into the west had created expensive garrisoning responsibilities. Nor were the garrisons anywhere near self-sufficient; taxation on the scant local population paid for barely 9 per cent of the expense of having a garrison in the first place, forcing the Tang emperors to subsidise the military presence with payment from their own coffers, inevitably sent west in the form of silk. By the 740s, the combined Four Garrisons of Anxi were costing the emperors 900,000 bolts of silk a year.

An army largely comprising Turkic and Persian allies of the Tang won several victories in the far west, but was decisively defeated in 751 at the Battle of Talas in what is now Kyrgyzstan. The 'Chinese' force, led by a Korean general and dominated by soldiers from the 'barbarian' borderlands, was beaten not only by the resolve of its foes from the Abbasid Caliphate, but also by disorder in the ranks, when several units switched sides.

The Battle of Talas was not regarded at the time as a key moment in Central Asian history. In hindsight, we know that the Chinese would not fight further to the west, but it was a relatively minor incident, and both sides expected a rematch. We also know that events back at the capital would lead to the Chinese soldiers being recalled closer to home. Talas was the last time that the Tang Dynasty had the military wherewithal on the frontier to challenge Islam. Although there was no physical Abbasid invasion of China, the lands west of Kashgar would be *culturally* lost to China. For generations, the region had been slowly favouring Chinese culture and Chinese contacts. Now, as Chinese influence ebbed back towards the east, the region drifted ever closer to Muslim ideals, norms and culture. The Battle of Talas marked the end of China west of the Pamirs, but also the firm beginning of Islamic influence in that region.

Supposedly, the battle also transformed the Middle East, and subsequently Europe, by introducing the Muslim world to Chinese paper. While undoubtedly some paper artefacts had made it along the Silk Road in years past, Talas is believed to have resulted in Chinese captives introducing their captors to paper-making. In using wood pulp rather than hard-to-find papyrus, and with an absorbency that made printing far easier than on expensive and ink-repelling parchment or vellum, paper was a medium with truly transformational potential. Its impact has led the scholar Jonathan M Bloom to playfully question if we should not call the trade route a Paper Road rather than a Silk Road, since silk, for all its legendary properties and value, is little more than a commodity, whereas paper initiated a revolution that changed the world for centuries to come, making knowledge itself replicable and affordable.

The tragedy of Yang Guifei

Back in the capital at Chang'an, the aging Xuanzong had found other things to occupy him. Asides in dynastic annals point to a growing interest in the good life, as the old warrior enjoyed the spoils of the Silk Road: Persian grapes, transplanted to Turfan and tramped into wine; petals of the desert rose, plucked and strewn in baths; silk robes draped on the scrubbed body by dutiful servants... all these things were to be found at the Huaqing hot springs outside Chang'an. It was there, so the story goes, that Xuanzong, mourning the death of his favourite concubine, caught sight of Yang Yuhuan.

Yang Yuhuan was legendarily one of the most beautiful women in Chinese history. She came from old money, with an ancestor who had been a powerful official in a previous dynasty, but who had backed the wrong contender for the throne in the days of the early Tang. She had also married into the imperial family, wedding one of Xuanzong's sons at the age of 16. Xuanzong wanted her for himself, and took her as his new favourite, elevating her to the newly created position of *Guifei*, or Imperial Consort.

The 'love story' of Yang Guifei and Emperor Xuanzong, one of the big iconic heritage narratives in modern Xi'an, is regularly likened by Chinese tour guides and brochures to that of Romeo and Juliet. This is a remarkably ham-fisted comparison, which only serves to demonstrate how thin on the ground actual stories of romantic love are in China. Yang Guifei was in her early twenties when she caught her father-in-law's eye. Xuanzong was at least 52 when he decided that he had to have her, and curtly ordered his son to give her up, spiriting her away for a nominal period as a Daoist nun in order to conceal any impropriety (as if), before smuggling her back into the palace as his new bedmate.

Nobody comes out of this story particularly well. There are occasional attempts to plead mitigating circumstances – that Xuanzong was distraught by the death of his favourite concubine – as if the late lady's son was not grieving himself, and just about to have his wife stolen from him. The whole 'love story' comes across as ridiculous and rather perverse.

Behind the scenes, it also points to the fervid politicking that characterised much of the early Tang Dynasty. The names that enter the historical record are the generals and the emperors, with the occasional wife, concubine or celebrity scattered among them. Enduring throughout, and much harder to see, are those old, rich families who continued to prosper while dynasties came and went. Regardless of what happened on the battlefields, sealing the fates of the Sui and the Tang, the Southern Qi and the Northern Wei, there were bystanders who simply waited to discover who the new ruler was. So long as you were never associated with a failed rebellion, so long as you paid your dues and kept your head down, your family might bear witness to a dozen short-lived dynasties, only coming to the notice of chroniclers when a particularly pretty daughter married a prince, or when one of your less idle sons became a minister.

The old families were often connected to Buddhist or Daoist monasteries, to which they had nominally donated their lands in avoidance of tax. Even more were deeply connected with the silk trade. Since it took many decades for mulberry trees to grow to their full size, mulberry groves were often tax-exempt, favouring those families with enough capital to play a long waiting game while the trees grew.

When Yang Guifei attracted the attentions of Xuanzong, she brought her relatives with her to her new social position. Her sisters all married swiftly into the aristocracy, while one of her brothers became an imperial son-in-law. There were, inevitably, mutterings among the courtiers that the Yang family had commanded a position that was not theirs by right, simply because Xuanzong was in the throes of what modern readers might call a midlife crisis, but he had immense power and capability to bring his fantasies to life.

Chinese chronicles characterise Yang Guifei as a wilful, capricious soubrette, cluelessly unaware of the power she wielded over the alleged ruler of the world. There are stories of the poor little rich girl, sending out for her favourite fruit, unaware that they are out of season, and that her simple request will tie up dozens of post-riders in a mad gallop south. Yang Guifei and her coterie tuck into ice cream, uncaring that the effort of creating a frozen dairy product (using the chill of underground storage rooms) occupies immense amounts of imperial resources while commoners starve. However, Chinese chronicles invariably despise women, unless they are one of a handful of ridiculously compliant paragons of virtue. This is because Chinese chronicles are written by misogynistic Chinese chroniclers, who are themselves invariably raised on Confucian histories that warn against the influence of pretty girls, some of whom were indeed used as enemy agents in ancient times.

Perhaps coincidentally, the story of Yang Guifei is entwined with that of another figure in Chinese history, which has not done her any favours. She was, it seems, very friendly with An Lushan, a man whose official Chinese name hides his origins, far to the west on the Silk Road. *An* is one of the 'jewelled surnames,' denoting his stepfather's homeland in Sogdiana; his own place of origin is likely to be somewhere near Samarkand. *Lushan* is likely to be a Chinese attempt to parse the Turkic name Rokshan.

The young An Lushan had been a refugee in Tang China, fleeing unrest among Turkic tribes, and finding a new career in Xuanzong's military. He put his mixed heritage and early travels to use, first as an interpreter for Xuanzong's horse traders. Falling on hard times, he was sentenced to be beaten to death for stealing a sheep, but was spared by the presiding judge, who admired his bravado and his imposing physical form – he was, so it was said, built like the proverbial outhouse.

Stripped of any titles, he swiftly rose through the ranks, and won plaudits fighting China's wars in the north-east. He also demonstrated a canny ability to target imperial envoys for entertainment and gifts, ensuring that every single government inspector returned to the capital fulsome in praise for the new cavalry leader An Lushan, often at the expense of higher ranking officers with less time or inclination to wine, dine and press the flesh. He certainly seems to have liked his food, and by the time he was summoned to Xuanzong's court, was legendarily fat.

'What does that barbaric belly contain?' Xuanzong once said.

'Nothing but a faithful heart,' Lushan replied – if the story is true, it speaks volumes about his personal charm. Surviving tales of Lushan often mention his ignorance of courtly customs, but his recurring ability to spin things in his favour. Once, he even cheekily bowed to Yang Guifei before acknowledging the emperor himself, and explained that among his people, sons bowed to their mothers before their fathers. Xuanzong lapped it up, and pronounced it to be a sign of even greater loyalty and honesty.

Reading stories of Lushan the man, it is hard not to like him. Even through the deadening fog of classical Chinese prose, he sparkles through the history books as a hearty, rakish character not afraid to laugh at himself, and disarmingly innocent among the po-faced, cynical courtiers. His military record, however, suggests that the brinkmanship of his edgy humour, which had got less charismatic figures kicked out of the court, was also applied on the frontier with less welcome results. He provoked several border conflicts in order to demonstrate his prowess, inadvertently causing far more serious reprisals that cost Chinese lives. He also burnt a lot of Xuanzong's diplomatic bridges, in incidents such as a banquet with surly tribesmen where he poisoned the leaders – perhaps pre-emptively putting down a revolt, but also creating yet more bad feeling and mistrust among China's enemies.

Back in the capital, Lushan and Yang Guifei hatched an elaborate prank, wherein the corpulent Lushan was dressed in a diaper and paraded as if he were a giant baby. A boggled Xuanzong laughed at the sight, although vicious tongues wagged that the intimacy and ease of Lushan and Yang was the outward sign of a secret affair. Seemingly in reaction to similar accusations, Xuanzong presented Lushan with an iron tablet, exempting him from punishment for any crime *except treason*. The final clause turned out to be awfully prescient.

Xuanzong was already in his sixties, and his children lacked his good humour towards Lushan. In particular, the crown prince, the future Emperor Suzong, had borne a grudge against Lushan ever since the barbarian general had facetiously refused to bow to him, claiming not to know who he was. Other members of the younger generation, which is to say, the likely officials of Xuanzong's heir, had similarly little patience with Lushan, whose charms seem to have been entirely aimed at the top echelons of the court, and often accompanied by jokes at the expense of the lower but up-and-coming ranks.

Not yet 50 himself, Lushan seemingly began to fret over what would happen to him when his patron died. He created his own elite company of 8,000 former prisoners of war, and successfully lobbied, much to the horror of many of Xuanzong's advisers, to replace many high-ranking Chinese officers in the army with his own non-Chinese appointees. He was suspiciously absent from court on several occasions, and suddenly, in December 755, rose up in revolt.

The An Lushan Rebellion lasted for 13 years, cost millions

of lives, and would cause the Tang Dynasty to lose its suzerainty over the Western Regions. Lushan's army seized much of north China and, swelled with Chinese captives who were persuaded to switch sides, was soon marching on Xuanzong's capital. The emperor fled with his court, only to discover that many of his soldiers were, if not persuaded by Lushan's proclamations, certainly sick of taking orders from Yang Guifei's family. At the inn on Mawei Hill, not far from the modern-day site of Xi'an airport, Xuanzong's soldiers refused to go any further in the company of Yang Guifei.

His dominion now diminished to a small group of embittered soldiers at a roadside tavern, the aging Xuanzong consented to the most brutal of their demands. Yang Guifei was grabbed among the horses, and strangled. Her brother was ordered to commit suicide. Reaching relative safety in Sichuan, Xuanzong abdicated in favour of his son, Suzong, who would recall all the troops from the Western Regions in an attempt to regain control of the centre.

An Lushan's bid to become a new emperor soon collapsed in recriminations and knifings among his own supporters. Emperor Suzong eventually regained his own capital, but only with the help of Uyghur mercenaries from the steppes. He was restored to power heavily in hock to Uyghur moneylenders, after several years of neglected harvests, social upheaval and consequent starvation among the people. The great Tang melting pot turned sour, with reprisals against many foreigners in China. It became dangerous to have a 'jewelled surname' like An, and many of An Lushan's countrymen changed their names. Those that did not risked purges and pogroms. In the Beijing area, a famous general, himself ironically of foreign origin, offered a reward for anyone who could kill a 'barbarian', wiping out all of An Lushan's ethnicity remaining in north China.

Meanwhile, the Four Garrisons of Anxi were lost, having been occupied by Tibetan soldiers soon after the Chinese pulled out. Ironically, this thereby preserved many sacred

Buddhist sites in the region when the religion fell out of favour in China proper.

The Tang Dynasty limped on, eventually becoming so cash-strapped Emperor Wuzong, skint after a war against the Uyghurs, began a series of proclamations in 843 designed to snatch resources back from unwelcome foreign religions. Buddhist holdings were drastically reduced to a lone temple with only 20 monks per region. Similar proscriptions effectively banned other foreign religions, such as Christianity, in a drive to eradicate a 'long-standing pestilence' that, according to Wuzong, threatened to 'confuse the customs of China.' More crucially, he felt that they leeched off the labours of good-hearted working men, and deprived the state of subjects, fathers, soldiers, farmers and tax-payers. Priests and monks were ordered to return to lay life, while their treasures were seized for government use. The state commandeered not only valuable donations, but the physical constructions of the temples, stripping them of metals and lumber. Notably, Islam went unmentioned in the anti-religious proclamations, seemingly because the Muslims in late Tang China had kept to themselves and made no attempt to proselytise.

Wuzong was dead within three years, possibly as a result of the avowedly 'Chinese' Daoist potions he had been quaffing in a quest for immortality. Although Buddhism was swiftly reinstated, the damage was harder to repair for smaller and more vulnerable sects.

Later Tang emperors struggled to maintain their grip on the country, and only did so by ceding ever-larger amounts of control to local warlords on the fringe. As had happened on several previous occasions in Chinese history, the local warlords became increasingly powerful and the power of the centre ever weaker. Within a century, the warlords were proclaiming themselves dukes, and then princes... and before long several made bids to become new emperors. Tang China collapsed into the 'Five Dynasties and Ten Kingdoms' and China's medieval heyday was over.

But China's contacts with the west were even stronger as its power faded, and later Tang emperors came to rely increasingly on the friendship and support of a new power in the region. The Turks' influence had faded, too, to be replaced by the Uyghurs, the richest of all steppe nomads, and swiftly regarded with glowing approval by Chinese chroniclers as immensely 'civilised'. The Uyghurs might still have been barbarians, but they built themselves an unmoving capital, married numerous Tang princesses and offered much-needed military support whenever the going got tough in the Tang heartland. Once the rulers of a wide steppe empire right along China's northern border, and all the way to the oases of Turkestan where they traded with the Sogdians, the Uyghurs were supplanted in the 9th century by another tribe, the Kyrgyz. With the fall of the Uyghur empire, many of its residents fled south-west to the Tarim Basin, settling around Turfan, and further increasing the ethnic diversity of the Silk Road.

5

The Uyghurs and the Mongols (907–1408)

FAR FROM THE SILK ROAD, in the Chinese coastal city of Hangzhou, there is a statue of a bearded white man. He is draped in an odd, toga-like robe and has a squashed cap on his head not unlike a turban. But he is plainly European, and carries a massive old-fashioned book, like a leather-bound album. In his right hand, he brandishes a quill. He seems to be frozen mid-sentence, as if haranguing passers-by, his weight uneasily shifted onto his sandalled left foot, as if he is insisting on some obscure fact, yet not quite believing it himself.

This man, Marco Polo (1254–1324), is memorialised here because of a series of bizarre upheavals that saw northern China lost to barbarians, and Hangzhou briefly reorganised as China's emergency capital. Mongols conquered all of China, but also all of the Silk Road, leading to one of the most sudden moments of hybridity in human history. Chinese soldiers laid siege to Budapest. Muslim voyagers set sail for Japan. And Marco Polo, an Italian man, found himself working as a civil servant for an occupying power, in a Chinese city. When he returned home, many people refused to believe his stories.

WITH THE COLLAPSE of the Tang Dynasty in 907, the

lands of the Silk Road fell under new masters. In the west of Xinjiang, the Turkic 'Qarakhanids' ruled the region around Kashgar in two occasionally rival bloodlines of 'lion' khans and 'bull-camel' khans. Linguistically and ethnically tied to Central Asia rather than China, the Qarakhanids were heavily exposed to the rising popularity of Islam. According to legend, a prince in the bull-camel branch, Satuq, took note of the devotion displayed by Arab merchants when they stopped all activity to pray several times a day. Intrigued by the religious power of the calls from muezzins, he acquired a copy of the Qur'an, and soon decided that he had found the one true religion. Another more folksy version has Satuq out hunting, and encountering a shape-shifting rabbit that tells him there is no god but Allah. Transforming into a bearded priest, the rabbit gets Satuq to recount a series of Buddhist stories about the various torments awaiting in hell, only to gently suggest that Islam would guarantee him eternal life in paradise, with all the wine and women he could handle.

Whatever the actual vectors for belief, Satuq converted to Islam some time in the 930s. His father, disapproving of this foreign heresy, ordered him to build a temple to prove that rumours of his Muslim conversion were not true. On the advice of his imam, Satuq commenced construction of a 'temple', fully intending to turn it into a mosque when it was finished. However, he need not have worried, as a conveniently-issued fatwa from his Muslim allies gave him an excuse to murder his father and proclaim himself khan.

Now an Islamic state, the Qarakhanids of Kashgar extended their influence across the southern desert to Khotan, eventually incorporating the jade-mining hillside town in the early 1000s. The history of the bull-camel khans proudly announces that Satuq 'converted the infidels to Islam by his sword, and established the laws and religion of the Holy Mohammed, the Messenger of God.' They also sallied out through the mountain passes further to the west, attacking and overthrowing the local Persians, taking their capital of Bukhara. For a time, the Qarakhanid realm encompassed the western half of Xinjiang and stretched all the way across the mountains as far west as the Aral Sea, carrying Islam to what is now Uzbekistan and Afghanistan.

Satuq died in 955, although the momentum of his conversion continued throughout the region. Five years after he died, local sources recorded that some '200,000 tents of the Turks' followed him by converting to Islam, suggesting an entire region at least nominally accepted the Muslim faith.

The Qarakhanids would persist in some form until the 13th century, although the mountains soon divided them once more, into a western realm that drifted ever closer to the Turkic or Persian world, and an eastern one in Xinjiang that was soon re-incorporated back into the Chinese world. It was one of those nations that inconveniently straddled the borders of several modern countries. But in bringing Islam en masse to Xinjiang, the Qarakhanids would transform the intellectual and spiritual foundations of the entire region, particularly in terms of a new 'foreign' religion to challenge the Buddhism which, although originally also an import from elsewhere, was now widely regarded as 'Chinese'.

The number of Muslims in modern China is still open to debate, with estimates ranging from one to two per cent of the total population. Most accounts suggest a number approaching 20 million, clustered heavily in the western regions, particularly Xinjiang, but stretching across the entire country. The most visible concentration on the tourist trail is in modern Xi'an, where the lively 'Muslim Quarter' in the town centre is a mandatory inclusion on all guided tours. Islamic communities elsewhere in China, and indeed, even elsewhere in Xi'an, are much less visible to the outsider, and sometimes are only noticeable by restaurants displaying the badge *qingzhen* ('true and pure') to indicate they serve halal food, or by the occasional onion-shaped archway or Turkic sign. However, they all trace their origins in some form back to Satuq Bughra Khan and his fateful encounter with Islam somewhere near Kashgar.

As in stories of early Christian conversions in pagan Europe, we might quibble with the speed and ease with which the faith spread. It is very unlikely that entire communities would voluntarily and unilaterally embrace a foreign religion unless they were somehow being incentivised to do so – the suggestion in Satuq's own biographies that he threatened to kill those who did not convert goes some way to explaining things. But as noted above, there was also a certain similarity between the modes of worship of Islam and Nestorian Christianity, and the suggestion that there was a new prophet, a successor to Jesus, may not have been all that earth-shattering a revelation for many believers out in the sands. Nor can Islam's focus on heaven for believers, when set beside Buddhism's emphasis on another round of suffering, have been unpersuasive among many sectors of the local population.

Barchuq switches sides

While the conversion of the Qarakhanids in Kashgar created a new set of memes that would spread and grow throughout the region for centuries, their rise in western Xinjiang came at the same time as that of another group, which would eventually adopt Islam as well. However, at the time of the fall of the Tang Dynasty, the rulers of eastern Xinjiang were no more Muslim than the Chinese they supplanted.

The name 'Uyghur' is another of the slippery diachronic terms that make studying the Silk Road so difficult. It is likely to have been *uyughur* ('the united') originally, a term of self-identification for a scattered group of tribesmen from the region around Lake Baikal, later applied to anyone who lived within the vast compass of the Uyghur Khanate. The name fell out of use over the centuries, only to be resurrected by Russian ethnologists seeking to label the people of the Xinjiang region who were not nomads, but stayed in one place. The name was later appropriated by the Chinese, and conferred upon the entire Xinjiang area, which is today a 'Uyghur Autonomous Region'. Modern Chinese also tend to confuse the terms for Uyghur and *Hui*, which is often used to mean 'Muslim'. Although most Uyghurs today *are* Muslims, that was certainly not the case in the medieval period, when most of them were Buddhists and Manicheans.

As with 'Tibet', the term 'Uyghur' is hence applied both to a modern part of China, and a historical empire that was, in the distant past, far greater in power and size than its current incarnation. The term is occasionally employed for territorial demands by 'nationalists' who hail from the former but allude in their arguments to the latter. This has led to a heavily politicised debate over the 'original' inhabitants of Xinjiang, in which the simplest of statements by either side come loaded with wider-ranging implications, and attempts by archaeologists to unravel the complex historical transformations of the region often uncover unwelcome facts that suggest both sides are wrong.

To confuse matters further, there were several overlapping groups of Uyghurs in China's high Middle Ages. Some moved south and simply assimilated into the Chinese state. A minor Uyghur nation flourished in the Gansu region for a century or so, before being brutally conquered by the Tangut tribe. However, the most successful group of Uyghurs came to dominate the Xinjiang region for several centuries in their own name, and for substantially longer as the agents of a new overlord.

The Uyghurs who settled on the Silk Road were fleeing an even more powerful group, the Kyrgyz. Persian chronicles dispassionately report the matter-of-fact arrival of the Kyrgyz tribesmen, and their blunt orders for the Uyghurs to move on, pushing them out of their original settlement in the Orkhon River Valley and southwards, ever southwards, over the mountains and into the notorious sands of the Taklamakan.

However, while the Kyrgyz seized the grasslands, at least

one group of the fugitive Uyghurs found themselves in a new region that, while often searingly hot or bitingly cold, belied its desert location. They settled at Gaochang (Qocho) in what is now the Turfan Basin in the late 9th century – the ruins of this capital can still be found some 30 kilometres outside the modern city (see Gazetteer: Turfan). They found, as had many others before them, a paradise amid the sands and a firm basis for the generation of agricultural wealth. Whoever controls the 1,000 square arable kilometres of the Turfan Basin is in a powerful position to steer the politics of the surrounding region, and the Uyghurs extended their influence both east and west on the Silk Road, west to Kucha and east to Hami.

This largely Buddhist kingdom lasted for several centuries, supporting new carvings at the nearby 'Thousand Buddha' holy sites, and also admitting many Persian visitors into its society. Manicheanism flourished among the Uyghurs, alongside Syriac Christianity, as attested by the discovery in the 20th century of a Christian library at Turfan, containing some 945 manuscripts in Turkic, Persian, Syriac and Sogdian, including fragments of the Old and New Testament, lives of prominent saints (particularly Saint George, always popular with Turks), and a didactic dialogue between a Christian and a Jew. The nature of the surviving documents suggests close contacts between the foreign community in Turfan and Mesopotamia, the epicentre of Nestorian Christianity.

Before the Uyghurs arrived, Gaochang had been a Chinese colony, and much of the society of the new kingdom seemed to run on Chinese models. What little evidence there is of legal statutes before the coming of Islam suggests that the Uyghurs in Gaochang largely copied or sampled Chinese laws, either themselves or through the hiring of Chinese scribes.

The Uyghurs were enormously influential in the history of the Silk Road, even after the supposed disappearance of their empire. With China still torn between several rival successor states to the fallen Tang Dynasty, the Xinjiang region came into contact with the Western Liao (also known as the Black Khitans), the remnants of a state that had briefly ruled northern China before itself being kicked out by stronger opponents. Rather than fight the Western Liao, the Uyghurs of Gaochang simply accepted their rule in 1130, which meant business as usual with occasional interference from an embedded Liao supervisor.

Unlike other conquering dynasties, the Khitans lacked both the will and the manpower to establish garrisons in subject territories. An official oversaw tax and administration while the locals got on with their daily lives, and soldiers only arrived in the event of a revolt. The Uyghurs soon exerted an influence upon their supposed rulers, particularly since Uyghur intellectuals were tasked with teaching many of the ruling elite to read and write.

The Black Khitans managed to maintain a shaky control of Xinjiang for a century, before pressures from both within and without brought their empire crashing down. In 1209, Barchuq, the local ruler of Turfan, turned on the Khitans with lightning speed, murdering the local supervisor and, depending on which source one reads, either throwing his head out of a window, or pulling a stone tower down on top of him. Seemingly understanding that the Khitans' days were numbered, Barchuq then went straight to the new rising power on the steppes, a Mongol tribe led by a man called Temujin, the Genghis Khan.

Barchuq's interest in surrendering to the Mongols is a matter of some conjecture. It certainly wasn't without consequences – Barchuq was obliged to hand over hostages to the Mongols to secure their good faith, and would have had to pay tithes and tributes, as well as a human tithe of experts and slaves. But he had already been presenting similar fees to the failing Black Khitans, and clearly saw which way the wind was blowing.

By presenting his entire domain to Genghis Khan,

Barchuq became the first bloodless acquisition by the Mongols. His act propelled Uyghurs into high places in the newly-forming Mongol administration, as the first and most senior officials of the new regime. With more than a century of Chinese or proto-Chinese organisation, the ability to read and write, and linguists who could deal with all the disparate races of the Western Regions, the Uyghurs from Turfan arrived within the Mongol realm as 'volunteers', without any of the stigma of a conquest or battle. Barchuq even received one of Genghis Khan's daughters as a bride, and the honorific title of 'Fifth Son'. His realm was largely spared any contact with the fearsome Mongol hordes of legend, and prospered in relative autonomy like the calm at the centre of a rippling pond, while the rest of Asia was plunged into chaos by the ever advancing frontline of the Mongol conquests.

The arrival of the Mongols was a disaster for most of the regions they touched – an apocalyptic spate of murder and theft that destroyed all trade in the surrounding area. However, trade of a sort would swiftly pick up again, not least because the Mongols themselves soon acquired a taste for luxury, and a desire to rid themselves of all their plundered wealth by spending it on quality items. Genghis Khan said of his lieutenants, wives, concubines, and daughters: 'my desire and intention for all is... to delight their mouths with the sugar of benevolence, to adorn them front and back, top and bottom, with garments of gold brocade, to sit them on fluid paced mounts, to give them pure and delicious water to drink, to provide verdant pasture for their herds.' The Mongol conquest dragged the Silk Road palpably north, so that it no longer ran in a horizontal line east-to-west, but up from both Persia and China towards a northern point on the steppes.

In the alcohol-averse lands of the Muslim world, Chinese tea and the porcelain used for drinking it flourished as a new export commodity. The distinctive tricolour *sancai* ware that flourished in the Tang Dynasty was off-loaded during the Mongol era, seemingly in large quantities, to Arab merchants, possibly as a result of impoverished Chinese families trying to make some ready cash. Transported on Arab sea routes out of southern Chinese ports, it shows up in Persia soon after the Mongol conquests, and by the late Middle Ages was being copied by potters in Syria and Cyprus.

Spices and luxury goods gravitated to the Mongol heartland, where baffled nomads paid for them in handfuls of stolen booty, often none too sure of the going rate. Artisans and craftsmen, some kidnapped along with their families, were spared the slaughter of the Mongol conquest and instead resettled at strategic points along the Silk Road.

While it is difficult to point at specifically Mongol-period fashions or designs, the century of the Mongol Empire is distinguished by an immense and wide-ranging admixture of styles and ideas, as Chinese potters were resettled in Persia, and Persian weavers brought east to add gold-threaded flashes to the cuffs and collars of Chinese silk clothes. Genghis Khan had grown up in an environment where simply owning iron cooking pots and a pair of good stirrups was a mark of wealth. Now he seized upon luxuries with all the fervour of a lottery millionaire, determined, for example, to dress his whole entourage in silks shot through with golden threads.

At some point in the Mongol conquests, one of the loutish *nouveau* noblemen snatched up a gift that was already absurdly over-wrought – a fur coat with a silk lining. However, by luck or judgement, possibly even by blunt and boorish ignorance, he put it on inside-out, with the gold-flashed *nasij* brocade on the outside, and the fur on the inside. The new fashion caught on (well, who was going to tell him he was wrong?), and can still be found in traditional ethnic costumes over much of western China.

History remembers the 'Mongol' conquests, as over the next century they would carry the sons and grandsons of Genghis Khan all over Eurasia, from the shores of Japan to the walls of Budapest. It remembers the great Mongol

Empire that briefly united that same region under one ruler. It is all very cinematic to tell stories of the great battles, the rains of arrows and the blood-soaked sieges, but that was merely the savage leading edge of the Mongol world. The horsemen fought and died, but their administrators and scribes, teachers and officials were recruited from the realms they conquered. As the first and most agreeable civilisation to hitch itself to the Mongol wagon, the Uyghurs gained permanent seniority in the Mongol administration. For the next 100 years, they would form the middle-management of an entire empire, second only to the Mongols themselves, who were soon thinly spread across their far-reaching lands.

The Uyghurs are also likely to have formed part of the 'Mongol' army that marched to conquer other parts of the Silk Road. Arriving in the wake of Qarakhanid persecutions of the Muslims in Kashgar, the Mongol forces swiftly gathered up proclamations of surrender from the locals, although Khotan held out and was annihilated as per the Mongol fashion. The last of the Qarakhanids fled over the mountains and, in a certain sense, Xinjiang became a Uyghur province, hidden beneath the banners of the Mongols.

Barchuq himself served as a Mongol general, leading a company of 10,000 over the mountains into Central Asia, and playing a key role in 'Mongol' conquests there. He also fought as one of the generals that brutally wiped out the nearby Tangut kingdom. The story of the fall of the Tanguts has become muddled in later accounts, since it was supposedly the site of the death of Genghis Khan himself, who either fell prone to disease during a siege or, according to a later Mongol account, was fatally and intimately wounded by the Tangut princess he was trying to rape at the time. The subsequent destruction of the Tangut kingdom is hence often regarded as some sort of Mongol revenge, although to the Uyghurs who formed a substantial part of the 'Mongol' army, it amounted more to assisted payback for Tangut persecutions of their Uyghur cousins two centuries earlier. Often dismissed in a single line in accounts of Mongol expansion, this Uyghur retaliation was tantamount to genocide, leaving less than one per cent of the Tanguts alive to be enslaved.

Shortly before the death of Genghis Khan, his lands were divided among his sons. Unfortunately for Xinjiang, the line of division between two heirs ran right through its middle, with Turfan in the east and Khotan in the south supposedly the property of the khans of China, while Kashgar in the west was beholden to the khans of Central Asia. As under the previous regime of the Black Khitans, each Mongol province was left to run its own affairs, under the supervision of a 'resident' cadre, or *darugha*, who represented the distant khan. With divide-and-rule being the order of the day, many educated Uyghur officials drifted eastward on assignments as *darughachi* in the newly conquered realms of north China, while the Uyghur homeland fell under the authority of Muslim *darughachi* from over the mountains in Central Asia.

Marco Polo

Genghis Khan did not live to see the conquest of China, but his grandson Khubilai, attended by a ready-made administration of officials from the Western Regions, would famously proclaim himself as the new Emperor of China in 1271. This was somewhat presumptive, as it would be another five years before Khubilai's multi-ethnic army finally brought down the last forces of the Chinese in the south. But it also imposed the Mongol administration, already functioning for a generation on the Silk Road, on the rest of China proper.

If the Tang Dynasty had marked the height of Silk Road opulence and material culture, the Yuan Dynasty founded by Khubilai Khan was the high-water mark of its political influence. For a brief century, the insular Chinese system, effectively closed to anyone who had not grown up steeped in Chinese culture and language, was dismantled by an occupying military power. China had ruled the Silk Road for centuries, but now the Silk Road ruled China.

Since their lands had been conquered by the Mongols a generation before troops had reached China itself, the Uyghurs and other western races were more fully assimilated into the Mongol system, and swiftly appointed to powerful cadre positions within Chinese society. The Chinese dismissed them disparagingly as 'people with beards', although the official term for them was *semuren* – literally 'persons of various categories'. A coincidental double-meaning also led to the popular gloss 'people with coloured eyes.' A Muslim was appointed as the governor of Yunnan province. Uyghur tax inspectors and administrators worked in Chinese cities as far east as the coast of the China Sea. The man appointed to oversee temple restoration in the river-delta city of Hangzhou was a Tibetan. Most famously of all among these people with coloured eyes was Marco Polo, a minor official in Yangzhou and a wide-eyed visitor to Hangzhou, and one of the few travellers thought to have travelled the Silk Road in its entirety.

Mongol wars disrupted trade at their leading edge, but gave way to an unprecedented state of peace in the aftermath. As in the fall of the Tangut kingdom, Mongol atrocities also quelled local enmities, and swiftly occupied thugs and brigands with military enterprises. That is not to deny the terrible human cost to those cities, like Khotan, that resisted, but to those like Turfan that swiftly accepted Mongol authority, the dawn of the 14th century offered immense opportunities for trade.

The Polo family of Venice hoped to capitalise on this by striking out on their famous journey to the east. Marco Polo was a mere youth of 17 when he left Venice with his father and uncles, and in his early twenties by the time the travellers reached the court of Khubilai Khan. The elder Polos seemingly hoped not only to acquire lucrative trading contacts, but also to exploit intellectual capital, with an initial plan to bring some Christian missionaries to debate and preach at Khubilai's famously eclectic court. But they lost their missionary companions en route, failed to bring along many of the holy books that Khubilai had been hoping to see, and eventually ended up in Khubilai's court with very little to offer except their own service. Although little is known about the activity of the elder Polos, Marco appears to have joined the ranks of the Mongol administration, and functioned in a relatively low-level capacity somewhere in China.

We know this, of course, because he would live to return to Europe and write up his experiences in *The Travels of Marco Polo*, which became one of the prime medieval sources on the Far East. Polo seems to have intended his work as a rather grim gazetteer of towns along the route – it is likely to have been his collaborator Rustichello, a balladeer and former crusader, who provided a lot of the vibrant local colour and tall tales for which the *Travels* is often derided.

Polo's book is most famous for its account of China itself, although arguably he saw remarkably little of distinctly Chinese civilisation, since much of his experience of it was as a clerk or manager of an occupying military force. Polo himself does not seem to have ever learnt Chinese, since the lingua franca of his fellow administrators was Persian. South China in particular was under martial law for decades, and the locals were careful to lock their daughters away from any predatory passers-by – Polo speaks fondly of whores in his *Travels*, but complains of rarely seeing any *Chinese* women. His dealings with Chinese people seem very limited, to the extent that he never appears to have noticed foot-binding, chopsticks or tea, and makes several omissions in his otherwise thorough memoirs sufficient for one historian, Frances Wood, to write her provocative book *Did Marco Polo Go to China?*

However, his concentration on the journey rather than the arrival means that a substantial part of his narrative is actually spent on the Silk Road, presenting an eye-witness account of life in Xinjiang. He reached Xinjiang through the mountain passes that he regarded as the 'highest place in the world', and reported on *Cascar* (Kashgar), which he believed had once been a kingdom, though it was then under the authority of the Great Khan. Polo goes on to describe the cities of *Yarcan* (Yarkand) and *Cotan* (Khotan), firmly siting western Xinjiang as a Muslim region by this point, and reporting somewhat impoverished conditions, particularly in those areas that had been punished by the Mongols for resisting.

Polo's grasp of the towns and oases of Xinjiang, which he called *Iuguristan* (Uyghuristan), suggests that he crossed it by the southern route as far as Ruoqiang, before heading north through a town he calls Lop, and across the desert at one of its narrowest points, along the occasional course of the Tarim River.

Polo also found the desert daunting, revealing that its winds and drumming sands could cause travellers in the cold desert night to lose their bearings.

> When travellers are on the move by night, and one of them chances to lag behind or fall asleep or the like... he will hear spirits talking, and will suppose them to be his comrades. Sometimes, the spirits will call him by name; and thus shall a traveller often be led astray so that he never finds his party. And in this way, many have perished. Even in the daytime one hears these spirits talking. And sometimes you shall hear the sound of a variety of musical instruments, and still more commonly the sound of drums.

On the north side of the desert, Polo stopped at *Carachoço*, his attempt to write Kara-khoja, the name used by the local Uyghurs to describe their capital, a day's walk to the north of modern Turfan. There, he complained about how cold it could get in winter – little knowing that in summer it would also have been unbearably hot. He writes approvingly of the religious melting pot of the peaceful Uyghur capital, noting that Muslim 'Saracens' live among Chinese 'idolaters' and Christians, and that the latter two groups are even known to intermarry.

He also comments on the 'excellent wine' of the region, something that he seems to have experienced on-site, and has an exotic beverage at the Mongol court. Although Polo does not mention this himself, amongst the various Silk Road commodities of the Yuan Dynasty, wine would prove to be one of the most ruinous, mainly because the Mongols were entirely unused to it, and were soon drinking as much of it as they could find.

The descendants of nomads on the Silk Road favoured *koumiss* (Chinese: *suan ma-nai*) or sour horse milk, a mildly alcoholic beverage that tastes like runny, slightly fizzy yoghurt. Fermenting the milk was not a weird hobby, but a physical necessity, since adult Mongols were lactose intolerant, and unable to digest raw milk – butter, cheese and *koumiss* are created by the introduction of bacteria which break down the lactose. As there was no immediate access to any wells, *koumiss* was often the main drink for many families, and was mild enough to be fed to children with impunity. *Koumiss* rarely has an alcohol content of more than 1 per cent; for the Mongol herdsmen looking for a buzz at the end of a hard day on the steppes, it was necessary to quaff *koumiss* in truly heroic quantities. After the Mongol conquests, the nomads were brought into contact with far stronger brews, including Persian wine and Chinese *baijiu* (see Chapter 9: Eating and Drinking), but seemingly kept up their drinking as if they were still knocking back low-alcohol horse-milk.

The results among the rank and file are largely unrecorded, but we can get an idea from the annals of the Mongol khans, which list a series of alleged curses, ailments and poisons that sound suspiciously like medieval scribes' attempts to report the onset of severe alcoholism, as the conquerors of Asia celebrated just a little too hard, and found themselves unable to stop. Ogodei Khan died enfeebled and incoherent, supposedly with a body 'at war with the spirits of earth and water'; his brother Tolui tried to save him by taking on his demons, drinking himself into a ritual stupor. Tolui's son, the famous Khubilai Khan, was already suffering from gout in his thirties.

By the time of Khubilai's old age, we do not even need to read between the lines. The chronicler Rashid al-Din faithfully reports that Khubilai's grandson and heir, Temur, was 'extremely fond of wine', and persisted in hopeless binges despite stern interventions from his family. There is often a degree of sly admiration in historical accounts of Temur's condition – he ordered his bath to be filled with booze in order to get around restrictions on drinking, and commissioned a tankard twice the usual size, so that he could honestly report that he was drinking half as many cups. But Rashid al-Din's pages on Temur are unmistakeably, tragically familiar in modern terms – a conniving, deceitful alcoholic and his enabling cronies. The only sentence that does not ring true is the happy ending, written while Temur was still on the throne, in which Rashid claims, somewhat hopefully, that the prince's drinking ceased when he succeeded his grandfather.

The Muslims

The Mongols' Yuan Dynasty barely lasted a century before the resurgent Chinese shook off their overlords and chased them back to their steppe heartland. But for much of the short-lived Mongol imperium, Xinjiang was cut off from the Chinese world, beholden instead to masters in the north, in particular to Khaidu, the Mongol prince who was the de facto ruler of the region in the late 13th century, despite several attempts by Khubilai to regain control.

As the power of the Yuan Dynasty waned, Xinjiang found itself once more as a contested border region caught between several rival warlords. The break-up of Mongol authority came accompanied by religious rifts, as many Mongols in the south and west embraced Islam, finding new connections with local peoples, and new enmities with their cousins in other khanates.

One such figure was Tughluq Temur (1329–63), a descendant of the second son of Genghis Khan, who legendarily converted to Islam after one of those all-too-common hunting encounters. This time it was not with a talking rabbit, but with a Persian priest, who shrugged when Tughluq called him a dog, and admitted that all men were dogs without the one true faith. This supposedly impressed the young Tughluq, who promised that in the unlikely event that he ever became khan, he would convert.

The priest was Jamal al-Din, a performer of miracles and preacher of the Muslim faith who had supposedly already called down an all-consuming sandstorm on a Xinjiang town where locals had not accorded him due respect. The sole survivor was the local muezzin, the man responsible for issuing the call to prayer, who sheltered at the top of his tower, emerging when the storm passed to discover the whole town buried in the sand beneath him.

When Tughluq did become khan, Jamal was long dead, but his son Arshad was conveniently on hand for the risky business of reminding him of his oath. This he did by sneaking up to Tughluq's tent and bellowing out the call to prayer one morning. Tughluq supposedly remembered at last, and declared not only that he would accept the peace of Islam, but that all his princes would also do so, on pain of death. Only one refused, although in what seems to be a relatively standard story template for the region, he soon changed his mind after his wrestling champion was bested by the weedy-looking Arshad.

Folktales about impressed khans and magically-persuaded princes hide more prosaic conversions among the lower classes. Although we should take the story of Tughluq's conversion with a pinch of salt, he, and many of his tribe, did embrace Islam during the 14th century, undoubtedly taking many of their vassals with them. The 'Mongols' of Xinjiang and Central Asia transformed gradually into the Islamic 'Mughals', and almost all of Xinjiang, with the exception of the Buddhist heartland around Turfan, became Muslim. Many of the Mughals, despite coming from nomad roots, had become city-dwelling people by the end of the era's great transformations. However, they retained a nostalgia for steppe tradition, which often found expression in their habits of worship in their newly-acquired religion, with many choosing to spend their leisure time in symbolic silk tents. With images of human figures often forbidden under Islam, they favoured patterns and symbols, at first on rugs on the floors, and then as floor space ran out, on rugs hung vertically as tapestries. What had once been a campsite-influenced need to have removable flooring became a new fashion in urban furnishing. The rug became a ubiquitous feature in the Central Asian home – silk clothing was forbidden for men, so weavers found a new business niche making carpets. As vital items, not only in decoration but in Muslim worship, rugs survived throughout the period, even during occasional Islamic austerity drives.

Before long, an emir north of the Tianshan Mountains, in the region often identified in the period as Mughalistan, declared a holy war on 'the Chinese'. Although this might have sounded like a recipe for disaster for a land sharing a border with the young Ming Dynasty, it instead focused its efforts on former Chinese possessions, namely the Turfan region. Turfan, too, soon became an officially Muslim area, although seemingly its conversion took substantially longer than the overnight bullying reported back to the emir. For centuries to come, the Turfan region retained its Buddhist idols and Confucian temples, although Islam did also gain prominence.

History remembers the wars. Or rather, for the next few

centuries in Xinjiang, the sources largely report a series of further reversals, betrayals and putsches, as cousins and uncles from several interrelated tribes knife each other in the back over control of the region. In Central Asia, the infamous warlord Tamerlane (1336–1405) proclaimed himself the Sword of Islam, but effectively carried out expansionist wars in a very Mongol style. Tamerlane never called himself *khan*, since that title was reserved for descendants of Genghis Khan. Instead, he married Tughluq's daughter to associate himself with the Mongols by marriage, and continued his campaigns beyond the mountains in the west.

The campaigns of Tamerlane were a disaster for the remnants of the Silk Road, as they united many Central Asian Muslim regions, at the cost of millions of lives. The sectarian violence bled through into Xinjiang at the turn of the 15th century, when Tamerlane's grandson, Mirza Alexander, launched a campaign against the 'Six Cities' of Xinjiang, marching as far as Aksu. There, he spared the city on the understanding that the residents would hand over certain merchants who dwelt there – which amounted to the lynching of the non-Muslim residents, variously written off as 'wealthy' or 'Chinese'.

The rise of the Mongols and the diaspora of their descendants had married itself to the rise of Islam, entirely transforming the region. From this point on, much of the region's sense of its own heritage is primarily Islamic, rich in mosques and *mazars* (tombs), tales of Muslim charity and religious fervour, and steeped in references to the Qur'an and the Hadiths. Islam is a vital, crucial element in the heritage of Xinjiang, but it shines brightly in the desert, driving its predecessors into the shadows.

Genghis Khan was largely indifferent to multicultural faiths; Khubilai Khan welcomed them and displayed a deep interest. But their successors, as multiple tales of swordpoint conversions should suggest, soon embraced an intolerant, brutal Islam that had no patience for other faiths.

Indeed, in the west of Xinjiang, little evidence remains of those other religions. Tamerlane and his sons had killed most of the Christians in Central Asia who had not already converted, and the remaining Buddhists were second-class citizens – many of their descendants adopted Islam. Infidel graveyards were soon left unattended; ruined infidel temples were broken up to make other buildings. Abandoned infidel communities drowned in desert sand.

Trade itself also changed. The continental Silk Road fell apart after centuries of Mongol and Mughal wars. Instead, Turfan, the Silk Road city closest to the Chinese heartland, sent a tentative embassy to the new Ming Dynasty in 1408, acknowledging a vassal status towards China, as an excuse to trade through the system of regular 'tributes'. The Chinese still needed horses. The Turfanese had raisins to move on in large quantities, but also jade and spice that had arrived from other communities in Xinjiang. This mass of trade now pooled once a year at Turfan, before being sent as a massive 'tribute' to the new capital at Beijing. The extent to which the Chinese had any real authority in the region would be a matter of constant argument for the next two centuries.

6

The New Frontier (1408–1912)

THERE IS NO STATUE of Afaq Khoja, the Master of the Horizons, in Kashgar. As a holy man of the Naqshbandi order, 'engravers of the heart' in Sunni Islam, he would have considered it an insult against God for his image to be carved in stone for others to worship. The local celebration of him is confined to the intricate designs of his beautiful mausoleum, which he shares with many other famous and infamous members of his family – such as his father, who was poisoned by his own cousins; or his widow, the 'Butcher Queen' and the heir she murdered.

The fate of Xinjiang's Muslim aristocracy is a perfect allegory of the region's gloriously chaotic history. Their own culture forbade their commemoration in terms that would be familiar to the Chinese or the Europeans, but to fellow believers, their legacy is a striking, living part of the region's history. It thrives in the richly appointed architecture of numerous opulent mosques, rising above the hovels of authentic old-towns, or tucked into cul-de-sacs behind modern skyscrapers. It is celebrated in ancient manuscripts and histories in Persian or Uyghur, rarely translated into Chinese and rarer still in European languages. Their ethnic and religious ties to Muslim lands outside China forever kept them focused beyond the mountains. Their sectarian spats played havoc with Islam's self-image as a unifying, pacifying force, as they frequently collapsed into rounds of poisoning, putsches and skirmishes over remote oases.

China has a habit of celebrating its rivals. There are stories of entire races being wiped out, of kings burned and their ashes scattered to the four winds, but far more tales of battles won without fighting, of local rulers invited into the Chinese system, or poachers sent to catch thieves. China prefers to co-opt its foes into its own ongoing narrative. It marries them to its daughters and ennobles their grandparents. It gives them Chinese names and teaches their children Chinese. Many a pirate, rebel or steppe chieftain has been subtly brought down by diplomacy, handed a dukedom or a commission and invited into the existing order. This even worked on some in Xinjiang, who found an accommodation with Chinese power, often taking the surname 'Ma' in homage to Mohammed, but otherwise fading into the mass of the general population. But it did not work on everybody.

The Mongol flood destroyed the old Silk Road, in part by allowing many technologies and craftsmen to traverse its length and install themselves closer to once-distant markets. The story of the Xinjiang region for the next few centuries is as one of the places *where once the Silk Road was*, now more of a backwater than ever before, its people inwardly focussed and struggling for subsistence.

As many early dynasties had discovered, politics in Xinjiang often demanded a local perspective. It was relatively simple to maintain control over a single oasis and the limited fields and pastures it supported. There were occasional skirmishes and unifications when rulers tried to expand, but any local ruler deciding to wage war on the next oasis would find the burden of victory entirely on his shoulders – oases had the desert itself as their natural defence, against tired attackers who had to bring their own supplies and precious water. An oasis, once captured, could only be held by hostage exchange or the thinning of one's forces by local garrisoning, since any punitive expedition sent to deal with a revolt would have to deal with the same harsh operational conditions as before. As a result, the political administration of Xinjiang largely returned to extremely localised townships, some proclaiming lip service to a distant authority, but for the most part left to their own devices. Turfan continued to send annual 'tribute' to Beijing on behalf of the region, allowing map makers in the distant east to colour it as a Chinese possession. Within the desert cities themselves, local authority often derived from an uneasy stand-off between Mongol and Muslim heritage, uniting the descendants of Genghis Khan and the *khojas* ('masters') claiming descent from the Prophet Mohammed. These twin dynasties often intertwined or shared power, although by the 17th century it was largely understood that the secular princes were mere figureheads, and the *khojas* were truly in charge.

Kazakhs, Kyrgyz and Kalmuks

Further to the west, in-fighting among the Mongol descendants of the Golden Horde would divide another nomad group. The victors remained in Central Asia, and would eventually be known as the Uzbeks. The vanquished fled eastwards, and would eventually be known as the Kazakhs. Some settled in the region now known as Kazakhstan, although many bled over into the Ili valley north of the Tianshan Mountains, which remains ethnically Kazakh-heavy to this day.

Similarly, some of the Kyrgyz tribesmen that had migrated into Xinjiang in the middle ages, forming a sizeable component of various armies of conquest, settled in what is now Kyrgyzstan – but the borders were undefined, so they also bled back across the mountains into Xinjiang. Poor, hard-to-find and literally holding the high ground, this group remained politically independent for centuries, although spiritually they embraced Islam at the end of the 16th century. As in other tales of conversion in Xinjiang, the credit goes to a

Sufi mystic master, in this case Ishaq Wali (d.1599), who ridiculed the thousand idols to which the Kyrgyz were praying in the hope of curing their leader Seyrop of an unspecified illness. Instead, Ishaq counselled faith in God, praying with his followers at Seyrop's bedside. The ailing chief sneezed and sprang to his feet, bellowing the Muslim proclamation of faith, causing his tribesmen not only to convert to Islam along with him, but also to smash up their most precious idol and present the silver fragments to Ishaq.

However, Ishaq did not speak for all Islam. Just as Christianity shattered into contending sects in Europe, some of which went to war with one another, Ishaq was himself part of a split in local Islam, between his own supporters and those of his elder brother Amin. Ishaq's group, the 'Black Mountain', differed in some obscure doctrinal way from Amin's, the 'White Mountain'. For the next few generations, their descendants would quarrel in eastern Xinjiang, with the divisions largely establishing themselves along geographical lines, between the foothills of the mountain regions north of Kashgar (White) and south towards Yarkand (Black). Since both groups of mystics had recently acquired tough Kyrgyz converts, they often fought their battles through nomad proxies, putting the horsemen to use defending matters of their new faith.

For a long while, it seemed as if the White Mountain had the upper hand, particularly since Afaq Khoja (d.1694) integrated Islam firmly into secular life in the region when he abolished the old Mongol statutes and replaced them with Sharia law. While the aforementioned legends and folktales might breathlessly suggest that Xinjiang became Muslim many centuries earlier, more grounded sources, such as the *Encyclopaedia Iranica*, cite Afaq Khoja's reign as the time when the multi-ethnic, multi-religious tribes and polities of the region finally 'began to develop a common identity based on allegiance to Islam.' It is for this reason that his tomb in modern Kashgar (see Gazetteer: Kashgar) is one of the most striking and sacred sites in modern Chinese Islam, although tour guides are likely to gloss over this particular element of his legacy.

In addition to his reforms and accomplishments in Kashgar, Afaq Khoja had a far more wide-ranging impact on Xinjiang politics, through his tense and dangerous relationship with a new group of nomads in the east of the region – the Kalmuks, a group of Mongolian nomads not directly related to the forces of Genghis Khan. Pushed away from the borders of Ming China, they, too, settled along the flanks of northern and western Xinjiang. In the early 17th century, a group within the Kalmuks known as the Zunghar Mongols achieved prominence, and formed the last steppe empire of pre-modern times.

The Zunghars were not part of the Chinese or Muslim worlds, but were throwbacks to the medieval period of Tibetan dominance. The heir of the Zunghars, Galdan Khan (1644–1697), was raised in Lhasa as a Buddhist under the authority of the fifth Dalai Lama, returning to the steppes only after the murder of his brother in 1671, and claiming his authority not only by birth, but with the religious support of Tibet. In 1677, Afaq Khoja, the leader of the defeated White Mountain faction, called upon Galdan for aid against his cousins, escalating the wars of these nomads in the service of Islam by introducing champions who were not even Muslims.

This led to the Zunghar conquest of Xinjiang and points as far as Tashkent to the west and southern Siberia to the east, after which Galdan decreed that all the subject cities were to be left to conduct their own affairs, except in such matters as involved their dealings with the Zunghars.

However, there had been changes in China. The declining Ming Dynasty had been replaced by the Qing Dynasty in 1644, a military occupation of tribesmen from Manchuria. The new Manchu leaders regarded themselves as successors of a sort not only to Genghis Khan but also to the medieval non-Chinese conquerors such as the Western Liao. As in the days of the Mongol-ruled Yuan Dynasty, the installation of a northern nomad emperor in China inevitably dragged the Chinese deeper into conflicts on the steppes.

By the 17th century, China had also found a new foreign contact. The empire of the Russian tsars had expanded ever eastwards, and eventually ran into a shared border with China. Silk, porcelain and tea for Russian samovars were traded across the once impassable steppes, causing the Central Asian routes to fade even further into obscurity. Qing Dynasty China stretched westward – in part to hold off Russian expansion from the other direction – and embarked upon a genocidal war against the Zunghars.

The tale of the Chinese stand-off with the Zunghars bears an uncanny resemblance to many previous points in the region's history. Despite the fact that the story ends in mass-murder, for much of the period the Zunghars were more important to the Chinese as trading partners than as potential enemies. Just as with the Xiongnu of old, the Zunghars were far more sophisticated than Chinese chronicles gave them credit for, even to the extent of having an artillery division of cannon-carrying camels. Instead of doing the traditional thing, and treating the Chinese like they were the centre of the world, the Zunghars concluded a number of deals with other states, settling territorial claims with the Russians, exacting tribute from Xinjiang city-states, and even meddling in the political affairs of Tibet. No caravan of tribute reached China from Xinjiang without the consent of the Zunghars, who often chanced their arm by sending vastly more 'tribute' than was required, forcing the Chinese to pay in kind for goods they did not necessarily want.

The Manchu emperor hoped to follow the same policy he had already successfully pursued in Mongolia, dividing and ruling by supporting several smaller tribes, with each khan looking to him. This would reduce the danger of truly massive population movement or warfare in the Zunghar region, and also ensure that much of the Zunghar energies would be taken up with fights among themselves, instead of directed against the Chinese. The big chance came in 1745, when the death of a powerful unifying leader caused the Zunghars to break into several factions.

China's Emperor Qianlong came to the 'aid' of one such faction, sending an army into the lands north of the Tian-shan Mountains in 1755 and swiftly occupying a region that had already been weakened by years of internal fighting. All went well until the Chinese departed, leaving only a few garrisons in strategic towns, and expecting the Zunghars to continue as four separate clans. Amursana, the leader who had called for Chinese aid in the first place, announced that he intended to become the ruler of all the Zunghars, and did so not only with a forceful proclamation that circulated all around the empire, but with the sudden massacre of all the Chinese troops in the region.

Livid, not only at the betrayal but at the expense of dealing with it, Emperor Qianlong declared war on Amursana, who was ironically already in retreat from the more invisible enemy of a smallpox outbreak. Even though the epidemic had already broken the Zunghars into many smaller groups, Qianlong was determined to ensure that there would be no repeat of the Zunghar revolt. Since he could no longer trust any Zunghar 'surrender', he ordered his soldiers to exterminate them. This plainly surprised his generals, who made several requests for clarification, only to have it restated for them in unequivocal terms. The old and the 'weak' (in classical Chinese, this can often be a euphemism for women) were to be spared, but the men were to be wiped out. Qianlong meant it, and the combination of slaughter and smallpox wiped the Zunghars off the map, while others starved on the run or fled across the border into Russia. A few thousand survived as slaves, but in such conditions that they had no chance of maintaining their ethnic identity, possessions or territory – they were not even permitted to keep their original names. The Zunghars disappeared, and exist today only in a few isolated place names, with meanings that often elude modern residents.

Emperor Qianlong's brutal decision marks a turning point in the involvement of the Manchus (and hence, the Chinese in general) in the region. Whereas policy in the past had favoured setting 'barbarian against barbarian', this direct, military intervention in steppe affairs signalled that the Manchus were in the region to stay. It recalled similar massacres carried out by the Manchus in their original conquest of China, when cities that refused to submit were annihilated. Just as the Manchus had occupied China and stayed, they now firmly incorporated the Western Regions within the same sphere. There was to be no more doubt or equivocation, no more nods and winks and vaguely defined tributary relationships. It has been suggested that the rather un-Chinese atrocity perpetrated by the Manchus on the Zunghars was in part because, in old-fashioned Chinese terms, this literally was a case of 'barbarian against barbarian'. Whereas Chinese dynasties had often valued even their enemies as potential suppliers of horsemen and horses, the Manchus already had ample horsemen of their own. In edicts that cited 400 years of trouble from the Zunghars, a triumphant Qianlong defended his actions, proclaiming that he could now face his ancestors in the afterlife and report the border problem crushed for good.

However, this opened a whole new can of worms to the south of the Tianshan Mountains, where the Zunghars had formerly settled disputes and preserved peace among the quarrelling city-states. At the fall of the Zunghars, Chinese troops had rescued two descendants of Afaq Khoja, who had been living under Amursana's protection as hostages to guard against any revolt or welching on tribute from the desert oases. Qianlong had rather hoped that they would accept him as a new master. Instead, they ran back to their homeland and fomented rebellion, claiming that this was their one chance to 'create an independent state'.

It would take years to clear up the mess. Even in the first flush of freedom, several major cities refused to support the new rebels, far preferring the authority of the Chinese. Eventually, their stronghold amounted to little more than the cities of Kashgar and Yarkand, and even then, it was the Khojas who did more damage than the Chinese, despoiling the areas around the cities in order to ensure that no besieging army had ready access to supplies. The reporting, even from sources sympathetic to the rebels, suggests that even the Khojas' local 'support' was coerced. One local ruler, however, enthusiastically welcomed the Chinese, and helped them in their campaign to restore order. It is for this reason that the fabled Emin Khoja not only has a beautiful commemorative minaret that has come to symbolise the architecture of the whole region, but also a distinctly un-Islamic statue (see Gazetteer: Turfan).

The Manchus were the last imperial dynasty to rule China – lasting until the famous 'Last Emperor' who gave way to a Republic in 1912. Their legacy would be the incorporation of many outlying regions securely within the nation of China itself, starting with their homeland of Manchuria, which is now known simply as the three provinces of the 'North East', but was outside China proper for many earlier dynasties. Their desire to secure their inland flanks from the Russians, but also from fellow nomads, saw them direct significant energy and resources towards wars along the Silk Road, eventually pushing as far west as Kashgar, and establishing, once and for all, a recognisable *modern* Chinese border.

The Manchus effectively ended their border problems by pushing the borders outwards to incorporate all those liminal or doubtful regions that might have previously caused trouble. Tibet was locked into the Chinese sphere, the Muslim outlands were brought to heel, and even Mongolia was signed up as a Chinese subject. However, history does not remember the Manchus' Qing Dynasty as a great success, mainly because in its supreme effort to solve a series of medieval problems it failed to realise that a whole set of new, modern problems was just about to arise.

It is important to remember that for the mandarins of the Qing Dynasty, and indeed many dynasties preceding them, the Western Regions *were* the site of foreign contact. Throughout most periods of Chinese history, the Silk Road and its attendant regions were the only places where China had real foreign relations of any kind. The Silk Road, with its emphasis on trade, difference, slippery deals and unreliable promises, false proclamations of fealty and half-hearted commands of obedience, represents the vast majority of China's experience of the non-Chinese world. It should, then, not be much of a surprise that it took the Qing Dynasty so long to realise just how drastically the world had changed when new 'barbarians' from even further west began appearing, and failed to play by the rules that had endured for many centuries.

This is not the place to recount the history of the 'Century of Humiliation' that saw China laid low by the Opium Wars, the Taiping Rebellion, and by a succession of 'unequal treaties' that parcelled out Chinese territory to foreign powers. But as Europeans and Americans exploited the weakening powers of the Manchus at the coast, China's hold on its own outer provinces began to waver. Hong Kong was lost to Britain; Macau to Portugal; Shanghai became a 'foreign' city. Is it any surprise that similar disruptions were threatened deep inland, among the desert cities?

Yaqub Beg and Kashgaria

The Western Regions were renamed Huijiang, 'the Muslim Frontier', and then Xinjiang, 'the New Frontier' in the 1880s. This shift in nomenclature reflects attitudes in China, which first regarded it as an area defined by a different ethnicity and religious belief, but later saw the potential for colonisation and exploitation. However, the 19th century saw a series of upstarts and rebels causing trouble in the region, often using Islam as an excuse, and leaning on support from beyond the borders in Central Asia, particularly from the Khanate of Kokand (1709–1876, a Muslim state centred on the Ferghana Valley).

They were never successful. Khoja Wali Khan, a distant descendant of Afaq Khoja, was a constant thorn in China's side through the 1840s and 1850s, attacked Kashgar on several occasions, and all but captured it in 1857, enjoying 77 days of murder and rape, and amassing a pile of skulls by the riverside. But even this legendary assault failed to take the city's fort, which held out until reinforcements chased Wali Khan away again. Nor did it win him any friends elsewhere, scandalising his former supporters when they discovered that he had sanctioned the execution of fellow Muslims. As with earlier conflicts among the people of Xinjiang, Wali Khan's predations are often remembered as a fight against China, when local Muslims suffered just as much, if not more, at his hands.

Wali Khan would try to involve himself in unrest once more in the 1860s, but would die in suspicious circumstances, seemingly at the order of a figure even more ruthless than him. Yaqub Beg (1820–77) was an adventurer from Kokand, who led an army into China in 1867, deposing the last of the White Mountain *khojas* and declaring himself an emir, at first as a vassal of his homeland, but soon afterwards as an independent ruler.

His short-lived state, sometimes referred to as Kashgaria, was also tied up with internal conflicts in Islam. He marched as far as Urumqi on a *jihad*, but it was a war against fellow Muslims; Yaqub's army notably contained Chinese soldiers, fighting alongside the Muslims of his own sect. Hoping to conquer the Ili region north of the Tianshan range, he fought several battles against the local inhabitants, pushing large numbers of Kazakh and Kyrgyz tribesmen into Russia.

With Xinjiang now in his hands as far west as Hami,

Yaqub imposed a harsh version of Sharia law that soon proved unpopular with his new subjects. The Uyghurs, it turned out, had been rather liberal in their adherence to the Islamic faith, and Yaqub's enforcers were scandalised to discover women without veils in Urumqi, men without turbans, and pork and wine on sale in the marketplaces. Floggings were meted out to the offending parties, and Yaqub made a great and pious display of donations to the mosques in the region, all the while using money taken from the people through heavier taxes.

The same monetary issues that had irked both the Han Dynasty and Tang Dynasty had not much changed over the centuries. Xinjiang cost more to hold than it generated in income. Lines of communication, soldiers' salaries, infrastructure and wear-and-tear, all ended up costing substantially more than Xinjiang appeared to generate on paper. Its true value was only clear to the long-term strategist, in terms of wars never fought, and armies never fielded. This was known to the Qing Dynasty, which had happily garrisoned Xinjiang at a loss, in the knowledge that the region had an important geographical and strategic function for China as a whole. But it seemed to be news to Yaqub Beg, who had no interior provinces from which to draw his funding.

He had no help from his native Kokand, from which he had rashly claimed independence. Nor was there a steady stream of silver from China. The supposedly independent Kashgaria was a financial folly of epic proportions. Yaqub Beg's blinkered religious utopia had put an end to trade, hampered farming, and murdered many local leaders. Now he had troops to pay and a state to run, and no means of raising further money. It is thus no surprise that his beleaguered new state soon attracted the attention of the British and the Russians, both of whom saw it as a tantalising scrap of real estate with a murderous despot in charge – an excellent potential addition to either empire! Both swiftly recognised Kashgaria as an independent state, but backed down again when it became clear that Yaqub Beg intended to take on China. Both the Queen and the Tsar would have been happy to make friends with a new Asian state; neither wanted a new war against China over desert wells.

General Zuo Zongtang, the man who eventually took control of Xinjiang from Yaqub Beg, summarised the region's invisible value to the Emperor. The steppes stretched right across Asia, but came perilously close to Beijing – within 300 kilometres of it. In order to ensure a strategically secure Beijing, any Chinese ruler needed to fully control Inner Mongolia. But Inner Mongolia was open to assault from the west, and could only be adequately protected by whoever owned the strategic choke point of the steppes north of the Tianshan Mountains. In other words, Xinjiang was not a money pit so much as the first defensible point on the steppes.

Yaqub Beg was a global celebrity in the 1870s. The Islamic world, which only heard that he was devout, praised him as a great Muslim leader. The Turks hailed him as an ethnic brother; the British and Russians, briefly, as a new desert king. Among most of the residents of Xinjiang he was regarded as a brutal foreign invader, with local Muslims even musing that life had been better under the Chinese.

The excitement over Yaqub Beg was swiftly forgotten. When the news came in 1875 that General Zuo Zongtang was on the march to recover the lost province, Yaqub's foreign support evaporated. The Russians, who had occupied the Ili valley in part to hold off the tide of refugees, allowed themselves to be talked out of holding onto it, on the understanding that they got some trade deals and a consul in Kashgar. Yaqub himself died, seemingly of a stroke, in 1877, although rumours soon spread that he had been poisoned by rival Muslims who had been corrupted by the Chinese. His desert empire collapsed, his followers fled or were executed, and those of his sons and grandsons who survived were imprisoned. Some were castrated and made to serve as eunuchs back in Beijing.

The international interest in Yaqub's revolt faded away as Xinjiang was left once more to the Chinese, although one small fragment of this historical oddity survives in the suburbs of London, a brisk walk south from the Woolwich Ferry. Just off Plumstead High Street, SE18, turn left at Lakedale Power Tools, and you will find yourself among the semi-detached houses of Kashgar Road. Where once were orchards and marshes, this residential area sprang up in the 1870s, and appears to have gained a street name evoking the headlines of the day, and the aspirations of the Victorians in the far, far east.

The tomb raiders

Xinjiang was not merely a new frontier for the Chinese. Among European explorers, it also came to represent one of the last parts of the world map that lay uninvestigated. For the British and the Russians, in particular, it was an alluring sweep of territory, clearly within the Chinese orbit but possibly available for the taking. Both these powers took hesitant steps to assess the region for its strategic value, as the Great Game ran its course in Afghanistan and moved up into the areas around Kashgar and Khotan.

This led to an influx of largely unsuccessful Christian missionaries, and a number of intrepid explorers and archaeologists. One, of course, was Ferdinand von Richthofen, who surveyed parts of the region in the 1860s, rather presumptively attempted to name a mountain range after himself, and stumbled across the dry basin of the Lop Nur. He returned to Europe and published his atlas of China in the year of Yaqub Beg's death, coining the term Silk Road. One of his students, the Swedish explorer Sven Hedin, mapped parts of the Taklamakan in the 1890s, becoming at one point the iconic desert madman, crawling through the sand, almost dying of thirst, towards a lake that turned out to be a mirage. It was one of Sven Hedin's expeditions that first uncovered the oldest relics of all in Xinjiang – dinosaur bones. Dating from a period when Xinjiang was far closer to the sea – the shores of the ancient Tethys ocean started at what is now the Himalayas – the bones were relics of giant reptiles, grazing on prehistoric ferns, and of fleet-footed, light-boned lizards now thought to represent a missing link between dinosaurs and birds. Unsurprisingly, dinosaur remains were never far from the residue of the forests and ferns on which they once feasted, crushed by the ages into the coal seams and oil fields that would bring Chinese miners into the remotest parts of Xinjiang during the 20th century.

Hedin's account of his travels, *Through Asia* (1898), inspired many others, including the Hungarian-born archaeologist Aurel Stein, who undertook several digs among the ruins of the Silk Road in the 1900s and 1910s, the German Albert von le Coq, who fell upon the frescos of the Thousand Buddha Caves like a man possessed, the Japanese Buddhist Kozui Otani, and the French polymath Paul Pelliot, who rode right through Xinjiang on an epic expedition from 1906–8. All wrote gripping accounts of their investigations, uncovering in Stein's words, the 'ruins of desert Cathay', and revealing the largely forgotten roots and routes of the region. It is their reports, filed no more than a century ago, that first introduced the rest of the world to the many places and peoples detailed in earlier chapters of this book, uncovering the ruins of Loulan, the first of the Tarim mummies, and the ruins of once-great Khotan.

The Chinese regarded them, rightly, with suspicion. Despite the climb-down over Yaqub Beg, both Britain and Russia remained interested in the Xinjiang region as a potential strategic location in any future war with China; many of their subjects who wandered through the area turned out to have hidden agendas.

In the case of the 'Swede' Gustaf Mannerheim, archaeology and anthropology were only a cover story. Mannerheim was a Russian agent, hand-picked for his two-year mission because as a Finnish nobleman he spoke perfect Swedish, and could pass as a Swedish explorer. Mannerheim's job was to ride the length of the Silk Road, ostensibly as part of Paul Pelliot's mission, but actually checking on the status of Chinese military installations, mapping the unmapped regions, and observing the degree to which Japanese 'advisers' had already infiltrated the region.

When Mannerheim returned to St Petersburg, he filed a long report in 1909 describing the rotten, corrupt state of the Qing empire, and the improbability that it would ever offer any threat to Russia. He wrote a cunning plan for seizing Xinjiang by occupying certain strategic oases, not as a plan for colonisation, but as a means of swiftly winning a huge area on paper. An invading force, he suggested, could nominally seize hold of Xinjiang in mere weeks by grabbing a handful of oases, but what would they really have? Nothing but sand and storms, and no genuine control over the fractious locals. Mannerheim saw Xinjiang as a strategic side-show, a scrap of territory that could be snatched and then sold back to the Chinese as ballast in treaty negotiations, in return for more useful concessions elsewhere.

His own souvenirs from his trip, including a striking Tibetan scroll of a god riding a horse, a Chinese desk and assorted other knick-knacks, remarkably survived the turbulent years of the First World War, the Russian Revolution and the Finnish Civil War, and can still be found at his house-museum in Helsinki.

When such explorers first arrived, it was with the attitudes of European colonialism. They regarded Chinese antiquities as far too good for the Chinese themselves, and fully deserving of a place in a European or American museum, where they might be best preserved and studied. We might forgive them or even agree – after all, thousands of shattered statues along the Silk Road are testament to the spiteful piety of Islamist vandals, and the Chinese themselves had observed the calculated destruction of many inscriptions by Chinese rubbing-sellers, determined to increase the value of their sheets by ruining the original. And we see such attitudes elsewhere in the modern history of archaeology. The Rosetta Stone, for example, was little more than a paving slab to generations of ignorant passers-by – one might argue that it was only 'discovered' in the British Museum in 1822, when Champollion began to truly decode it.

However, this is not how things look to the Chinese. They see, instead, wave upon wave of snooty gatecrashers – some, like Pelliot, true China enthusiasts, others little more than tomb raiders and fortune hunters – paying pennies to dumbfounded peasants for junk and flotsam that was not really theirs to sell. Aurel Stein wrote wistfully of accruing Buddhist 'merit' in the next life for all of his endeavours, clearly believing them to be honourable. But within a couple of chapters he is already gaming the local officials, arranging ruses to distract them and making time-wasting enquiries, all the better to allow him to poke around sites undisturbed. In part, this was because of a general and growing suspicion in China towards foreigners; he was, after all, on his mission to Khotan while the Boxer Rebellion rumbled on in distant Beijing. But there is the distinct sense in Stein's text that he felt the Chinese could not be trusted to know the value of their own antiquities, and that they were unreliable custodians. At the time, he was probably right.

A recurring issue in many of the arguments over ownership and heritage for the last 200 years is that it is unfair to hold the departed archaeologists to today's standards and values. This holds just as true for the locals as for the Europeans, since many Chinese seem to exercise a remarkable amnesia regarding the conditions under which the foreign archaeologists were working. Albert von le Coq, more likely to be cited today as a vandal than an archaeologist, believed himself deeply committed to the *preservation* of Chinese heritage, and reported with head-shaking despair the sight of Chinese yokels scraping priceless pigments from the Bezeklik caves to use as fertiliser on their fields. These fields were often newly broken ground, and became arable only after the removal of inconvenient stupas, temple ruins and graves. What little survived below ground was then ruined by irrigation, while any extant religious images in nearby caves were subject to ruin at the hands of ignorant peasants. Albert von le Coq was sure of his own nobility of purpose when he chipped murals from the walls of Bezeklik with a pickaxe. If he 'defaced' the grottoes, he did so with the intention of rescuing the sacred images, since many others had already had their eyes and mouths gouged out by would-be Taliban. There is, then, a certain awful irony that most of the murals rescued by von le Coq were annihilated during the Allied bombing of Berlin, and now only exist as photographs. They might have fared better if left in their caves, but probably would still be lost by now, all the same.

The most notorious of the items spirited out of China were the scrolls found piled high in a hidden room at one of the Mogao caves (see Gazetteer: Dunhuang). Possibly walled away for safe-keeping during an enemy attack, possibly a dumping ground for religious texts that could not be destroyed, this pile of old documents lay undisturbed until 1900, when they were uncovered by Wang Yuanlu (1849–1931) a priest who had taken it upon himself to sweep away some of the sand that had drifted into the many caves.

In one alcove, he found a hollow wall, and behind it a subsidiary 'Library Cave'. Aurel Stein would later see it himself, and wrote in *Ruins of Desert Cathay*:

> Heaped up in layers, but without any order, there appeared in the dim light of the priest's little lamp a solid mass of manuscript bundles rising to a height of nearly ten feet, and filling, as subsequent measurement showed, close on 500 cubic feet. The area left clear within the room was just sufficient for two people to stand in.

Wang is an interesting figure in the history of the Dunhuang sites. He was a Daoist and an amateur archaeologist, who had notified the Chinese authorities of his discovery of the Library Cave, and applied for funding to preserve it. Given the brush-off by his own people, and ordered to re-seal the cave in what sounds like a very Chinese passing of the buck, it is perhaps easy to see why the arrival of foreign explorers, offering him money for what others might have literally described as waste paper, proved incredibly tempting.

Aurel Stein laid it on thick, claiming to be following in the steps of the legendary Tripitaka, and seeking to take sacred scrolls back to a sacred site in India. It is difficult to know, a century later, who was swindling whom – Wang kept up the performance of the reluctant devotee who might be persuaded by 'donations', even though he was not actually a Buddhist himself. Stein continued his act of pious Buddhist belief, and seems to have been economical with the truth regarding the scrolls' final destination – not India, which was merely a staging post, but India's colonial master, Great Britain.

Eventually, Wang caved, and let Stein run off with a stack of scrolls. Although undoubtedly worth far more than Stein paid for them, the scrolls in question were chosen more for their condition than their content. Stein couldn't actually read most of the texts, and inadvertently came away with dozens of copies of the same sutra. One of them, however, turned out to be the oldest printed document in existence, a text of the Diamond Sutra dating from AD 868. Today, it is rolled out in all its glory in the British Museum, London.

Arriving only a few months later, the gifted linguist Paul Pelliot was far more meticulous, often plumping for the most moth-eaten and torn manuscripts, particularly when he realised that they were over-written on even older documents, or contained languages unrepresented in European archives. The Dunhuang scrolls have since become one of the most famous literary finds in world history, including priceless religious texts – rare scriptures of Nestorian Christianity including the 'Jesus Sutras' – but also a manual for playing the game of Go, star maps, history books, dictionaries, medical treatises and songs. In many cases, a Dunhuang manuscript is the only copy of the text in existence, and opens up entire new areas of study in medieval history and culture. Many of the documents are in Chinese, but others are in Tibetan, Sogdian, Uyghur and a number of other scripts, not all of which have been deciphered. In enlightened modern times, the entire stock of Dunhuang manuscripts, from all over the world, has been digitised and made freely available online for researchers the world over, marking a departure from the spirit in which they were originally taken – snatched by foreign imperialists and smuggled out of the country.

The Chinese soon wised up. Within a couple of years, it became much more difficult to acquire antiquities, and the state began concerted efforts to keep Chinese artefacts in China. The Nestorian Tablet, for example, that ancient proclamation of Christianity in Tang Dynasty China, was moved to the Forest of Steles for its own protection, after the Chinese authorities realised in 1908 that several foreign trophy-hunters were sniffing around it. Its original remote location, literally open to the elements in the middle of a field, was scant protection against tourists, and its Christian credentials were catnip to foreigners. Already, there were accusations that interfering Jesuits had tried to alter the inscription to make it more relevant to their own order, and that the sheer number of rubbings taken had worn some of it away. The telltale crucifix at its apex, for example, has been hard to see since the 19th century, worn down by countless reverent fingers. The Danish explorer Fritz Holm arrived in Xi'an with the express purpose of carrying the tablet away for the British Museum, only to discover that the Chinese had had enough. Instead, Holm commissioned a duplicate, and sputtered in indignation when a group of mandarins went to inspect the original, in order to ensure that he had not switched them. It was, Holm bitterly observed, the first time that the Chinese authorities had bothered to even look at the Tablet, even though it had been sitting in place for 300 years.

The Nestorian Tablet today is in a rather inconvenient spot, just one of the many slabs in the Forest of Steles in Xi'an. Its back is to a wall where one cannot see the obverse inscription, its front protected by a sheet of grubby perspex that makes photography pointless. It is difficult to stand too long and observe it without impeding the passage of others. Where a European museum might have placed it literally on a pedestal, in a chamber of its own, its position in the Forest of Steles reflects its position in *Chinese* history, as merely one of many, many important inscriptions. The fact that it is not in a bespoke museum gallery in New York, Berlin or London represents something else – a turning point in China's own sense of its heritage, the moment when the Chinese began to realise that their antiquities deserved to be kept in China, and not flogged off in a yard sale to covetous foreign literati. The fact that there is anything at all for modern travellers to see on a trip to the Silk Road is at least in part a result of this historical moment. However, largely unremembered today is the role that other foreigners played in the story. One of the first tourists to see the Tablet in its new home at the Forest of Steles, Gustaf Mannerheim, wrote that it was Protestant missionaries who had alerted the Chinese authorities to Holm's alleged plot: '...and one of them is reported to have said that the stone belonged more to him, who had lived in China for 20 years, than to [Holm], who had only arrived a day or two before.'

7

Autonomy and Hegemony (1912–2012)

YOU USED TO BE ABLE to count on finding a statue of Chairman Mao in every city in China. However, today, although you'll find replicas by the dozen in antique markets and jumble sales, he has largely sneaked away from public places. As most Chinese regions turn away from homogeneity and go in search of local colour and local heroes, Mao has ceased to be a great unifying influence. His face is already on all the banknotes, does he have to be in the town square as well? In many town centres, local officials discreetly bundled him off into retirement during the 1990s, often in midnight removals to prevent any photographers snapping the moment when he literally came off his pedestal. He has largely been replaced with more ancient historical figures, or by abstract, quasi-mythical icons that might have once been called river-goddesses or Muses, but now, in a secular state, are more likely to be described as personifications of various Communist virtues and aspirations. There are crowded, bustling representations of the People, and spiky sweeps of steel like corporate logos. But there are a few Mao statues holding out. There's one in Chengdu, in front of the science museum in Tianfu Square. There's one in Beijing, at the University of Geology. And there is one in Kashgar, just before the Silk Road winds up into the mountains and out of China.

The Kashgar Mao faces People's Square, standing on a

pillar that is as tall as he is, looming over a squat, four-pillared arch, as if he is planning some sort of gymnastic feat. Like most other Mao statues, he is clad in a bulky overcoat designed to keep out a Beijing winter, incongruously buttoned up in the hazy Kashgar heat. But Kashgar's Mao seems a little tired. His coat, which is normally shown flapping in the Communist wind of change, sits rather drably by his sides, as if the breeze has let up. His arm is raised in a gesture of resigned invitation, as if he is showing you the town centre and saying: 'That'll have to do.' His mouth is closed, the lips grimly pressed together, as if this is the last big photo-op before he can get home for some rest.

The turbulent 20th century is as important a part of Xinjiang history as any other, although its heritage is both more readily apparent and yet harder to appreciate. Although many of its reversals and putsches mirror similar events in the Han, Tang or Qing dynasties, the presence of living people whose parents or grandparents lived through it all keeps memories raw.

The sights of modern tourism are similarly alive and personal. There might not be all that much to see in Shihezi, but the *entire town* is a monument to the 20th century, and coalesces around a series of agricultural colonies – the most recent in a series of veteran resettlements dating back to the Han Dynasty. The town is also home to a museum of military history (see Gazetteer: Shihezi), which is far more immediate for the locals, many of whom are descended from those same former soldiers. Visit Xinjiang today and you will find the 20th century still playing out, with its renewed promises of the region as a 'new frontier' for the Chinese, a place of abundant mineral wealth and untapped agrarian capacity. One still gets a sense of can-do 1950s technocracy, in bold claims and massive schemes to open up new land and tame wild desert.

What made the 20th century different was the scale of the population. Han Chinese settlers arrived not in their thousands, but in their millions. Communications, particularly roads and rail, connected Xinjiang more directly to the Chinese core than in any previous era. Post-colonial authors talk of 'hybridity' – the inevitable wash in both directions as two cultures affect one another. Without question, the Chinese see Xinjiang as a treasure trove of oil, gas and mineral deposits, a true frontier of potential profits. But conversely, deny the presence of the Han Chinese in Xinjiang, and you deny some of its modern marvels. The fact that the Ili valley is Chinese at all, and not some forgotten Russian backwater, is at least partly thanks to the Han settlers. The highway to Ruoqiang, the wine groves in Turfan and the wind farms in Dabancheng are products of Communist-era development projects and foreign investment.

The foreign press makes much of locals outnumbered by outsiders, and the threat to minority cultures from a tidal wave of homogeneous Han; less is written about the massive, invisible exodus from Xinjiang to the east, as Uyghurs and other ethnic minorities are tempted by the bright lights and business opportunities of the big cities. Such modernity is the product of the 20th century in China – its cause and its bugbear, its great hope and its bitter disappointment. Modern life itself lures believers towards the secular, and tempts traditional craftsmen with industrial alternatives. Some tourists want everything to remain primitive and 'authentic', as long as it does not affect the tourists themselves. It seems odd to arrive on a plane and sit in an air-conditioned hotel bar, drinking foreign beer that is cold from a fridge, and to then complain that Xinjiang is losing touch with its past.

The Republic of China

When the Qing Dynasty was toppled in 1911 in a Beijing revolution, the capital had other things on its mind than the distant desert. In Urumqi, the local viceroy carried on regardless, as if the Emperor were still on the throne. North of the

Tianshan Mountains, the Ili valley, crammed with resettled veterans, proclaimed itself for the Republic, partly out of genuine sentiment, and partly because many of those same veterans were members of the Gelao ('Brothers and Elders') secret society, devoted to overthrowing the Manchus. Fighting between rival factions poisoned the winter of 1911–12, but left neither side dominant.

It was, of course, highly possible that the new regime would behave in an entirely Chinese fashion and simply rebrand the existing authorities as new 'Republican' bureaucrats. Seemingly in anticipation of such a compromise, Gelao agents assassinated a number of Qing officials.

The motivation of the rebels eludes easy rationalisation, depending on to what extent local rivalries were co-opted within a story of a 'national' revolution. Some of the Gelao, for example, hated the Manchus, but were not necessarily hoping to overthrow the imperial system as a whole, merely to restore a Chinese emperor to the throne. Some of the Uyghurs clearly believed themselves to be fighting against the Manchus, others against the Chinese as a nation, and others were caught in local power struggles against fellow Muslims. In Hami, the 'Chinese' governor was overthrown, but he was a Muslim despot, granted authority in thanks for helping the Chinese in their 19th century campaign of conquest. The several hundred rebels who attacked him hid out in the mountains, but later signed a truce with the Republican army, which they joined as a cavalry unit. But in order to secure their cooperation, the general sent to hire them had to swear on the Qur'an that his intentions were honourable. He used similar tactics with other rebels in Turfan, but made no real attempt to address the grievances of the Uyghurs, who complained that they were still treated like serfs by their Muslim leader, while Chinese colonists had better rights.

As the Republicans had failed to radically alter the Qing-sponsored status quo, a new revolt broke out in the region in 1913. This time, the 'cavalry units' of the Republican army came out in support of, or were *accused* of coming out in support of, the rebels. Their ringleaders were executed, being now substantially easier to find than when they were hiding in caves.

Soon, the new Republican master of Xinjiang was revealed as Yang Zengxin (1867–1928), an official who swiftly asserted his authority as a mandarin in the old Confucian style – just, fair and stern. This, at least, is how the imposition of his rule was spun in his territories; a secular authority that did not genuflect to old local power bases or religious affiliations. However, Yang did have powerful local connections, and might be better regarded as another of the many warlords who sprung up in the Chinese hinterland in the chaos after the Republican revolution. Certainly, he filled a power vacuum of his own making, having killed many lesser rebels and the most powerful members of the Gelao. His forces included mutually hostile Muslim Black Mountain and White Mountain factions, the former pro-Chinese, the latter still quietly favouring an independent Islamic state. But despite the support of these forces, Yang was less a government official than a tolerated dictator – even his contact within the government had been given secret orders to have him replaced if at all possible.

Yang was one of the last Xinjiang rulers to hang onto his authority with a bloodstained dinner party. When he heard, in late 1915, that a group of restorationists were plotting to overthrow him, he had the messenger executed. This, however, was a ploy designed to lull the plotters into a false sense of security. At the Chinese New Year, he invited them to a banquet, where three of them were beheaded partway through the main course. With steely composure, Yang went on eating, ignoring the dwindling fountains of blood as they seeped into the floor.

He also leant on a staff of Muslim enforcers, some of whom seemed to see themselves as new emirs. One, Ma Fuxing, was put in charge of Kashgar, where he imposed a harsh interpretation of Sharia law, bedecking the city walls with amputated limbs, and cavorting with a harem of terrified local girls. This was largely ignored by Yang's administration for as long as it did no harm in the wider political scene, and was only terminated in 1924 when Ma's predations seemed to be encouraging a backlash in other cities. On Yang's orders, Ma was murdered by one of his own subordinates.

If Yang's policies seem medieval, he was at least good at running a medieval state. His brutalities kept the fractious ethnic groups in line, and he successfully opened up new agricultural land using medieval technology, setting an army of men with shovels to work. Xinjiang gradually slid back into the middle ages, and while there were some successes, the administration was unable to mount health or education policies, and drifted further into debt – as ever, Xinjiang cost more to govern than it brought in from tax. Refusing to be swallowed up by debt like Yaqub Beg, Yang simply began printing money, creating four separate currencies in Urumqi, Kashgar, Turfan and 'Ili' (i.e. the region north of the Tian-shan range). This helped to keep Xinjiang divided into four distinct economic zones, although all four of them suffered from ballooning inflation.

The chaos had many consequences. For a number of white imperial adventurers, who felt sure that their European credentials afforded them bulletproof invulnerability while the Chinese shot at each other, Xinjiang became a tourist destination of some cachet. One certainly gets the impression from several of the travelogues of the time that anyone with a pen and a pair of eyes could get a book contract if they were willing to peek into the romanticised desert region, now the site of power politicking between the Chinese, Russians and 'Turks'.

Sven Hedin had no qualms about exploiting the situation in Xinjiang, returning with hard currency in 1927 to conduct geological surveys, fixing the location of oil, iron, coal and gold beneath the desert sands. He found himself appointed by the Chinese government to investigate the possibilities of building a road through the desert, bringing him into direct contact with several warring factions in the supposedly pacified region. Eventually, many of the trucks in his expedition were commandeered by a Chinese warlord who needed them in the fight against Russians who had invaded the Ili region.

Aurel Stein also returned to Xinjiang in the last days of 1930, in what he had hoped would be a glorious fourth expedition among the ruins of desert Cathay. However, he was there for barely three weeks before his visa was cancelled. The story of Stein's ill-fated expedition offers an interesting encapsulation of changing attitudes among what he called 'the Young Chinese', and within the British establishment.

Stein had already been warned that the Chinese attitudes towards the pilfering of antiquities had changed in the years since his last trip. He had trouble securing funding from British institutions increasingly conscious of tensions in the region, but eventually wangled some money out of the Boxer Indemnity, a fund that could only be used for activities that would be 'mutually beneficial' to China and Britain. To officials of the preoccupied Republican regime in Nanjing, he claimed to be only interested in the contents of 'ancient waste-paper baskets and other rubbish dumps', and would not be taking away anything of interest to the Chinese themselves. But whatever Stein's stated aims, as a foreigner he had enemies within the administration, who soon published a newspaper article claiming that he had said:

> Sinkiang [Xinjiang] is not Chinese territory, and there is no central government in China. Sinkiang is not fully civilised. I think I can do with Sinkiang officials today what I used to do with those of the old regime. If you give some additional money with which to bribe them, I can have everything my own way in Sinkiang.

Stein's biographer, Annabel Walker, notes that the phrasing and vocabulary is so unlike Stein's extant correspondence that she is sure the quote is a fake. But as a summary of Stein's attitude towards Chinese authority, it is probably not all that far from the truth. The comments on the absence of government seem calculated to provoke a response, which came in the form of the revocation of Stein's licence to be in China at all. He left in a hurry, and rarely spoke again of the debacle.

By the time Stein arrived in Xinjiang, Yang had been assassinated (with poetic irony, at a dinner party), and the region was split once more into warring groups of pro-China Muslims, pro-independence Muslims, pro-China-non-Muslims and Soviet sympathisers.

Peter Fleming, elder brother of the more famous Ian, foresaw in Xinjiang the 'blue riband of inaccessibility', and took great pride in his *News From Tartary* (1936) of a journey right along the southern route and then through the mountains to Kashmir. Although not a spy like his sibling's creation, 007, Fleming travelled ostensibly for *The Times* of London, and concentrated with deep interest on the political and humanitarian situation in the region, almost as if preparing a report for other masters.

Nestled within Fleming's travelogue is a different perspective on Aurel Stein's legacy, as reported by an official in the remote desert outpost of Cherchen, halfway between Khotan and Ruoqiang.

> Of the very few white men he had met the one he liked best to talk about was Ishtin Sahib, a super-human figure whom, after initial perplexity, we identified as Sir Aurel Stein. All through the southern oases this great explorer is still spoken of with respect and admiration.

It would not be the first time that Chinese officials had told credulous foreign visitors what they wanted to hear, but Fleming's report is backed up by similar comments from as far away as Kashgar. There, the consul CP Skrine observed that a number of entrepreneurs among the local Muslims saw themselves as *Taklamanchis,* or explorers of the ruins, and made periodic trips out into the desert to comb for buried treasure. They would keep any gold they found, but any other artefacts, from statues to scrolls, were piously set aside for Ishtin Sahib's long-awaited return. Was this out of respect for seekers of knowledge, or a wily swindle at the expense of gullible foreign antiquarians (see Gazetteer: Khotan)?

It is possible for both perspectives to have an element of truth. A few 'snobs', in Fleming's phrasing, might have been dazzled by Stein's European *hauteur* and profession of Buddhist faith – a welcome change in an environment that was increasingly bitterly iconoclastic. For local peasants, who appraised old idols and scrolls as worthless trash, there was certainly likely to be some local mythology about the crazy white man and his yappy dog, riding into town to pay money for worthless old junk. Nor should it be that surprising that, in a territory riven by war and deprivation for over a decade, the locals might have other priorities on their mind than the possible heritage-value of a few old caves. While foreign explorers remained focussed on Xinjiang's historical antiquities, new history in the making had the inconvenient habit of breaking out in the middle of their expeditions.

Fleming also observed the human cost of Yang's underfunding of health and education, noting that the arrival in some communities of a foreigner with a travelling medicine kit was welcomed as if a fully fitted hospital had rolled into town. He interviewed several of the warlords jostling for control, and wrote of the shock of familiarity when seeing something from beyond the desert, a feeling still familiar to travellers today.

> Here everything that was not of local manufacture had a history behind it, a long itinerary and an outlandish pedigree of owners; you could weave romance for hours on end round a tattered jacket of European cut or a tin bearing the name of a firm in a distant city.

Yang's death had been a sign of the slow approach of Chinese authority from the east, although the arrival of agents of the Republican government (specifically the Nationalists or *Guomindang* who were competing with the Communists for control of China), actually made matters worse. One Chinese official, Jin Shuren, blundered into the complex regional politics of Xinjiang with little thought to the consequences of his actions. He placed Han Chinese bureaucrats in charge of village communities that had previously been allowed to choose their own ethnic leaders, and disastrously replaced the Buddhist religious leader of one tribe with an atheist civil servant.

When a peasant revolt broke out in Hami, Jin sent in the troops. Whereas Yang had been brutal but successful in cutting off the heads of the leaders, Jin's soldiers killed indiscriminately in reprisals for atrocities against Chinese settlers. Instead of cowing the population of Uyghurs, this action merely showed them that surrender was pointless, fanning the flames of suicidal resistance. Even in attempting to assert the authority of the Chinese in Xinjiang, Jin created new excuses for the locals to push back.

The 'Republics' of Xinjiang

By 1933, an elusive group of anti-Chinese factions had accumulated into a notional entity proclaimed on 12th November in Kashgar as either the East Turkestan Republic or the East Turkestan *Islamic* Republic, and celebrated in its first coins as the Republic of Uyghuristan. The confusion over the names, present even in documents from the time, reflects the lack of consensus among the participants, some of whom saw themselves as republican democrats, while others saw themselves as supporters of a new Muslim emirate. The nominal president was a *khoja*, former vizier of the ruler of Hami, but he was deposed only a few months later, with the arrival of a supposedly Muslim army, which overthrew the occasionally

Muslim government. The blink-and-you'll-miss-it rise and fall of the East Turkestan Republic has been seized upon as a rallying cry for modern separatists, who see it as a thwarted attempt to establish independence for Xinjiang. However, it is also a matter of some interest to the pro-Chinese lobby, which sees in it yet another example of the hopeless infighting among the region's petty sects and factions, who could not even agree on the name of their state, let alone the degree to which it was 'Islamic'. James Millward, in his *Eurasian Crossroads*, observes that the formal proclamation of the East Turkestan Republic invokes God less often than a modern US presidential address, and the extent of its Islamic devotion seemed to vary wildly depending on what one's correspondent wished to believe.

There have long been rumours that the ETR was somehow the result of foreign espionage and meddling, although its limited foreign contacts offer no evidence of this. Although Britain's consul in Kashgar was cautiously optimistic about an administration that promised freer trade for foreigners, his government offered no material support, clinging to its official relationship with the Republic of China. Nor did the Soviets react with enthusiasm to the creation of what they saw as yet another Islamic hothouse.

The East Turkestan Republic was not the only upstart state that winked in and out of existence in the 1930s. In one of the most bizarre events amid the chaos, mullahs from Khotan approached a pickle-maker's son from London, and asked him to be the king of 'Islamistan'. Bertram Sheldrake (1889–1947) was a Londoner in his forties who had converted to Islam along with his wife Sybil. Now known as Khalid and Ghazia Sheldrake, they became pillars of the international Muslim community, supporters of charitable works and public-speakers with an avowed interest in popularising and demystifying the Islamic world.

Doing himself few favours with his toothbrush moustache and a ludicrous fez, Khalid Sheldrake roused suspicion among his fellow Muslims, some of whom wrote him off as a deluded orientalist rich kid, in particular after some of his crazier stunts, such as an attempt in 1927 to translate the Qur'an into Esperanto. But while he was certainly an English eccentric and something of a braggart, he was also a deeply devout man, a doctor who ministered to the Muslim poor, a tireless speaker on inter-faith issues, and a prolific contributor and editor of journals and articles. Although he never visited Khotan, and hence had little appreciation of its awful dust storms or impoverished conditions, he jumped at the chance to become, in his words, the 'King of Islamistan.' He sent a message to Mrs Sheldrake in Forest Hill, to tell her that their two sons were now oriental princes, but did not have the opportunity to take up his new post.

It seems that Sheldrake was not the only potential ruler approached by Khotanese envoys, who had made the same offer to a Turkish prince, newly powerless after the rise of Atatürk. Nor did the 'Emirate of Khotan' last long in the political ferment of 1930s Xinjiang, where it was soon subsumed beneath the power of another local warlord. This, however, did not stop Sheldrake, a man who had already been warned by fellow Muslims that true glory awaited in heaven, and not in earthbound honours, from billing himself at numerous speaking engagements as 'His Majesty King Khalid of Islamistan'. Nor did he bother to explain to many of his followers that the grandiose-sounding Emirate of Khotan was a single oasis, already consigned to the history books as an independent state, instead allowing his audiences to believe that he really spoke for the millions of Muslims in Xinjiang. He didn't.

The last flash of separatism in 1930s Xinjiang was of an altogether different stripe, in the form of Sheng Shicai (1897–1970), a general supposedly loyal to the Chinese government, but actually working for the Soviet Union as the military governor of a notional Soviet satellite state. Sheng seemed to be operating in the belief that when matters eventually settled down, Xinjiang would become the Soviet Republic of Uyghuristan.

Sheng enjoyed military aid from the Soviet Union, but faced resistance from Xinjiang locals, particularly those who considered themselves Turks, who objected to being designated as Uyghurs. A man under siege, who had machine guns mounted outside his residence and who locked all his filing cabinets every night, Sheng remained quietly loyal to the Soviets until the early 1940s, when he came to believe that the Communists would collapse. Never one to stick to his principles, Sheng deported his Soviet advisers and executed several Chinese Communists in his retinue. When, following the Battle of Stalingrad, it became apparent that the Communists were not in trouble after all, Sheng turned once more on the Nationalist Chinese and demanded help from Stalin. Stalin refused, leaving Sheng at the mercy of the Nationalist Chinese, who removed him from his post in Xinjiang, but made him a minister in their government. In 1944, he left Xinjiang for good, with dozens of trucks full of his ill-gotten gains. Without his Soviet support, he was hitched inextricably to the Nationalist wagon, not the least because he was unlikely to make any friends within the rising Chinese Communist Party – one of the Communists he had executed was a brother of Chairman Mao.

As Sheng abandoned Xinjiang, he would soon abandon mainland China, fleeing for Taiwan with the other Nationalists as the Communists took hold of China as a whole. Soon after he departed, a second East Turkestan Republic was proclaimed, this time in the Ili valley around Yining, once again in a confusion of contradictory clauses. Despite early claims that this was an Islamic republic that had overthrown Chinese rule, the Ili Rebellion soon backtracked on this assertion – seemingly because the whole thing was being orchestrated by the Russians, who had just agreed at Yalta not to interfere in Chinese affairs. So what might have been a Soviet puppet state suddenly changed its mind, and began negotiations with the Chinese against whom it had been rebelling, over the chances of rejoining the Republic of China.

For the next few years Xinjiang was ruled by Zhang Zhizhong (1895–1969) a Chinese Nationalist with an unprecedented interest in giving self-determination to the Uyghur majority. He appointed three prominent Muslims as his advisers, including a man who had once been the emir of Khotan, incorporating much of the old order within his administration. By 1946, it was widely agreed that the Ili rebels were now the official administration of the 'Xinjiang province' of the Republic of China.

The People's Republic of China

With the victory of the Communists in China proper, the Ili rebels began negotiations to re-integrate Xinjiang into China as a whole. The Nationalists were persuaded to surrender, and many were settled in situ, as veteran farmers. Leading representatives of the Ili rebels, including a Chinese, a Kyrgyz, a Kazakh and a Uyghur, were invited to a consultative conference in Beijing in 1949, but never arrived. The circumstances of their disappearance remain a controversy to this day, and have been variously blamed on a plane crash, a surgical removal of potential independence advocates by either Mao or Stalin, or possibly both.

The second ETR, or what remained of its government after the heads had been removed, ceded control to Xinjiang in the 'Peaceful Liberation', and the last of many armies arrived in the province in 1949– the People's Liberation Army, arriving not to fight, but to establish government structures and rebuild.

During the 1950s, the Xinjiang area was slowly turned into a series of enclaves organised along ethnic lines. The Chinese Communist Party refused to consider requests for Soviet-style 'republics' under Chinese suzerainty, instead carefully wording its documents to confer 'autonomy' on districts, counties, and eventually on the entirety of Xinjiang. Hence, to this day, the traveller in Xinjiang finds themself within Chinese hegemony, but also within an area that might be a Mongol, Kazakh, Kyrgyz or Tajik county, among others. In all cases, the divisions were designed to represent the majority ethnic group in a particular area, although populations did not always fit this requirement, and many single-ethnicity districts naturally contain other racial groups. In particular, there was a degree of complaint when in October 1955, the province as a whole was renamed the Xinjiang *Uyghur* Autonomous Region. Non-Uyghurs objected, but Chairman Mao was adamant – he could not grant autonomy to a place, only to a people.

'Autonomy' within the People's Republic means recognition as an official ethnic minority, and certain dispensations for religious or cultural practice, including the use of minority languages on signage and in schools. This is often most noticeable in regulations on family size; where Han Chinese were encouraged to have only one child, ethnic minorities were often permitted two or three. However, Xinjiang was also the site of massive Han settlement programmes, often under the auspices of the Xinjiang Production-Construction Military Corps (XPCC, or *bingtuan* for short in Chinese), a colonial entity largely comprising demobilised soldiers, and intensively involved in resettlement and reconstruction.

The most famous Xinjiang tune from the Mao era was, and still is, '*Xinjiang Hao*' ('Xinjiang is Good') by Ma Hanbing, set to music by Liu Chi – it is the author's favourite song.

Our Xinjiang is a good place, ah!
With good pastures south and north of the Tianshan
The sands of the Gobi transformed into fine fields
Snow melts to irrigate the farms
Our beautiful pastures
Our beloved home.

The song is ubiquitous in Chinese media coverage of Xinjiang, and sure to be part of any modern performance relating to Uyghur culture. Its writers, however, were Han Chinese from Shaanxi and Fujian, who answered a call in 1951 for new songs that could form the repertoire for a Frontier Soldiers Choir. '*Xinjiang Hao*' is a three-verse advert pleading for settlers to go west, ticking off all the available natural resources, including iron and coal, gold, melons and grapes, cows and sheep. It exhorts everyone to leap to their feet, banging on drums, singing and dancing, promising 'a grand union of all races, praising our leader Mao Zedong.'

The *bingtuan* colonies are the most crucial element in Xinjiang's 20th century history. In the 1950s, they afforded a vital means of integrating the Communist's former Nationalist enemies into the system, turning them from potentially dangerous foes into useful farmers and labourers. As the years passed, the XPCC became a valuable institution for public works, road-building and agricultural settlement, maintaining its quasi-military organisation even when its direct ties to the military had faded. Its unofficial motto, 'one hand on a pickaxe, one hand on a gun' neatly encapsulates its own sense of frontier pioneering and its ready militia, warding against border incursions or local unrest. In a repeat of the resettlement programmes of many historical dynasties, the XPCC also funnelled convicts to the new frontier, both genuine criminals and exiled dissidents. By the 1960s, the XPCC was actively recruiting among the eastern urban population, sending officials to the big cities, particularly Shanghai, to lean on youthful patriots to go west.

Soviet contacts soured and faded, to be replaced with Mao's own brutal attempts to drag China up by its bootstraps in his notorious Great Leap Forward. China plunged into a new form of chaos amid the reversals of the Cultural Revolution, and Xinjiang was not exempt. The great frontier experiment was caught up in the over-optimistic developmental targets issuing from Beijing, and saw many failed attempts to conquer the natural order. Kazakh herds were dragged from the pasture and fed grain in a vain attempt to increase productivity. The national hysteria over steel production saw the construction of many local furnaces, which distracted locals from their actual work. As Mao's greatest follies led to shortages and famine, cross-border connections encouraged many Kazakhs in particular to consider defecting, prompting the XPCC to establish military farms in the border zone to police for emigrants.

In the most ludicrous turn of events, archaeologists in Astana near Turfan were caught up in the era's frenetic demands for increases in productivity. How did one rate the 'productivity' of an archaeologist? Why, in artefacts recovered, of course, leading the excavation of Astana to proceed at a break-neck pace, with objects torn from the ground by the truckload. This was a disaster – so often in archaeology, the where and the how of an object's interment can be as, if not more important than its material existence. In a bizarre form of rescue archaeology, the cash-strapped researchers gave up digging their own pits, and instead picked and pecked in the wake of ditch-diggers at roadsides, like seagulls following a fishing boat. This certainly yielded sufficient *quantities* of artefacts to impress Party scrutineers, but like many other achievements of the Great Leap Forward era, the findings lacked quality, certainly in archaeological terms.

Xinjiang was not spared the worst excesses of the Cultural Revolution – indeed, ethnic and religious differences often magnified the tensions as China turned on itself. Scarcity in resources even led to a split within the XPCC, as cadres argued over who was the better revolutionary, leading to open battles over strategic sites and food reserves.

In the aftermath of the Mao era, Xinjiang has been picking up the pieces. Its touchstone has been a 1957 speech by Mao's rival and colleague Zhou Enlai, who called for the people of Xinjiang to fight the twin dangers of 'local nationalism' (a common complaint throughout history) and 'Han chauvinism.' It is for the latter point that Zhou Enlai gained immense popularity in the region – they have literally built statues to him for daring to suggest that his people might have a bias of their own. In suggesting that the Han way is not always the best way, Zhou has secured himself a position as something of a local hero, and a touchstone for debates on the future of Xinjiang (see Gazetteer: Shihezi).

Whose song is it anyway?

Wang Luobin (1913–96) is a case in point. Lionised and celebrated by the Chinese, his face and his iconic cowboy hat are associated in the Chinese mind with a lifetime's output of songs inspired by and drawing upon local musical traditions. But he also blundered, late in life, into a controversy over whose music it really was, in particular when he demanded performance royalties from a pop musician who covered some of his best-known songs. This, in turn, ignited several debates over colonialism, appropriation and privilege. Was Wang really the 'author' of his most famous tunes, which can be heard noodling in the background of every railway carriage, nature documentary and airport, or had he commodified and usurped folk songs that were not really his? And what did it say about cultural attitudes in China that his biggest hits, like 'Dabancheng Girl' (1938) amounted to insistent declarations by a Chinese man of sexual interest in a Uyghur girl, as if China were the active, patriarchal, domineering force, and Xinjiang the passive, ethnic Other waiting to be possessed?

Wang himself pleaded that the world's sound libraries contained thousands upon thousands of tapes of ethnic music, none of which had topped the charts. It was the role of adaptors like him to pick out and refine the gems. Such songs did not become hits until they had an amanuensis that brought them to the public, sanding off the rough edges perhaps, or sifting them into the right degree of the exotic and familiar.

The ethnomusicologist Rachel Harris, in her study of the Wang Luobin case, notes that things get even more complicated, in a carnival of finger-pointing that finds the moral high-ground trumped on several successive occasions. Albert von le Coq, the infamous despoiler of temples, had also collected songs in Turfan in the 1920s. There, he recorded a 16-year-old girl singing a song that he filed as the 'Love Song of Daban-cîng', with transcribed lyrics in Uyghur that are sufficiently close to Wang's in Chinese for them to be one and the same. This not only put the shoe on the other foot with the Uyghurs (it's okay for *them* to lust after Uyghur ladies, it seems), but also opened a whole new can of worms regarding the song's origins, which le Coq claimed to have been a declaration of doomed love by one of Yaqub Beg's fundamentalist warriors to a local girl, shortly before the Muslim separatists were defeated by the Chinese army in the 1870s. This not only placed the origin of the song 60 years before Wang Luobin's version, but also revealed it to be a song intimately connected to tales of Muslim rebellion. Perhaps, it was argued, the only way to tell for sure would be to dig out le Coq's ancient phonograph from the Berlin Institute of Psychology... which turned out to have been bombed flat by the Royal Air Force in the Second World War.

It is easy to find 'folk music' all over China. Any record store, from Beijing to Hong Kong, is sure to have triple CD sets of Xinjiang hits or Tibetan ditties, usually featuring a lissom super-model on the cover, dolled up in ethnic clothes. The fast-track to a recording contract, it would seem, is to be a pretty girl from a minority like the Qiang or the Kazakhs, who can be rolled out on the talent shows to fulfil a quota of ethnic songs. Half of the new records on sale seem to have titles like 'Tibet This' and 'Grasslands That', suggesting a passionate interest in folk music from the hinterland among the yuppies and students of the big cities. Many, however, take old tunes and repurpose them as 'Red music' in the service of the Party – even 'The East is Red', that stirring 1950s paean to Chairman Mao, began as a Shaanxi farmer-girl's ballad about a brother who is missing at dinner.

It has been suggested that, Red reversionings or not, the entire 'interest' of the Han Chinese public in folk music is merely a cunning plan to co-opt the broad cultures of the ethnic minorities into the narrative of Han history, marking them as little more than happy, drumming tribesmen and sexually-alluring belly dancers. We'll do the politics and the money; you can have a sing-song, leaving us, for example, in a situation where the town of Hami shows up in playlists not as a site of ancient kingdoms or Muslim devotion, but as the subject of Tian Wenjun's inadvertently suggestive grocer's song 'Please Taste My Melons'.

Honestly, the argument is exhausting. One wonders if the Han can ever do anything right in the eyes of the minorities, or if the minority activists would only be happy if they were totally ignored... which would then be another sign of oppression! Wang Luobin's compositions are masterpieces of popular music, and while many of them are indeed better described as arrangements and translations of existing folk-songs, he was very good at what he did. Later attempts to modernise and popularise Uyghur songs have all too often devolved into predictable Euro-pap models, with perfunctory key changes and synthesised instruments. Others, imitating Wang's middle-brow approach, have successfully imported old-time rhythms and melodies into modern pop, but always as participants in compilation albums. Ask in one of the aforesaid record stores for an album solely comprising songs by Xinjiang artists such as Wu Zuobao or Kelim, and you will receive nothing more than a shrug and the offer of another *Now That's What I Call Desert Music*. The hand-pressed, rough-and-ready CDs of local musicians on sale in the bazaars of Urumqi and Kashgar are the closest thing you are likely to get to authenticity. Tellingly, many of these local, 'unspoilt' artists are often still found to be doing cover versions of some of Wang Luobin's hits. For some notes on Uyghur music *before* Wang Luobin, see Gazetteer: Yarkand.

8

The Silk Road Today

HONGSHAN (RED MOUNTAIN) PARK takes its name from the dark, sandy Permian outcrop that forms the highest point of modern-day Urumqi. It is home to the Temple of the Heavenly King, built during the Tang Dynasty, and the Zhenlong Tower, a relic of the Mongol conquest. Visitors twirl parasols, and lean indolently on the balconies that look out over the lush forests, down towards the Ferris wheel in the nearby fairground. The city itself squeezes past below, in the narrow gap between Hongshan and the nearby peak of Yamalike (Monster Hill) – local legend holds that the two hills are the corpse of a defeated dragon, and the river valley between them is the slice of a divine sword.

Both Hongshan and Yamalike are covered in trees, a lovely view that is entirely modern, since both were little more than bare crags only 60 years ago. The effort to cover both mountainsides with forest was an entirely artificial government endeavour, arranged as part of the general effort to transform Xinjiang in the 1950s from a desert region to a more habitable, temperate area.

Near the top of Hongshan there is a statue of an official. He is draped in a long scholar's robe, arranged as if to suggest that he has one foot raised possessively on the plinth where he stands. He seems stern and thoughtful, his goatee beard trailing wispily onto his chest. The front of his bare head is shaved, while his hair is gathered in a long braid down his back, identifying him as a figure from the Qing Dynasty, when all subjects of the Manchus were obliged to show their allegiance in such a manner.

This is Lin Zexu (1785–1850) a Chinese civil servant also commemorated in his native Fujian, and in New York Chinatown, where he stands in the middle of Chatham Square, his hands behind his back as he stares up in contemplation at the modern skyscrapers. He is best known to English-speakers for standing up to British drug-dealers, when he confiscated tonnes of illegal opium, setting off the infamous Opium Wars in 1839. His open letter to Queen Victoria, scolding her for allowing her subjects to pursue such criminal acts, was published in *The Times*. The day on which he began the long process of dumping his confiscated opium in the sea near Hong Kong, 26 June, has been celebrated since 1987 as the United Nations International Day Against Drug Abuse and Illicit Trafficking.

This is not the reason why there is a statue of him in Urumqi. He is remembered in Xinjiang because of the embarrassing aftermath of the Opium Wars, when his attempt to take a noble stand against the imperialists was defeated by superior forces and corruption within the Qing state. Discredited and demoted, Lin was packed off into internal exile like many other failed officials, troublesome princes and dissident writers, and served several years as a governor in Ili (see Gazetteer: Yining).

Ever the eager manager, he embraced his new command with gusto, and initiated a number of audacious land reclamation and irrigation schemes. Lin gets pride of place in modern Urumqi, even though he can hardly have done much more than pass through on his way somewhere else, because he is a famously good-hearted figure, who took a great interest in the local peoples, championed Chinese projects that provided a better life for all, and in his way, stood up to the dual bugbears of pre-Communist China – the imperial system and the foreign invaders. He looks down in stern approval at modern Urumqi because it is a multicultural city, thick with green-leafed trees, where there was once little more than windswept wasteland.

Lin Zexu is the kind of man that the Chinese government wants to represent Xinjiang – incorruptible, fearless, loyal and industrious. Even though he died a century before the arrival of the Communist era's military colonists, he stands as a harbinger of their transformative efforts.

Millions of Chinese flock to the eastern cities in search of their fortunes, and the inhabitants of Xinjiang are no exception. Even without official permits, they have joined the ranks of unsanctioned migrants, as kebab sellers and walnut bakers on the streets, short-order cooks and casual labourers. Such an exodus from the heartland, of course, threatens the culture of Xinjiang itself, particularly when its tourist value is strangely bipolar – visitors are welcome, as long as they like the whirling dances and the glittery silks. Travel further afield, to the more obscure corners of Xinjiang, is discouraged and obstructed, in part by officialdom, but largely by the simple logistics of getting around such a wide, inhospitable place, when even Mandarin-speakers are in shorter supply, and the unwary traveller is apt to blunder into a waterless desert or a radioactive bomb-testing site.

Ecology and erosion

The desert is growing. While there may have been colder spells in the millennia since the people of Lop built their lakeside villages, the world is still getting warmer, and today the snow cover on China's mountains is rapidly declining. Without a let-up in global warming, China will have lost two-thirds of its glaciers by 2050, and by 2100 there will be no glaciers at all. That will shut off *all* the water that feeds the Xinjiang region, and expand the desert conditions of the Taklamakan, that notorious Place of Ruins, far beyond their current borders. As well as being steeped in history, the realms of the Silk Road have a new, doom-laden role to play, as a glimpse of how the future might look for many other countries in a resource-scarce, parched world.

The rhetoric of Party propaganda since the 1950s has been in line with the message of '*Xinjiang Hao*', that green pastures and rich arable land await colonists on the new frontier. But that is only partly true. Like other desert regions, Xinjiang is a fragile ecosystem. If it has been sparsely populated for most of its history, it is partly because of the unattractiveness of the land, but also because its population reached a state of equilibrium. The vast numbers of 20th century colonists have broken new ground, opening up immense areas of irrigated agricultural land, but in doing so, they have ripped out the guts of organic structures that had run for centuries. Massive tamarisk root systems, that once held fragile, powdery soil in place, were torn out by tractors, briefly creating flat ground for crops, but later whipping up a dust-bowl of unprecedented proportions. Xinjiang has always been plagued by *qara-buran*, the black sandstorms that so frightened Marco Polo, but now they are more frequent, and farther-ranging. In recent memory, Khotan was wreathed in choking sandstorms for two days out of every three, for a whole year. Thick clouds of red dust, the result of similar efforts in the nearby Gobi Desert, have blown as far as Beijing, turning the capital into a Martian vista, with a pale sun peeking through gritty air.

Xinjiang was not designed to sustain so many millions. Increases in populations, not only of Han colonists, but also the local Uyghurs, Kazakhs and Kyrgyz and even the vastly enlarged herds of sheep and cattle, have placed severe new burdens on the water table, to the extent that wells must now often be sunk thrice as deep as they once were.

It is not unusual to find place-names in China that allude, in one language or another, to historical lost lakes, phantom rivers or buried ruins. Today it is increasingly common in

Xinjiang to find modern-day signage that points to a pasture that has already disappeared, or to a forest that has already vanished. The poplar trees that once held together the northern foothills of the Kunlun Mountains are gone. One of the most common 'trees' in the rest of the region was the saxaul (*Haloxylon ammodendron*), a hardy, shrubby Central Asian bush that once covered huge areas of the Ili valley north of the Tianshan Mountains. But the resinous, knotty wood was often the only fuel available to Kazakhs and colonists alike, and most of the saxaul trees in the Ili district have been cut down. The government is now frantically trying to reverse the process, with saxaul trees being replanted in barren areas in an attempt to hold the ground together and push back the desert.

The oases were a delicate balance. Xinjiang was not ready for whole new cities conjured out of nowhere, like Shihezi. Nor could the rhetoric of the Cultural Revolution, which saw in technology and elbow-grease a victory over nature, magically make the region support more cows than it already did. Such efforts and expansions have diverted water that once went elsewhere. Lakes, already down from their historical heights, have shrivelled further. The treeline has retreated from hillsides. Rivers that once watered marshes and wetlands at the desert's edge, now no longer reach so far. The incredible *karez* system of Turfan has been made a protected site, at least in part because only a third of its tunnels now carry any water at all – it is thought that all of them will be dry by 2030. Despite the amazing agricultural achievements of the mid-20th century, a fifth of the newly created agricultural land has already been reclaimed by the desert.

The Chinese remain undaunted. In a state that is unafraid of truly huge macro-projects, there are multiple efforts underway to transform Xinjiang. In Dabancheng, near Urumqi, where explorers once complained that 'all the winds of Asia' seemed to howl through the gap in the Tianshan Mountains, iconic wind turbines harness the elements to create power (see Gazetteer: Urumqi). Local authorities continue to experiment with the potential of solar power, on the understanding that Xinjiang's baking sun might also be turned into a force for good, although solar panels are notoriously prone to damage from dust and sand, which Xinjiang also has in abundance. Excited geologists discovered in 2003 that many of the lost rivers of the Taklamakan had not evaporated at all, but had instead sunk into the sands to create a giant underground lake. This aquifer is sure to be exploited, but is also a finite resource.

There have been worrying discussions of water-engineering schemes that mirror disastrous Soviet efforts. Party cadres have suggested a 60-mile super-*karez* – an underground canal diverting an entire river into the region in order to create new prosperity. Two even put forward the fantastically dangerous idea of an 800-kilometre channel, carved through the Tibetan plateau with atomic weapons.

Current schemes are somewhat less bonkers, although no less likely to cause trouble internationally. When Chinese engineers undertake a huge macro-hydrology exercise on the Yellow River or Yangtze, such as the famous Three Gorges Dam, the coverage focuses solely on the consequences for the Chinese. But Xinjiang's intersection with international borders intimately exposes the Chinese to foreign concerns. A scheme to divert water from the Irtysh River, north of the Tianshan Mountains, might water new pastures for the Chinese, but also reduces water levels in Kazakhstan and Russia, into which the Irtysh eventually flows. The Ili River itself, which gives its name to the region north of the Tianshan, flows out of China and into Kazakhstan's Lake Balkash, which is now shrinking, partly due to Chinese reallocation of its upper waters.

Nor are local schemes necessarily without consequences. In Gansu (see Gazetteer: Lanzhou) it is now possible to take a boat from Lanzhou to the Bingling-si grottoes, thanks to a dam that has created a new lake. But the benefits of such messing about in boats are offset by other schemes with less welcome results. In 1970, the 'East is Red' hydroelectric dam secured water and power for northern Xinjiang, but also raised the level of the nearby river. This, in turn, threatened the Kumtura grottoes (see Gazetteer: Kucha), which had survived undamaged for centuries. They are now a protected site, but that tends to mean that nobody can see them at all.

Religion and races

It is still difficult to find areas with a mutual accommodation of Chinese culture and Muslim culture. Even if one lives in both spheres, as many locals do, one cannot reject both. And in Xinjiang, there are always religious calls from the distant desert – brothers in Islam in need of charity or assistance against bandits, disputes that call to be settled by the law of Sharia rather than that of the Chinese overlords. Secular life and secular prosperity often lures the individual away from religious concerns, leading to a faith that favours the have-nots and the dispossessed, the down-at-heel and the uneducated. There are family and business ties across the mountains to territories that are now Uzbekistan, Afghanistan and Pakistan, and this makes the government nervous.

Such concerns, of course, are not unique to the Muslim faith. The Chinese have similar suspicions about the Catholics and their allegiance to a distant god-king, connections between Protestant believers and foreign espionage, or the influence of certain Buddhist leaders over their Chinese flocks. What distinguishes Islam is its firm combination of belief, home and family in Xinjiang, where the majority are Muslims. Today it unites the descendants of multiple tribes and clans that were once at each other's throats. China in the east has for years presented a united front to the world about what it means to be Chinese, glorifying what it calls the Han culture. Within my own lifetime, however, political correctness has assaulted this notion – my Chinese teachers originally claimed to be teaching me *Hanyu*, the 'Han-language', but that term has now been entirely supplanted by terms meaning 'National language' or 'Chinese language'. This, in turn, reflects a growing awareness among the Chinese that there is a value in diversity.

Nevertheless, Chinese ID cards still specify whether the holder is one of the 90 per cent Han majority or one of the 100 million or so ethnic minority citizens, many of which are clustered in the west. They need to do so primarily because certain minorities get several special dispensations denied the Han, waivers on tax or on the number of permitted children, for example, but to some this simply paints the minorities as 'Others'. It has been suggested among modern policy makers that the way to solve this problem would be to abolish all ethnic distinctions. Take that box off the ID card; cancel all special dispensations for minorities, and just say that hereafter, everybody is just Chinese. But that would not make everybody the same; it would simply deny any existing differences.

Tourism and tradition

China's growing awareness of heritage has also rehabilitated many ethnic minorities. Particularly for those tourists whose visit is an unrepeated, single holiday of a lifetime, there can be immense appeal in subcultures and something other than the products of the Han majority. That tiny 10 per cent of the Chinese population has produced entire worlds of arts and crafts that can season the tourist's haul of souvenirs – Hui Muslim hats, Tibetan bags, Kazakh carpets, colourful Qiang dresses... Such articles provide status for tourists; you have seen more than just the Great Wall and the Forbidden City.

The ethnic minorities themselves have mixed feelings about this. Such attentions do not necessarily preserve and support local cultures so much as they can carnivalise and belittle them. Today's young Xinjiang man, studying information technology in a Kashgar college, doesn't necessarily want to spend his life selling carpets. He wants the same chances as any other Chinese boy, to go to the big city and wear Hugo Boss while listening to the Beatles. His heritage might put food on the table, but it also risks becoming a new form of restriction. When he tells people he comes from Xinjiang, the last thing he wants to hear is a half-remembered rendition of '*Xinjiang Hao*' and questions about whether he knows the dance-steps. The most visible presence of ethnic minorities in Chinese media is on the endless TV talent shows, where you can be sure there will be a quota of Tibetan ballads and Xinjiang dance numbers.

The generation now in charge of China's antiquities was the first in decades to have the chance to study abroad – an opportunity previously only granted to scientists and engineers. Armed with American or European post-graduate degrees in art history and museology, the overseers of today's tourist sites have learnt many tricks of the marketing trade. Many famous Chinese sites are now dominated by vast, meandering paths that start up to a mile away from the antiquities, and have been deliberately designed to kettle tourists into a contemplative, docile state, ready to sample innumerable snacks and souvenirs.

Louguantai in Shaanxi (see Gazetteer: Xi'an) might easily be mistaken by the casual passer-by for Just Another Temple. But the mile-long preamble of statues and art installations subtly whispers of its place in Chinese history, in the hope that visitors will appreciate the momentous importance of the place where they stand – the place where the great sage Lao Zi wrote the ancient classic, the *Dao De Jing*. At least, that seems to be the plan. Tourists also have the chance to buy squid kebabs, Spider-Man masks and plastic guns from the numerous hawkers, none of which really does much to instil a sense of the sacred.

In part, such architecture is another facet of the same advance planning that has erected so many empty shopping malls – the Chinese middle-class is coming, and there will be *millions* of them that require crowd control. Six hundred million, in fact, which is the estimated number of affluent Chinese projected by the year 2015, according to Party demographers. Recent years have seen incredible reversals in policy and propaganda, as the Chinese government realises that it can generate immense wealth and tax revenue if it can simply encourage its newly affluent citizens to take a few holidays *within* China instead of blowing all their cash in Harrods. Such 'staycationing', of course, still encompasses an area the size of a continent, and has been made easier by the relocation of several official holidays in order to create 'Golden Weeks' when a couple of extra days off will give even the hardest worker a clear run at a week's trip. To where? Well, how about one of the old capitals, like Luoyang or Xi'an. Many A-list sites, such as the Longmen Grottoes or the Terracotta Army, are priced beyond the means of ordinary Chinese, but soon will not be. But these long outdoor foyers, these atria of experiences, are also designed to remind visitors why they are here in the first place. For many foreign tourists, particularly those with no prior grounding or reading in Chinese history, there is a common condition of diffidence and disinterest, a feeling of being 'templed out' by the sight of yet another place with curvy roofs and the pong of incense. What is so important about *this* temple? *This* statue? Such a class of visitor demands to be entertained. They demand to be led by the hand through history, and can turn resentful and bored if history does not leap out and explain itself. For such visitors, the modern additions to Chinese tourist sites can be a subtle exercise in education.

History and heritage

Because so many English-language books about Xinjiang pursue a deconstructive agenda, picking at the scabs of empire and ethnicity, few of them recognise the presence of the Han as another form of local heritage. How exactly can a Kazakh of the Ili Valley, whose family home is built on the bones of thousands of dead Zunghars, have the moral high ground over the new Han settlers? How can a Uyghur from Turfan, whose vineyards suck nutrients from the graves of forgotten Tocharians, Persians and Indians, complain that 'his' heritage is under threat? As Xinjiang sits at the crossroads of so many cultures, it is naturally a place where everyone might reasonably claim to come from somewhere else.

The question of heritage in Xinjiang is a thorny and political one. Russia, Uzbekistan and India are uncomfortably close at hand. Dig too deep into cultures and histories, and there are cross-border relations and revelations that can be unwelcome. The fortune-cookie version of Xinjiang politics defines it as an uneasy mix between Chinese and Muslims. And while that is true for some residents and modern activists, it imposes a bilateral, black-and-white view of a region that contains a dozen ethnic minorities, several autonomous regions with their own unique heritages and vast, hidden depths of earlier cultures, not least the Han Chinese themselves, who may well have arrived in their millions in modern times, but have also been a regular sight in the region for thousands of years. Thousands of *Muslims* in Xinjiang are actually descended from Han Chinese. Thousands of Uyghurs in Xinjiang are so secular-minded that they identify more readily with the Han than their own Uyghur nationality.

Chinese annals write off successive Central Asian occupiers behind the catch-all term 'barbarians', although that conceals, for example, the period that the region spent as part of the Indian and Tibetan empires. Islam has been a part of the region's heritage for 1,000 years, but it is a relatively *late* arrival, coming after millennia of Chinese traders and settlers – who had a rich Indian heritage, which in turn contained Central Asian influences, from Turks, Bactrians and Sogdians – and nomadic residents whose footprints are far harder to see. Like a tapestry of its most renowned commodity, the Silk Road's cultural makeup is a complex and multicoloured series of knots and threads, forming a picture that is so much greater than the sum of its parts.

Some visitors are surprised, for example, to discover booze in a supposedly 'Muslim' region (see Eating and Drinking: Alcohol) – the Kazakh-populated region of Ili is the site of many of the area's breweries and distilleries. Meanwhile, the supposedly secular city of Xi'an, hundreds of miles from Xinjiang, not only has 12 operational mosques and a thriving Muslim quarter, but an entire Muslim district tucked away behind the bustle of Chang'an Avenue. To put it another way, things are nowhere near as simple as many commentators would have you believe, and that includes many separatists, activists, Communists, Muslim, and non-Muslims. As Justin Jon Rudelson noted in his book *Oasis Identities*, Xinjiang's past and present are such cultural melting pots that it is very difficult to get a consensus on any aspect of its heritage, even among people who supposedly share a religion or race. Furthermore, as suggested by Blaine Kaltman in *Under the Heel of the Dragon*, blaming Islam for the social inequalities that can lead to crime and deprivation is often a case of putting the cart before the horse.

Heritage is a pin in a butterfly that is already dead, a quixotic attempt to preserve a moment in time that can be only accidentally relevant. Pick your moment to fix in time. The red-haired Tocharians at the shores of their lost sea? The medieval dancing girls of Kucha, famous throughout the desert for their exotic Indian moves? The pious Buddhist carvings, when they were first hesitantly made? When they multiplied into myriads of artworks by professional artists? When they were defaced and smashed by vandals? When they were hacked from their walls by European archaeologists? When they are recreated today by wealthy Buddhist patrons?

Similar issues trouble the arts and crafts, as silk, jade,

carpets and other old-world artisanal industries are left to the mercy of modern tastes and technological temptations. The Chinese government does what it can, for example shoring up the old industry of mulberry paper-makers by buying everything that the artisans cannot sell to tourists. That's all very well, but mulberry bark is tough to source, difficult to work and largely unappreciated when fortunes can be made by literally buying and recycling the waste paper of American offices. When smooth, blemish-free paper can be bought by the ream at any corner store, is it any wonder that the paper-makers of Xinjiang are eschewing their mulberry groves in favour of more profitable walnut trees? When there are no camel-saddles requiring felt blankets, is it any surprise that the felt-makers of Xinjiang are drifting into fake North Face gloves and Columbia fleece jackets?

Jade, too, has lost some of its mystical value in the modern age. Demand has not diminished; in fact, jade does a roaring trade among the *nouveaux riches* of China's rising middle class. But this demand has been met by a growing industrialisation of what were once handicraft professions of extraction, refinement and distribution. Part of jade's mystery once lay in its mythical hardness – difficult to cut or work with any material apart from other jades. But now it can be machine-tooled, leaving old artisans out of a job, and discouraging the young from even learning the trade. And it competes on the market place with many lesser, cheaper nephrites, some of which have been chemically bleached or restored with invisible polymers.

You can still sieve for pebbles of jade in the Khotan river beds, but it is plainly an exercise for tourists, while giant mechanical diggers gouge far larger chunks out of the landscape in search of industrial quantities nearby.

Not even the silk is necessarily the same. Some 35 countries produce silk today, and while the old ways of producing Chinese silk remain common, there are other concerns. Weaving has been industrialised, and not all silks quite match the fabled treasures of old. Tussah worms, bigger than the usual mulberry worms, produce substantially stronger and more enduring silk, but at a price. Tussah silk does not dye so well, and creates less even threads. Eighty per cent of the world's tussah silk comes from China, but dilutes many observers' concepts of what silk actually is.

Politics also comes to the fore in the logistics of modern archaeology. In cities, millennia of human habitation make rescue archaeology the norm, rather than the exception. Dig a hole anywhere, and you'll hit something – a Zhou Dynasty tripod, a Han Dynasty horse, Tang Dynasty ceramics. Familiarity can breed contempt, and it can also be difficult to decide where precisely to draw the line. Do we preserve the medieval mosque, or the dark-age temple ruins it was built upon? Or even the 1940s revolutionary headquarters it later served as?

During the 1950s, a disastrous excavation at the Ming Tombs outside Beijing ended with Chinese archaeologists dumping priceless silk artefacts to rot in a damp shed. Insult was added to injury during the Cultural Revolution, when fanatic Red Guards dragged the corpses of Emperor Wanli and his Empress outside and burnt them. Perhaps understandably, this has led to a certain timidity when dealing with important sites. The smart contemporary Chinese archaeologist knows not to charge pell-mell in search of buried treasures at the centre of any site. Whatever he finds, it will be downhill all the way thereafter. It is far smarter to pick at the outskirts – all the better to dangle promises of greater discoveries in front of the authorities and funding bodies. This is not the act of swindlers or conmen; it is a sensible, reasoned application of game theory and marketing. The site of the Terracotta Army is a vibrant, living archaeological site, with over 600 pits and more sure to be uncovered. But the First Emperor's tomb remains unopened and uninvestigated – imagine the let-down if it turned out to be empty.

Similarly, the mountain mausoleum of Empress Wu is untouched. Historians are divided as to what might be inside. The blank memorial stone outside her tomb suggests that her hateful relatives might have buried her with nothing. But, equally, fearful of curses from the afterlife, they might have sent her on her way with the most lavish grave goods ever found on the Silk Road.

At the turn of the 21st century, the authorities in Xi'an approved the buying and clearing of a vast area in the north-east of the city. Where there was once a drug addiction clinic, rundown tenements and corner stores, bulldozers created a park area twice the size of Pompeii. This is the Da Ming Gong ('Palace of Great Brightness'), site of the imperial complex that was home to 17 of the 21 rulers of the Tang Dynasty.

Today it is a park within a park – an outer area of trees and paths, free to all, and an inner sanctum that requires paid entry, preserving a few remnants of the place that was once the centre of the world and the terminus of the Silk Road.

The Da Ming Gong is a fascinating exercise in modern museology. Xi'an is making a bold and justifiable stab at becoming not merely *a* stop on the tourist's China itinerary, but the only stop worth making. In an effort to stop the tour parties that only pitch up for a day to see the Terracotta Army, it has invested in substantial monuments like the Da Ming Gong, seemingly in careful consideration of how to bring the past to life. Modern archaeological policy insists on the preservation of originals rather than their recreation in replicas, although sometimes in China, both approaches can co-exist. The great, towering gate of the Da Ming Gong is a modern, hollow facsimile, built over and around the drab remnants of the original, which can be seen from viewing galleries within. It is hence both a museum and a reconstruction, protecting the true artefact while also supplying context to explain just why anyone should care about it.

When entire capitals could be struck down, boxed up and relocated, as Xi'an itself once was, it should come as no surprise that so few original structures remain from the Chinese past. Far too many long quests to see ancient palaces and legendary castles end at disappointing hillocks. But the designers of the Da Ming Gong know this, and have concocted numerous ways to bring history to life, so far, mercifully, without the West's modern-day insistence on pallid interactivity. There is the inevitable introductory movie at the visitors' centre, but also on-site museums of ceramics and the site's reclamation and archaeology. There is the gate reconstruction, and a vast parade ground, a rival to Tiananmen itself, where occasional pageants of elfin palace guards in golden armour, attended by twirling dancing girls and stocky drummers, confound the casual passer-by. Past the anonymous plinths that once supported a great palace, the park itself is dotted with installations that *evoke* what was once there. There is a miniature replica, the size of a football field, of the whole palace in its heyday, even down to exquisite bonsai trees in its courtyards. There are statues of famous incidents and characters – dancing girls and Buddhist grandees, along with signs explaining what great historical moments and decisions occurred among these haunted lawns.

In the park's eastern quarter, near an avenue of kiosks and snack carts, is its most evocative artwork, a bronze statue of a riderless horse, grazing listlessly by the lakeside. Look closely and you will see that there are smaller statuettes around it, of broken swords and discarded sandals. This is an artistic representation of *absence* – the desolate aftermath in AD 905, when a usurper ordered the capital dismantled and relocated to Luoyang. It is a statue of the end of the Tang Dynasty, and of the moment when the Palace of Great Brightness became little more than a rubble-strewn meadow.

We live in a commercial culture, and often experience stories of the Silk Road through intermediaries who are trying to sell us something. Inevitably, this means that many popular accounts of the Silk Road focus on trade, and on commodities. As Valerie Hansen has provocatively argued, the Silk Road is probably one of the least travelled and least lucrative trade routes in world history, and a concentration on souvenirs – statues of camels for the mantelpiece, pashminas for your maiden aunt, or a Chinese scroll for your wall – too often encourage foreign observers to fixate on trade.

Among many historians, the Silk Road's importance is summarised in radically different terms, as a vital, world-changing conduit for people and ideas between the vastly different worlds of Europe, Islam and China – a pathway for entire religions, catastrophic bacteria and viruses, transformational inventions and entire gene pools of refugees. But what would tourists go and see if there were no things to behold and places to visit? The material items are what survive for us to see, in tombs and museums and replica forms, but it is the people of the Silk Road that were its true treasure, and the vast majority of them were not merchants at all, but farmers and herders, craftsmen, sons and daughters, monks and warriors. Fully experiencing the Silk Road requires more than a fridge magnet from the gift shop – break Shaanxi bread into small chunks and cast it into your mutton soup; hear the call to prayer outside a Kashgar mosque; feel your aching calves as you struggle up the steps to a Buddhist grotto; smell the faint rasp of sand in the air, even in a modern city. And then your souvenirs will truly be keepsakes, reminding you of those memories.

There is an undeniable romance to the Silk Road, but would you want to live there? The sand gets everywhere, in tough scratchy grains like biscuit crumbs, and in faint dust like talcum. The black winds make everything grubby and scuffed. The glittering towers of the new cities will soon turn brown and dull. The new mosques and temples of the devout will lose their bright tiles. Life on the Silk Road is a constant, Sisyphean struggle, as it is at Dunhuang, to keep the sand at bay. Travel on it, and know that the wonders you see, and now you, yourself, are but a fragment of its rich history.

More, much more is buried, faded and forgotten, because even those who remember have gone. You will be forgotten, like the lost city of Loulan. But you were there.

Part Two

BEING THERE

9

Eating and Drinking

Food

Chinese food is one of the true wonders of a trip to the region, and is an integral part of the experience – lunch and dinner at the very least should be pageants as exciting as the day's tourist trips. It should not surprise the visitor that the food known as 'Chinese' in the West is a catch-all term that foolhardily attempts to encompass an entire continent, as crazy an idea as a 'European' restaurant that serves Italian spaghetti alongside Icelandic pickled shark. Among the main Chinese regional cuisines – Sichuan, Beijing, Shanghai, Canton, Hunan – there are many minor variations. Xinjiang cuisine is less well-known abroad, but is sure to be regularly on offer to any travellers.

These different cuisines are cheap and ever-surprising treasure troves, not to be missed. Rice is commonplace, but rarely part of *local* cuisine – its cultivation requires much precious water that is better allocated to cotton or less thirsty crops. Seafood is a term rarely heard on the Silk Road, which begins and ends hundreds of miles from the sea. Marine produce is more likely to be farmed rather than fished, and while easily found in restaurants, sea fish do not form part of local cuisine, and lake fish are something of a luxury for special occasions. Restaurants in the hinterland often advertise River Food (*chuan cai*), meaning fish.

In Shaanxi province, the snack of choice is the Meat Sandwich (*roujiamo*), tender hunks of grilled meat and green peppers in a burger-like bun. Pork buns are known throughout China, but the true *roujiamo* is an Islamic variant, reflecting the presence of the 12 mosques in Xi'an by discarding pig meat in favour of lamb or chicken. Another local delicacy is Soaked Bun (*paomo*), in which the bread is broken into tiny morsels and scattered into a lamb or beef soup.

To the west, the Chinese love for roast pork diminishes drastically as the hinterland becomes progressively more Muslim. Beef becomes a garnish rather than a dish in itself, while increasing numbers of hawkers can be found with skewers of spiced mutton, barbecued over long, thin troughs of glowing charcoal embers. In a modernist variant, many can now be found offering halal hotdogs on sticks, cut in a spiral to make a corkscrew of meat, and dipped in chilli sauce. Chilli, the ubiquitous spice of Sichuan and Hunan cuisine, fades as the traveller heads westwards, in favour of cumin and turmeric.

One province over, in Gansu, the most popular dish is Pulled Noodles (*lamian*), so named because they are kneaded and stretched to create sumptuous, soft strings. Many restaurants make the hand-pulling of the noodles a feature of the dining experience, and get their cooks to fling their dough around in public view to attract gawkers and thus, customers. The noodles are then served in a bowl with a meat-based broth, usually beef or mutton, since most *lamian* cooks are Muslim, and the cafes are hence usually halal. Throughout China, these are usually known as Lanzhou noodles, named for the capital of Gansu, although in Japan they are perhaps better known by the Japanese pronunciation of *lamian*, as *ramen*. Lanzhou menus usually also offered a variant fried in a tomato sauce, but tomatoes are a relatively recent import, sneaking in from the Americas in the last few centuries.

In Xinjiang proper, the word *lamian* gives way to *laghman*, the soup ditched in favour of a stir-fry with vegetables and the ubiquitous mutton, spattered with incongruous tomato sauce. Contrary to popular myth, Marco Polo did not bring back pasta from the Far East. Durum wheat is a Persian variety that migrated both east and west along the Silk Road – dumplings are *manti* in Turkish, *manta* in Uyghur, and morph into *mantou* buns by the time they reach China.

'Big Plate Chicken' (*da pan ji*) is not to everyone's taste, and is derided by some as 'Tractor Chicken', since the recipe for it might be reasonably expected to read: 'First, run over your chicken with a tractor.' An entire bird, albeit thankfully plucked, is eviscerated and cooked for the table, presented in a saucy stew piled high with onions and peppers. The dish is, as the name suggests, *big*, and substantially more filling than, say, a Beijing Duck, since one must contend not only with the breasts and drumsticks, but also the head, feet, wings and assorted offal. Pick successfully at the carnage and snapped bones, and your waitress will swing past with succulent, chewy noodles, dumped into the remaining sauce as a final filler. *Da Pan Ji* is, to be sure, All You Can Eat. The best is supposedly found at Urumqi's Diyi Dapan (literally 'Number One Big Plate') on south Nanhu Street, but you will see the dish on sale throughout the region. If something seems inedible, it often is – certain body parts are so gristly that they are literally indigestible, but they are nevertheless munched by the Chinese to pass the time, like organic chewing gum.

Even odder is *apke*, or goat's head soup, which features much of the unfortunate animal's digestive system, from its lolling tongue still in its skull, all the way down to its reamed and re-stuffed intestines, which are turned into a long, meaty sausage coiled in a simmering broth.

With a long tradition of Buddhist abstinence, China is kinder to vegetarians than the casual tourist might first expect. Buddhist restaurants, particularly in the swisher temples, offer elaborate menus fashioned largely from mushrooms and greens, and often carved into representations of other things.

Although Chinese 'five spices', Sichuan peppers and soy remain as ingredients, the food of the Silk Road adds more Middle Eastern spices. Of black cumin seed oil, the Prophet once said: 'There is healing in it for every disease except for death.' Ever increasing numbers of restaurants west of Luoyang are *halal*, as indicated by unmistakeable Arabic script on their exteriors, and the characters *qing-zhen* ('clear and true'), one of several Chinese terms for Muslim. Many restaurants also serve curry (*ka li*), although this will often turn out to be a ready-mix variant more related to Japanese or Indonesian food than the Indian original. The Delhi Durbar, in the shadow of the Great Goose Pagoda in Xi'an, offers real curry, seemingly as an exotic flourish for pilgrims who have followed in Tripitaka's footsteps.

Flat, leavened bread is ubiquitous, and regularly forms part of a meal. The Chinese for it is *nang*, echoing the term in most other languages, including the original Persian, the Indian, the Russian and the English, *nan*. Some street sellers in Xinjiang favour the thicker, rounder Tajik variant, which is called *nong*. Traditionally, nan bread forms both the dish and the cutlery, although you are unlikely to be expected to eat with your hands. Although locals are liable to be forgiving towards tourists, a common custom holds that you should never leave nan behind. It is considered disrespectful among the devout to have to throw bread away, and it is better to order more when you need it than to order too much and then leave it. If you do find yourself with bread left over at a restaurant, honour is best preserved by asking to take it with you. If eating bread, break a piece off; do not lift the whole thing to your mouth.

Rice reasserts itself in the far west of China, as the Silk Road climbs into the Pamirs and dovetails with the culinary traditions of Central Asia. The standard dish is called *zhuafan* ('special rice') in Chinese, rice cooked in seasoned broth with vegetables and hunks of meat. It has many other names, many deriving from the Persian *polow* – *plov* in Uzbekistan, where it is the national dish, *pilau* in India, and *palau* in Afghanistan. Legend holds that it entered Europe, as did so many Silk Road items, with the returning soldiers of Alexander the Great, who brought the word *pilafi* into Greek after first tasting it at his wedding to the Bactrian princess Roxana. This story, however, seems unlikely, since recipes for pilaff do not seem to enter the European repertoire until the Middle Ages, and the term in Modern Greek derives from the Turkish *pilav*, not directly from ancient Bactria. You are unlikely to find yourself in a truly traditional setting, but if no cutlery is provided, it is customary to eat *plov* with your right hand, never the left. If no napkins are provided, you are expected to wipe your greasy hand on your boots.

The Xinjiang variant of Turkish Delight is palpably less delightful, with an oddly grassy, earthy taste reflecting the relative lack of sugar in the diet.

Drink

In winter, enterprising street merchants sell the hot juice of apples, crab-apples and berries, and there are often carts bearing fruit – oranges, satsumas, bananas and melons are all fair game for the hungry tourist, but only if you can peel them yourself to guarantee they have not been washed with bad water. The same hawkers will switch to other fare in summer, particularly shaved ice – a powder of frozen water, garnished with berries, fruit or candies. Traditionally, the raw material is harvested in blocks from frozen rivers in winter, and then stored for months, packed in straw, in icehouses until it is grated into your dish. This leaves it open to numerous opportunities for contamination, from the original river source, to the unhygienic shed, to the likely grubby transport and the hot, dusty cart on which it ends up. While shaved ice is a culinary joy in a hot Xinjiang summer, be wary of its source. If you trust a vendor, then few joys can match a cool *durap* on a summer's day – shaved ice, honey and yoghurt mixed into a thick smoothie.

Obtaining cold drinks can be a lottery. Some stores do not seem to bother using electricity unless absolutely necessary, turning many a corner-store fridge into little more than a glass-fronted cupboard for lukewarm bottles of tea. Ice in one's drink is a Western luxury best forgotten – even if it is offered, can you be sure that the ice was made from boiled water? Restaurants often serve tea or hot water (*kai shui*) – in both cases, the fact that the water has been boiled will assure you of its safety. Otherwise stick to bottled water, available everywhere, and occasionally with flashes of local colour, such as Kunlun Spring, which sports a logo actionably evocative of that of the more famous Evian, but has a point of origin deep in the Qinghai Desert.

Alcohol

Beware the extra power imparted to alcohol by high altitudes. A light beer drunk on a mountain top in Tashkurgan has much more of a kick than the same drink imbibed below sea level in Turfan. In a few places where Muslims remain in the majority, alcohol is usually tolerated but frowned upon as a habit that marks you out as a visitor rather than guest – and people with beers in their hands are Han Chinese, not Xinjiang Uyghurs. You can buy beer in Yarkand, for example, but only in a few hotels, and it is not ubiquitous in corner stores as it would be anywhere else in China. Drinking will not necessarily invite disapproval, although being visibly *drunk* certainly will.

Xinjiang has its own beer, Wusu, brewed in the town of the same name in the Ili Kazakh prefecture, but with a name that can handily also be taken to mean 'Welcome to Urumqi'. The same brewery makes Sinkiang Black Beer, 'made from local barley, Loulan Star hops and fresh meltwater from the Tianshan Mountains.' Another common sight is the Kingway brand (Chinese: *jinwei*), its English name and Cantonese-accented romanisation giving it away as an outsider, owned by a Cantonese brewery, itself part-owned by Heineken.

Wine has long been a traveller on the Silk Road. The Greeks left in Ferghana by Alexander the Great brought grapes with them, and appear to have grown the first local vineyards. Grapes migrated along the Silk Road from Ferghana to Turfan during the Han Dynasty, but appear to have been regarded as a food, not as the raw material for an alcoholic drink. By the Tang Dynasty, however, the locals in Turfan may have realised that grape skins contained the yeast necessary for fermenting the juice into wine. Evidence, however, is scant and circumstantial. There is little to support this in archaeological terms, but extant documents from nearby Dunhuang refer to penalties for latecomers to a Buddhist festival as incurring a fine of 'a horn of *jiu*', while no-shows are instructed to cough up 'half a jar of *jiu*.' *Jiu* is a generic term for all alcohol, but *could* be evidence of viniculture in the region – again, local Tang-era documents appear to distinguish between two kinds of alcoholic beverage, which suggests that one of them might have been wine. The Tang poet Li Bo, who probably never went to the region, imagined life on the frontier, and mentioned 'drinking grape wine' as one of the likely pastimes.

Strict Buddhists, of course, are not supposed to drink, and neither are strict Muslims (until they get to paradise), causing mention of wine in Turfan to fade from records as Islam took hold in the medieval period. However, under influence in particular from French investors in the modern period, Turfan has become increasingly known for its wine, particularly the Loulan brand, which produces a Cabernet Sauvignon and a crisp Sauvignon Blanc and takes its name from the most famous of the Tarim mummies, the Beauty of Loulan. Despite not being known internationally for viniculture, China is the sixth largest wine-producing nation in the world, in the face of odd 'high desert' conditions that force many vineyards to lower their vines and bury them each winter to protect them from subzero temperatures.

Today, 60 per cent of Xinjiang's wine grapes are Cabernet

Sauvignon, followed in decreasing quantities by Merlot, Chardonnay and Riesling. Many harvests of Turfan grapes (and those from other regions of Xinjiang, such as Urumqi and Heshuo) are sent to distant wineries in Beijing and Shanghai to be blended, forming a large component of the grapes used in many Chinese wine brands that are not explicitly from the region, such as Dragon Seal, Dynasty and Great Wall. Wine forms a major part of the Chinese government's plans for tourism in the region after 2015, so you can be sure you'll hear more about it.

Depending on whom you ask, wine is either a product made by the locals but not touched by them, or something enjoyed with great alacrity by all and sundry. Certainly, many Chinese Muslim restaurants still have alcohol on the menu, and some purportedly 'Muslim' families in the region will be affronted if a dinner guest turns down an offer of wine.

Far more common in the drinking culture of west China is the stronger *baijiu* (white liquor), a distilled drink with 40–60 per cent alcohol by volume. Fermented from sorghum, wheat or other grains, it has a strong standing in the archaeological record, going back 5,000 years, and remains a popular sight at modern Chinese banquets. Commonly knocked back in straight shots after a toast to some shared interest or experience, downing-in-one traditionally shows sincerity, and is a prime cause of the shouty drinking games played by many red-faced older Chinese men at the more boisterous restaurants.

Baijiu is one case in China where you truly do get what you pay for. A *sorghum rotgut* can be found in any supermarket for as little as 20 yuan, but it will taste like brake fluid. At the town of Shihezi, an hour's drive outside of Urumqi (just inside the borders of the Ili Kazakh Autunomous Prefecture), the Xin An distillery churns out the powerful and not unpalatable 52 per cent ABV firewater Xinjiang Gong ('Xinjiang Pride'), which retails at a boggling 65p for a 165 ml bottle. For half the price, you can pick up a bottle of Ili Tequ

('Ili Special'), notable in part because it has to be one of the only liquors in the world to come in a bottle decorated with Turkic script, an image normally associated with a teetotal world. But the interested traveller is advised to avoid blue-collar tests of endurance, and to instead invest in something a little classier. Exhaustive authorial experimentation suggests that the *baijiu* event horizon is somewhere around the 1,500 yuan mark (about £15), at which point it stops being revolting and becomes rather pleasant, with many delightful flavours and bouquets. At the Chinese end of the Silk Road, the most visible brand is Xi Feng ('Western Phoenix'), which invariably comes in intricate and attractive bottles and vase-like flasks, often packed in gilded boxes. The latter are often frustratingly difficult to open intact, reflecting the equally common role of *baijiu* as a form of gift-giving capital – a present to be admired and possibly surreptitiously recycled elsewhere, and only actually drunk when it ends up in the hands of a true fan. The large numbers on the bottle usually denote the age of the contents – a two-year age difference can add 20 per cent to the price, which rises exponentially in reflection of the troubled times and the scarce resources behind the production of anything more than 30 years old.

Despite thousands of years lubricating Chinese negotiations, *baijiu* has experienced a sudden and dramatic fall in sales, following Communist Party austerity measures in 2013, restricting all luxury banquets and specifically forbidding the consumption of *baijiu* at official occasions. An old man's drink, instrumental in the creation of many a Chinese alcoholic, it is shunned by many of the cleaner-living younger generation, and has come to symbolise some of the inequities of the current system – a Chinese McDonald's employee would have to flip burgers for weeks to afford a bottle of Xi Feng. The loss of the lucrative political junket market, and the liable fallout at any occasion with a Party member present, has caused a fall in the share prices of the major *baijiu* manufacturers, and is likely to lead to increased efforts to glamorise and diversify the product, possibly even in export territories. For the foreign traveller, this may mean tantalising airport offers – if you are a drinker or know one, leave space in your luggage for one final souvenir. It's probably a more effective use of your last few banknotes than the hit you'll take on exchanging the money back into your own currency. Airport *baijiu* stocks are understandably parochial – you will only find western Chinese brands at western Chinese shops, and not, say, at the Beijing Duty Free shop.

10

Travel Logistics

Before you go

There are a few necessities for a trip into Xinjiang, although since many travellers will embark on their journey after stops in larger Chinese cities such as Beijing or Xi'an, most can be sourced in China. If you are heading out of the cities, be sure you have good sunglasses, not only for the desert, but also for the glaring snow of the mountains. You will also need water purification tablets for emergencies, and a flask of your own water for the first few hours, before you can be sure where to get more. A torch is also essential, preferably one that can be mounted on a headband so both your hands are free – you will be grateful for this when looking for a latrine in the dark. You will need a pen-knife – for at the very least, you will be peeling a lot of fruit. And finally, a medikit – it is Murphy's Law that you are sure to be miles from the nearest plaster or disinfectant when you cut your finger.

Chinese pharmacies are plentiful and cheap, but unless you trust your own Mandarin-speaking abilities enough to explain what you need and read the instructions, bring your own supply of necessary medication. Even if you have a cast-iron stomach and avoid dangerous-looking foods, diarrhoea or mild discomfort can be a natural side effect of adjusting to new foods, so do not scrimp on the Imodium. As a rule, place no trust in Chinese ice cubes or condoms.

Experiment before leaving home with the best way of keeping your camera dust-free. Grime and dirt is a hazard even in the most modern of Chinese cities. Cheap digital cameras often have an iris that 'protects' the lens when not in use. Ironically, this can be the first thing to jam, creating black bars at the edges of the unwary traveller's snaps. More serious photographers are apt to have cleaning kits with them, but not necessarily any guarantee of a clean place to do the cleaning. In the worst desert conditions, consider keeping your camera permanently inside a transparent plastic bag.

The vast bulk of airborne particles throughout Xinjiang never rise more than a metre off the ground. Simply holding your camera up can keep it out of much of the worst exposure to dust.

Security issues

It is standard practice for your Chinese hotel to take a photocopy of your passport on arrival. This is to register your presence with the local police and has no other sinister purpose. This saves the foreign traveller an immense amount of faff; if you are staying in a private residence, you are obliged instead to present yourself in person at the local police station within three days, bearing your visa documentation and duplicate copies of your passport.

Security guards are ubiquitous in China, and represent many levels of authority and jurisdiction, from humble doormen to the full-on public security police (*gong-an*). Many such jobs are sinecures or low-level appointments that simply work out cheaper in the long term than fences, pelican crossings or other permanent measures – don't be surprised to see officious old men in high-visibility jackets, standing on street corners, and blowing whistles in vain attempts to stop the Chinese jaywalking. In many public situations, they are apt to be terrified of you, since if the foreign stranger falls over, walks on the grass or transcends some other unspoken petty rule, it is the guards who will lose face, even though they are probably ill-equipped linguistically to tell you any of this. If they spoke a foreign language, they wouldn't be security guards.

If hawkers suddenly bundle up their wares and run for the car park, don't panic. Many Chinese street markets or other unofficial sales pitches are illegal, and have to be regularly moved along by traffic enforcers (*zhifa*) simply to stop the pavements becoming completely clogged. Stay in any location for more than a couple of days and you, like the hawkers, will be able to time the arrivals of the next vanload of bored-looking policemen. Wait another quarter-hour or so after they have dispersed, and the sellers of rhinestone-spangled boots, musical toys and balloons will soon gravitate once more to their original pitches.

At the border zones, particularly on the Karakoram Highway, all travellers need permits from the local authorities before they can even get on the bus. If you are with a tour or booking a guide, they will usually do the paperwork for you. If you are a private traveller, expect to have to make, at the very least, a trip to the local police station with a passport photograph and photocopies of your passport and visa page.

Time

China exists in a single official time zone. When it's five o'clock on the Pakistan border with Xinjiang, and ten o'clock in Russia's Vladivostok, the Chinese towns of Tashkurgan and Mudanjiang are both technically at eight o'clock, even though each is only 100 miles or so from their foreign counterpart. Beijing sets the time for the entire People's Republic, and official business always runs on Beijing time. Local matters, however, from the time of breakfast, to opening hours at your favourite restaurant, to the time you agreed to meet your guide, might well run on an unofficial local time, so be sure to double-check anything involving a clock when in Xinjiang.

Shopping

Whether you visit the knife-making town of Yengisar (Yingjisha) or not, it is the source of most blades in the region, and a Yengisar knife is a popular souvenir. So, too, are the carpets made all over the region – as with antiques in general, if a price is too good to be true, it often is. Some carpets are literally too good to walk on, and are instead hung on the wall as works of art – a custom that has drifted into some parts of Russia from its Muslim connections in Central Asia. Look out in particular for completely mental modernist designs – portraits of Genghis Khan, or AK47s worked into the patterns. Such images, which might seem ironic or tongue-in-cheek to the tourist, often hide a more complex story, as artisans in threatened crafts embrace military or political subjects to attract new markets and powerful protectors.

If a price is not marked on an object, the seller is apt to decide on the spot what he or she wishes to charge for it. On such occasions, the decision is based on what the market (that's you) seems likely to bear, the time of day, time of year, and even the weather. Wander the bazaar sipping on a Starbucks latte that costs more than many people's daily wages, sporting a camera worth six months' hard labour in the fields, and you will be treated accordingly, as an eccentric millionaire with more money than sense. Prices will immediately be halved for Chinese speakers, but are still liable to be double what the seller would be happy to take. Decide before haggling begins what price you will be happy to pay, stay polite, and be prepared to walk away.

A mental note as to your own bottom line is important, as many travellers end up walking away from a trade feeling ripped off if the seller has agreed too readily. Many Chinese superstitiously believe that the first sale of each day is an omen for all further trade before sunset, and will try very hard to ensure that their 'first customer' buys something. Being the 'first customer' can hence lead to slightly higher discounts than later in the day.

Use common sense with 'antiques'. Most items on sale to tourists will be replicas (i.e. fakes). The Chinese genius of fakery will sell you a facsimile of anything you desire – statuettes, pottery and jewels, often caked with a layer of grime to make you think you are picking up a genuine artefact. True antiques are recognisable by a sudden ten-fold increase in price from a similar object. If you insist on the genuine article, also insist on a receipt, as without one you may be prevented from taking your dusty knick-knack out of the country. For this reason, you are advised not to buy 'antiques' from people in the street.

Postage and packing

It can be irritating, on a once-in-a-lifetime trip, to see a must-have article – a replica terracotta warrior, say, or a Buddha statuette – only to realise it is too heavy or bulky for your luggage. Posting souvenirs home from China is actually considerably easier than doing so from many European countries. Small street-corner post offices do not carry international mail, although they might be able to sell you stamps for postcards. The main district post offices in Chinese cities have a packing counter, where a staff member will assess your goods, pick out a box and pack it for you. This not only saves you the bother of finding the materials yourself, and puts your items in the hands of an artist with bubble-wrap and duct tape, but also helps you avoid any legal infringements. They will not accept ready-packed parcels, so you might as well go with the flow. The officials not only have to know the regulations for the Chinese postal service, but for your destination country, as well.

Chinese postal forms require details of both sender (on the left) and recipient (on the right), as well as a rough summary of the three largest or most numerous articles in the package. They require five carbon copies, so write firmly and clearly, on a flat surface. Surface mail to Europe takes three months, but the service is reliable and efficient.

National holidays and local festivals

Very few national holidays have a direct impact on Chinese life, since it is rare indeed that shops will close for all that long. Weekends often pass with no discernible difference in trading times or opening hours, while religious days such as Christmas mean little or nothing to the Chinese, despite incessant carols on in-store stereos, and incongruous snow and Santas plastered on the windows. Instead, as with much of the capitalist West, the religious calendar is now more likely to serve as a guide to a procession of advertising campaigns, combining Chinese tradition and foreign festivals in a series of excuses for marketing promotions and discount deals. There are moves in modern China to change this, and several government initiatives to make certain holidays *actual* holidays, in order to bolster the nascent industries of domestic tourism. But that still means someone on staff at the kind of places that tourists go, which means that even if the Chinese are on holiday, the average visitor's experience is liable to go unaffected.

In the interests of warning against those rare occasions when the corner shop might be shut for a few hours, or when a parade or funfair might suddenly appear to break out in the street, these are the main holidays you are likely to encounter.

1st January (New Year's Day)
Although officially a holiday, this rarely seems to pass with any impact, but do not be surprised if restaurants are a little more crowded as people splash out.

Late January/early February (Spring Festival)
This marks the first day of the first month of the lunar calendar, and is usually known around the world as 'Chinese New Year'. The residents of the People's Republic, however, often seem to take exception to the notion that their year is any different from anyone else's, and will often correct you by saying it's the Spring Festival. This is the most important festival of

the Chinese calendar, traditionally involving homage paid to one's ancestors, and bringing much of the same parental insistence on assembly as Christmas or Thanksgiving in the West. Hence it usually involves a trip back to the home town ('for all but the most heartless and ungrateful of offspring,' says my Chinese hairdresser's sulking mother), creating a mass exodus of the millions of migrant workers who keep China running smoothly for the rest of the year. Many stores and amenities will shut down or work on skeleton staff for the whole week, and public transport will be fully booked and crowded both before and after.

The Spring Festival will see a veritable apocalypse of fireworks, feasting and merriment, lion dances and vivid red celebratory clothing. People start to dress like Liberace for no apparent reason, and the edgier Chinese youth experiment with punkish haircuts that they can be sure to shave off or grow out by the end of the week when they have to go back to work in the iPod factory.

Fifteen Days Later (The Lantern Festival)

There is an itinerary of customs, foods and celebrations that technically lasts for the first two weeks of the Chinese New Year, but the most obvious iterations are on the first day (see Spring Festival above), and the 15th, which is known as the Lantern Festival. Households light candles to guide lost spirits home, although one wonders how this helps if *everyone* lights a candle. Fragile paper lanterns rise into the air, powered by the hot air from an interior candle, creating a poetic scene of dancing lights in the sky, and keeping the fire brigade busy when they tumble in flames back to the ground. Hawkers appear on the streets selling 'ghost money' – currency redeemable at the Bank of Hell, which may be burned in order to send cash to one's ancestors. Usually decorated with the image of either the King of Hell, or Chairman Mao (in the fashion of real Chinese money), ghost money is a wonderful souvenir of China, although the Chinese are aghast that gauche foreigners risk bad luck by collecting it; it is technically illegal because some of its bills are very similar to real money, and hence count as counterfeit. Because of the counterfeit designation, it is often illegal to post it home, so you will have to carry it in your luggage. The author has amassed several million pounds' worth of ghost money (usually bought at 20p a sheaf), but has yet to find a branch of the Bank of Hell where he can change it.

14th February (The Sweetheart Festival)
The secular Chinese state does not recognise religious festivals, so there is no such thing as a 'Saint' Valentine to have a day for. But the Chinese gift-giving, card-selling, spouse-appeasing and mistress-buttering apparatus would not miss out on this one. Nobody gets a day off, but expect a morass of hearts and flowers all over the place.

8th March (International Women's Day)
Some female employees may get a half-day off, although they are likely to have to make up the hours later!

c.4/5th April (Qingming Festival)
Supposedly the day when the Chinese traditionally visit their ancestors' graves, although this has been largely supplanted by the Spring Festival, which is most likely to get people travelling home. The Qingming Festival is unlikely to result in public closures, although it can often lead to an upsurge in foreign tourists of Chinese ethnicity, making the long trip to make sure the family tomb has been swept.

1st May (Labour Day)
Although the Chinese are usually too busy labouring to celebrate the international workers' day off, the apparatus of the Communist Party would be remiss in its beliefs if it did not. As a result, most government offices are closed on 1st May – not a good day to get a visa stamped or for any other

bureaucratic operation. If there is a parade, it will probably feature tanks.

Late July/Early August (Eid al-Fitr)
The Feast of Breaking the Fast marks the end of Ramadan, and is hence a likely source of celebration in Muslim communities. The Chinese sometimes get into the spirit by forgoing pork for the day and tucking into mutton, lamb or beef. Muslims supposedly have the day off in Xinjiang, although this seems to rarely apply to restaurateurs and cab drivers. There is increased activity around mosques and a carnival atmosphere at Muslim holy sites.

1st August (Army Day)
Military personnel get a half-day off. There is a reasonable chance of scattered parades and occasional fireworks.

Somewhere in September (Eid al-Adha)
The Feast of the Sacrifice, celebrating Abraham's willingness to stab his own son to death in the name of God. Xinjiang Muslims supposedly get the day off, but see Eid al-Fitr. Expect increased activity around mosques and a carnival atmosphere around Muslim holy sites. This occasion moves 11 days earlier each year, so will be in August by 2018 and July by 2020.

Somewhere in Autumn (The mid-Autumn Festival)
A harvest festival in the old agrarian year, this is a time of thanksgiving for the Chinese, which, for a change, is often marked by the letting off of a hundredweight of fireworks. Taking place at the full moon in the month of the harvest, it is also associated with romance and marriage among the Chinese – those taking trips to the more picturesque tourist sites may find them clogged by newlyweds trying to have some nice pictures taken. For the next few years, the festival mainly falls in late September or early October.

1st October (National Day)

The proclamation of the People's Republic, issued by Chairman Mao from the top of the Tiananmen gate in the centre of Beijing, marked the beginning of the modern era in China, and took place on 1st October 1949. Expect public art installations, parades and the usual fireworks.

11

Gazetteer

Aksu

Formerly known in the Han Dynasty as the 'kingdom' of Gumo, and in the Tang Dynasty as Baluka, Aksu's outskirts are attended by a swirling fog of dust. This once lent an air of mystery to the scattered Han ruins looming out of the gloom, but these have now largely been replaced by the usual concrete buildings. Aksu city is also the capital of Aksu *prefecture*, leading some guidebooks to lump many sites with it that might be better described as being part of a trip to Kucha, some 200 miles away.

The city sits at a crucial junction, where the road to the ice-bound Muzart Pass and fertile Ili beyond, leaves the main trading route, which is why the sacred **Sayram Thousand Buddha Caves** can be found on the city's outskirts, in the foothills.

The **Aksu Museum** (Y10) contains exhibits pertaining to the region's history, and to the two ethnic groups living nearby, the Duolang and the Guisi. Nearby, **Duolang Park** (Y10) has a fairground and an impressive modernist bridge that looks like threads of red silk, picked out in steel. There are several spots outside the town of natural beauty – **Yangquan Park** (Y15), which is supposedly 'the most delightful sight south of the mountains', and the **Tianshan Sacred Wood** (Y80), a fertile oasis surrounded by sands, which has inspired its nickname of 'the bright pearl of the Gobi.' Modern maps also note the presence on the outskirts of a 'Park of Queer Trees'. Enter at your peril!

Altay (Aletai)

Wedged into a spot where the borders of Kazakhstan, Russia (the Altay republic) and Mongolia are all within 100 kilometres, speaking English is a long way down the list of townspeople's priorities, which only serves to put this town even further off the beaten track. The city museum is compact, containing just 298 artefacts, while sites of interest favour nature – the **Birch Forest** (Y10), the fist-shaped rocky outcrop at **Five Finger Spring** and the **Altay Forest Park.** A 50-mile drive will get you to the **Koktokay Geopark** (Y120), which includes the 1931 **Fuyun Earthquake Fault** (a mile long, and as wide a football field) and its attendant museum, which highlights the area's geological oddities and mineral deposits.

Bortala Mongol Autonomous Prefecture

A remote spot that shares a border with Kazakhstan, Bortala encompasses the wilderness surrounding two lakes, Sayram and Ebinur. **Bole Old Town**, also known as Dalet, is a compact city built by Tang Dynasty administrators. Although part of the battlements have been worn away by the nearby river, some are still standing, and the area is a rich archaeological source of pottery fragments, bronze ware and other detritus of the Chinese colonists of 1,000 years ago. Bortala is best known for its fantastic **Stone Gorge** (Y20 – *guaishi-yu*) a valley of sand-blown stones 48 kilometres outside Bole, some of which are truly mind-boggling. Look out for one outcrop that seems to mimic the head of a roaring lion. The **Hariturege Scenic Spot** is a gorge lined with trees, although its name in Mongol means 'the Place Haunted by Black Vultures.'

The region is haunted by shipping containers in modern times, as the **Alashan Pass** (or Zungharia Gate) is a bustling trading post for rail and road traffic towards the west. Although this has little to offer the tourist directly, it has at least assured the presence of a local airport, which allows flights to come in from Urumqi and hence connects this otherwise remote region more firmly to the centre.

Bayingolin Mongol Autonomous Prefecture (Bayin'goleng; Bayangol)

Chinese guidebooks make this seem like a heavily-populated spot, but that is merely because of its sheer size – Bayingolin is the largest autonomous prefecture in China, with an area of 462,700 square kilometres, which is larger than Germany. It encompasses a massive chunk of Xinjiang, and much of it is nothing but sand. For greater detail on specific sites of interest, see the separate entries on its capital, **Korla**, and its minor township **Ruoqiang**, the closest to **Lop Nur.**

Changji Hui Autonomous Prefecture

Although it occupies a region the size of Ireland, this nominally Muslim area has a capital that nestles close to Urumqi, a mere bus-ride away. The snow-capped mountain peak of **Bogda Feng** (Y20), highest of the Bogda Mountains, is open to the public, and popular for climbers as a spot of natural beauty, and for the icy snowmelt that washes from its slopes into the Tianchi lake, where the locals cool off in the summer heat. The area's most famous feature is the **Five-Coloured Bay** (Y30 – *wu cai wan*), which, despite the name, is a series of rocky outcrops in the middle of the Gurbantunggut Desert. The rich, vibrant shades in the rocks were naturally created in the distant past, when lightning seemingly struck an exposed coal seam, starting an epic underground fire which sintered the surrounding minerals into a cascade of colours, themselves later revealed by geological processes. Visitors are advised to make a day of it, as the effect of the coloured rocks varies with the progress of the sun.

Predating the Chinese, the Muslims and even the Buddhists are the breath-taking **Shimenzi Cliff Carvings**, near the town of Kangjia (Y20). Etched into the rock 3,000 years ago, these distinctive stick figures with expressive faces appear to represent a forgotten fertility cult. Many are dancing, but others are clearly stripping off and copulating. The figures range in size from a mere hand's breadth to larger than man sized, with genitals to match.

Relics from before the time of humans are to be found at the region's **Dinosaur Valley** (Y20 – *konglong gou*); Changji remains one of the centres of Chinese palaeontology.

Dunhuang

Dunhuang, literally the 'blazing beacon', has been a site of pilgrimage and refuge since 121 BC, when the Great Wall was notionally extended in a line of beacon towers stretching into the west. Some of these towers are little more than dilapidated hillocks in the wilderness, leading some explorers to report that they weren't even sure they were looking at a man-made phenomenon. But Dunhuang had an oasis capable of supporting many soldiers, and soon flourished as a trading and resupply depot. Over the following centuries, a local custom developed of offering alms in thanks for, or in anticipation of, a safe journey on the Silk Road. The result was the 'great art gallery in the desert.' At the **Mogao Caves** (Y180), 25 kilometres outside Dunhuang town, hundreds of grottoes and wall carvings celebrate Buddhist saints and holy men, with a wide variation in size and detail.

Despite the predations of sand and wind, vandals and souvenir hunters, some 500 of the hand-carved caves remain in good condition. The price of admission is not as high as it may appear, since it includes a guide – English speaking tours are at nine, midday, and two – who will shepherd you to the main site, and through a handful of unlocked caves-of-the-day. The guides are flexible enough to agree to unlock other caves (for a fee) if you have an interest in a particular kind of fresco or statuary not represented in the day's exhibits. The more specialised your interests, the more likely you are to need your own torch. For the explorer in search of a truly rare artefact, keep an eye out for a sign near the entrance that chastises 'the thief' Paul Pelliot for his seizure of priceless sacred scrolls.

The town is surrounded by iconic, majestic sand dunes like something out of *Lawrence of Arabia*, sure to feature in any traveller's most photogenic memories. The picturesque **desert** is technically a nature reserve (Y120 – *mingsha-shan*, literally 'bright sand mountain'), and for that extra authentic touch, you can hire a camel ride for Y100. For the real Silk Road nut, Charlie Johng's Café in town can arrange camel treks in the desert. These are also flexible, from a sunset camp under the stars, depositing the camel-riders at the **Mogao Caves** in time for the next morning's tour, to a full-on seven-day desert wander. Expect to pay around Y400 a night, although discounts may be available for certain groups and conditions, on what is surely a highlight of any Silk Road trip.

Other sights in Dunhuang include the **White Horse Pagoda** (Y15 – *baima-ta*), which, like the White Horse Temple in Luoyang, commemorates the trusty steed who carried Kumarajiva's sacred sutras to China.

Hami (Kumul)

The **Hami Museum** (Y10) showcases the region's history as a nomadic trading post, and also proudly recounts its past as an autonomous Muslim enclave, with many exhibits of weaponry pointing to less than harmonious internal relations between the contending ethnicities represented – chiefly

Sarts (Uzbeks), Chinese and Uyghurs. Hami's 'royal' past, ruled by local despots, translated sometimes as 'kings' and sometimes as 'princes' depending on the prevailing political situation, is represented in two impressive sites, the **King's Mansion** (Y40 – *hami huiwang fu*) and the **Tombs of the Hami Kings** (Y40 – *hami huiwang ling*). The latter contains the remains of several of the region's nine rulers, with Islamic domes perched above Chinese roofs, symbolising not only the co-existence of two very different groups, but also the funding for the tomb itself. Determined to curry favour with the ninth king in the 1840s, the Chinese government stumped up much of the cash for the buildings. The park on Red Star (*hongxing*) Road is dedicated to the westward march of the Red Army, and features a brutalist monument of a fist firmly clutching a blocky red firebrand.

Marco Polo was more impressed with the scandalously open marriages of local residents of the town known to him as *Camul*, noting in his *Travels*: 'I give you my word that if a stranger comes to a house here to receive hospitality, he receives a very warm welcome. The host bids his wife do everything that the guest wishes. Then he leaves the house... and the guest stays with his wife in the house and does what he will with her, lying with her in one bed as if she were his own wife... And the women are beautiful and vivacious and always ready to oblige.' This doesn't come up in the museum, although it was a reported custom in many later sources, and the subject of some annoyance among several devout Muslim governors.

Several ancient sites can be found in the surrounding countryside – including **Wubi**, **Dahe** and **Lafuqueke**. All are in a state of considerable ruin, in part because of the depredations of time, but also because of the traditional Muslim aversion to idolatrous images, which has done for many of the Buddhist temples. The names of several archaeological sites in the area contain Chinese words for 'devils' or 'haunted', preserving echoes of local attitudes towards relics of the past before more enlightened times. The Dali-esque erosions of **Strange Stone Mountain** (*guaishi-shan*) and the **Ghost City** (*mogui-cheng*) demonstrate that these attitudes were not wholly unjustified.

Two hours' drive into the mountains (Y12 on the bus) will bring you to **Songshutang**, a ski resort with gentle slopes favouring the beginner, and seasonal ice sculptures to bolster the view.

Ili Kazakh Autonomous Prefecture

Starting at the edges of Urumqi, but extending all the way to the border of Kazakhstan, the Ili district is the size of Croatia, and incorporates its regional capital **Yining** (Qulja), as well as the cities of **Shihezi** and **Karamay**, for which see their separate entries. Its close connections to the Kazakh people brought it temporarily within the Russian orbit in the 1940s, which the Chinese countered with a massive resettlement programme to move demobilised soldiers into the area. Sixty thousand Kazakhs voted with their feet and moved to the Soviet Union, which today has resulted in strong family ties with what is now Kazakhstan over the border.

Close to the Kazakh border, in the hills above the town of **Huocheng** (Korgas), is the **mausoleum of Tughluq Temur** (1329–63), last of the Chagatayid descendants of Genghis Khan, whose realm at various times spanned what is now the border region on both sides. A trip there can also encompass the ancient **Almali City**.

Karamay (Kelamayi)

As the centre of the region's oil industry, the city of Karamay has benefited from the spending of petrodollars, although this has also created financial awareness and a slight rise in prices. It costs Y40 to go down and look at the river, and Y20 to get onto the bridge! That aside, it is fascinating to see **Black**

Oil Hill (Y10 – *heiyushan*) where oil still does seep from the ground in pools, as it did in Marco Polo's day. Similar geological fun is to be had at the **Mud Volcano** (Y30 – *nihuoshan*) where underground heat causes bubbling, suppurating pools of mud. **Nine Dragons Dam** (Y10 – *jiulong-piao*) presents an impressive ten-metre cascade of water, topped by a superstructure like the arcade of a Chinese temple.

A hundred kilometres outside of town is the region's most famous landmark, the **Urho Wind City,** better known locally as the Urho Ghost Town (Y20 – *wu'erhe mogui cheng*), with majestic, sand-worn rocky outcrops that look remarkably like America's Monument Valley.

Kashgar (Kashi)

Marco Polo's *Cascar* is still a vibrant city, with a massive bazaar said, in local parlance, to be the place where you can buy literally anything 'except for chicken's milk and cow's eggs.' It is steeped in history, from the **Ban Chao memorial** that celebrates the Han Dynasty conquest in bas-relief, to the largest mosque in China. But Kashgar is often as interesting for what one *can't* see than for what one can. Chinese guidebooks push the Ban Chao monument as one of the must-see sights, even though it is little more than a statue in a park, albeit one that reminds visitors how long the Chinese have been here. The area was the also the sight of fervid and often comedic Great Game competition between the British and Russian consuls, although Chini Bagh, the former residence of the consul Sir George Macartney and his wife, and a veritable home-from-home for many famous Victorian explorers, has lost its gardens and been turned into a couple of anonymous hotels – the original building is the Wake Hotel. The former Russian consulate is also now a hotel – the Seman.

The ancient, walled city of **Kashkar** (Y10 – *kashi shitou cheng*) is someway outside the modern city, and still has impressive ruined fortifications. Although it has a long history as the junction between the north and south Silk Roads, Kashgar is truly as far west as you can go and still be in a Chinese metropolis, and much of its appeal lies in its alien appearance. Kashgar's old town remains a largely Muslim area, with terracotta walls and tight alleyways like many a Middle Eastern souk. It is an active part of town, but visitors are expected to pay Y20 for coming in and gawping. It is possible to sneak in for free down one of the back alleys, but really, do you want to be one of *those* people? See old Kashgar while you can, as the Chinese authorities have proclaimed much of it, not without reason, as unsanitary and unsafe, and plans are afoot for 85 per cent of the mud-brick traditional buildings to be razed to the ground. There are promises of ethnically relevant facades in their place, but you can be sure that there will be more skyscrapers soon enough. Before long, Kashgar is going to look just like everywhere else.

Five kilometres out of town, Arabesque tiles and minarets decorate the holiest Muslim site in all China, the **mausoleum of Afaq Khoja** (d. 1694), scion to the Sufi 'White Mountain' faction, who introduced Sharia law in opposition to the Mongol Yassa code that was then the custom among the region's rulers. Despot of much of western Xinjiang, and the wounded party who summoned the Zunghar warriors to wipe out his rival cousins of the Black Mountain faction, he has been cited in retrospect as a monarch of what was once quasi-independent 'Kashgaria', and is buried here with 71 of his family and descendants. The building was originally designed as a resting place for his father, but it is Afaq who gets his name on the door.

His fame has been somewhat eclipsed by his granddaughter Iparhan, the 'fragrant princess', whose story differs radically in Chinese and Uyghur accounts. According to the Uyghurs, she was a beautiful Muslim girl, dragged off to Beijing as a concubine to Emperor Qianlong at the end of his wars of conquest in the region. She died in mysterious circumstances, possibly while planning to murder the emperor, possibly from suicide to preserve her honour. The Chinese version claims that she was the 'fragrant concubine' (*xiangfei*), a Uyghur girl brought to the emperor's palace disconsolate and homesick, who was eventually won over by increasingly lavish attempts to impress her with tastes of home. Her body was then returned to Kashgar after her death, as a symbol of enduring reconciliation.

Neither of these accounts necessarily relate to any identifiable coffin in the mausoleum, but the story of the fragrant concubine has taken on an iconic, popular significance. Although the Afaq Khoja *mazar* is the holiest Muslim site in China, the constant focus of secular tourism has undermined its sacred status, to the extent that the romantic legend has been entirely superimposed on its image and heritage. It is now more likely to be listed, and even pictured, in Chinese guide books as the 'Tomb of the Fragrant Concubine' (*xiangfei-mu*). The overwhelming majority of Chinese tourists come to see that story played out, and the signage in the mausoleum often reflects that.

The **Id Kah mosque** (Y15 – but for God's sake dress respectfully) is an active place of worship, China's largest mosque, with space for 10,000 believers. As a focus for the Muslims of Kashgar, it has also been the site of several iconic moments in history, particularly in the turbulent 1930s, when numerous local warlords ended up with their heads on spikes. It was here, too, in 1934, that the warlord Ma Zhongying told his fellow Muslims that their future lay with the Chinese, and not the Russians, although mysteriously Ma then slipped over the border and was never seen again.

Further afield from Kashgar there is the ancient city of **Hanoi** (Y15), a Tang Dynasty settlement with the sand-worn ruins of Buddhist stupas. The **Caves of the Three Immortals** (*sanxian-dong*), the oldest Buddhist caves in China, are marked on local maps but almost impossible to visit, as they are ten metres above the rushing water of a river. Organised tours can probably arrange a ladder and safety gear, but private tourists should not even attempt it.

Tushuk Tash, the 'Pierced Mountain' in Uyghur, or *Tianmen*, 'Heaven's Gate' in Chinese, is the world's largest natural rock arch, as high as the Empire State Building if one includes the drop from its western approach. It was first reported to the West by Eric Shipton in his *Mountains of Tartary*, and hence is often also known as Shipton's Arch.

> Before we reached the col we had seen only a very small portion of the Arch; now the whole vast structure opened before us. On the other side of the col, the ground dropped vertically into a profound abyss, so narrow in its lower portion that its floor was for the most part invisible. The Arch was about a hundred and fifty feet from where we stood, a quarter of its height above us, three quarters below... It was impossible to estimate its total height, but I do not believe this was far short of a thousand feet.

Getting there requires a four-wheel drive and three bumpy hours, but it is one of the most magical sights in China. There is no official entrance fee, but local entrepreneurs have brought ladders to make the climb substantially easier. If you don't give them the requested Y30, they will take their toys away and the ascent will take you hours.

Kizilsu Kyrgyz Autonomous County

Half an hour's drive out of Kashgar is **Artush** (Artux), main city of the Kizilsu Kyrgyz Autonomous County, which snakes along the border with Kyrgyzstan and Tajikistan and leads on to Tashkurgan. Satuq Bughra Khan (d.955), who first imposed Islam on the Kashgar region by force, is celebrated here in his elaborate tomb, although the current building is a late 20th century replacement for the original, destroyed in an earthquake.

This is where the Karakoram Highway snakes into the mountains and, eventually, to Islamabad in Pakistan, although the region requires permits to visit, and anyone without the correct paperwork, be they Chinese or foreign, will be turned back at the military checkpoints along the road.

Korla (Ku'erle)

Korla was once a mere stop on the northern Silk Road, although the Tarim Highway, built for the petrochemical industry, now cuts across the desert to reach it, and has turned it into a more crucial junction. As a result, it is now bigger and more important than nearby Karashahar (Yanqi), which was historically the seat of power in the region.

Korla is home to the multi-storey **Bayingolin Mongol Autonomous Prefecture Museum** (Y10), which emphasises its role as a defensive point on the Silk Road on the route to Yanqi (Karashahar), but also the strong presence of nomadic settlers in the region, including the Torguts (Kalmuks), whose Mongol ancestors settled in Russia in the 17th century, but who famously returned en masse a century later, to settle here and further north in Ili.

The **Iron Gate Pass** (Y10 – *tiemen-guan*) outside the city is a bottleneck in the hills where a single gate blocks the Silk Road, forming an important strategic site. According to legend, a burial mound in the gorge is the last resting place of a local princess and her herdsmen lover, who plummeted to their deaths while trying to elope.

The sheer size of the Bayingolin region can lead into some optical illusions on maps and in expectations. Some Chinese guidebooks file the famous desert ruins of Loulan and Miran as sites to visit from Korla – and although this is possible, they are over 200 kilometres away, and marginally closer to

Ruoqiang (qv). Similarly, while the Bayanbulak grasslands and Swan Lake are listed as a site of natural beauty 'near' Korla, they are actually 360 kilometres away.

As Hami is famous for its melons, Korla is famous for its peaches, and for having an actual, bona fide, honest-to-God river running through the middle of town, its banks transformed into a park and boulevards of cafés and kiosks. The Konchi River flows all the way to Lop Nur, although that can mean anything from the *town* of Lop Nur not far from the city limits, to the modern-day salt flats and marshes of the 'wandering lake' itself, which can be up to 500 kilometres away.

Kucha (Kuche)

An ancient centre of Buddhism, Kucha had strong connections in ancient times to the Indian-influenced towns on the far side of the desert. It is surrounded by several 'Thousand Buddha Caves' including those at the ancient city of **Subash** (Y15), Kumtura and Kizilgala, although the last two are usually locked, and can only be visited by prior arrangement. The most famous are the **Kizil** (Qizil, Qyzyl) **Thousand Buddha Caves** (Y50), 75 kilometres out of town, and said to be second only in size and importance to the grottoes at Dunhuang. Kizil was a working monastery, with its cliff-side caves divided into places of worship and humble monks' dwellings. Although Albert von le Coq's expedition ruined many of the 236 caves, some are still intact, and display strong foreign influences, including inscriptions celebrating Tokharian benefactors, references to Indian priests, and vibrant blue pigments derived from Afghan lapis lazuli.

Kucha itself has an attractive old town, to the east of modern city, where the local museum (Y15) can be found in the repurposed mansion of the former governor. Much of the region's archaeological treasures, however, were carted away during the great grab for antiquities by Victorian archaeologists from Europe. The local mosque (Y15) is the second largest in Xinjiang, after Kashgar's massive Id Kah, and the area comes alive on Fridays, when a market sets up on the western river bank.

Subash also has a Buddhist temple (Y25), which is largely worn away by the sands of time, while nearby Kizilgasha sports a ruined beacon tower (Y10) – one of the scattered vantage points for isolated groups of forgotten watchmen.

Khotan (Hetian)

A centre for jade since prehistoric times, Marco Polo's *Cotan* is still heavily associated with the stone – shops selling jade throughout China often promise it is *hetian* jade as a mark of quality. It is arguably the most crucial city on the southern routes, rivalled only by Yarkand for its importance to trade and history. There is, as local legend has it, something in the water, for the springs and snowmelt from the Kunlun mountains, supposed residence of the Chinese gods, famously imparts long life to the locals, and thick wool to the herds that supply the raw material for their carpets.

Once a centre of Buddhism, Khotan was subject to push and pull struggles between Buddhist and Islamic warlords in the middle ages, before being razed entirely to the ground by the Mongols for being the one oasis that refused to surrender without a fight.

Its proximity to British India made it one of the earliest sites for British archaeologists, with much local colour and information preserved in books such as Aurel Stein's *Sand-Buried Ruins of Khotan*. One enterprising local, Islam Akhun, confounded historians for years by inventing a series of ancient documents in an imagined language and then flogging them to the feuding British and Russian consuls in Kashgar. Ninety volumes of his forgeries now lie in the archives of the British Library.

The ancient sites nearby are often impressive ruins.

Melikawat (Y10), on the banks of the White Jade (Urungkash) River, is named for its discoverer, the farmer Melik Ahun who first uncovered its ruins in the desert in the 1930s – the city appears to have flourished between the Han and Tang dynasties. **Niya** (Y10), only discovered in the sands in 1901, has been called the 'Asian Pompeii', although the reasons for its abandonment have never really been established. **Yotkan** (Y10) is even more nondescript, although all these sites appear to have once been the seats of regional powers. Theories abound of foreign invaders, local conflicts, or simple sand encroachment, but the most likely explanation is surely related to the fluctuating availability of water, causing the site of 'Khotan' itself to shift every few centuries in search of better wells. 'Ever since human activity first created the oases of Khotan territory,' observed Aurel Stein, 'their outskirts must have witnessed a continuous struggle with that most formidable of deserts, the Taklamakan; while local traditions, attested from an early date, told of settlements that had been abandoned before its advance.'

The sites might be evocative and impressive, but they lack any place to exhibit archaeological findings. Stein wrote of the 'rich statuary' of nearby sites, but it has all been removed now from the site, and sent to foreign museums or to the modern **Hetian Museum** (Y25), which has nail-less wooden coffins containing dessicated Buddhist priests, ancient maps and coins.

The **Stupa of Rawak** (Y8) is the crumbling remains of what must have once been a wonderful Buddhist site. It remains an iconic image of the Silk Road, and somewhat difficult to reach. Whereas other ruins in the region have been cossetted with tourist roads and visitor centres, Rawak remains off the beaten track, requiring a four wheel drive to get within a couple of miles. Even then, the final approach must be made on foot across the dusty rocks. Perhaps this is why it remains a familiar site in Chinese imagery of the Silk Road, as it still requires a degree of effort to reach it, and invites a sense of achievement.

Khotan's handicrafts are under heavy threat from industrialisation and straightforward lack of interest, as China's growing middle class favours Ikea. There are discernible government schemes to encourage a sense of heritage among consumers, and if that doesn't work, to commodify the industry itself for tourist purposes. **Aidelaixi Silk Factory** is open to the public (Y10), so you can drop in to watch the 1,000 workers, who live and work in the industrial complex with their families, producing 150 million metres of silk a year, as well as nylons, velours and velvets. Visitors can also buy the wares at their source, as at the **Hetian Carpet Factory** (Y10).

Lanzhou

As the capital of Gansu province, Lanzhou is liable to be linked to Xi'an by high-speed rail by 2015, making it substantially 'closer' to the tourist trail than it was before. The provincial museum, free to visitors with valid ID, contains one of the most iconic statues of the Silk Road, the famous **Galloping Horse Treading on a Swallow**, depicting a rushing steed, so fast that it has apparently planted one of its hooves on a surprised-looking bird. Found in a Han Dynasty grave in 1969, this item is much imitated all over China, and is one of the most common replicas in museum shops as far afield as Beijing, cast in porcelain, bronze or even jade. Annoyingly, the version on display here is *also* often a replica, as the original is so famous it is regularly sent off to be displayed in museums abroad.

Thanks to an artificial lake created by a hydroelectric dam, it is now possible to take a boat upriver (Y200) in the summer months to reach the **Thousand Buddha Caves of Bingling-si** (Y50), which include a massive cliff-face statue of Maitreya Buddha, which resembles the now-lost giant statues of Bamiyan in Afghanistan.

Three and a half hours by bus from Lanzhou is **Xiahe**, a one-horse town in the Gannan Tibetan Autonomous Prefecture, one of the only sites outside Tibet proper that retains vestiges of the high-water mark of the medieval Tibetan empire. The town is all but dwarfed by the huge **Labrang Temple Complex**, an entire religious *city* of temples, pagodas and stupas, and a place of pilgrimage for believers from Mongolia to Ladakh. Established in 1709, it remains one of the most sacred sites in Tibetan Buddhism, and a working monastery. For anyone interested in Buddhism, there is a day or two's worth of exploration to be had here, and English-language tours that leave from the ticket office every day at 10 and 3.15. However, Labrang has always had an uneasy relationship with visitors – when Gustaf Mannerheim was there in March 1908, he found them most unwelcoming.

> The door of the next temple was closed in my face, and all blandishments proved unavailing. A large number of lamas collected to watch my departure and showed their hostility in various ways.... I saw two stones prepared to be thrown at me, and the door was banged in my face.... The bare-headed lamas, dressed in red, appeared on all sides like an army of ants. Hooting, jeers, stones etc.

Labrang remains a devout place of worship, and the residents ask visitors to respect their requests for no photographs, and not to interfere with ceremonies (Mannerheim appears to have blundered into one). There is no parade for the kids here, and no tour-oriented effort expended at giving visitors an 'experience.' There is no one-price-for-all ticket, so separate buildings often require nominal entrance fees (between Y10 to Y60). Labrang is the ultimate test of tourist motives. Don't go there if you want a photograph of yourself turning a prayer wheel. Do go there if you want to peek in at one of the holiest sites in the Buddhist world.

Do not buy any of the fur on sale in the streets outside – many items are poached, and sure to cause trouble for the tourist either leaving China or arriving back in their home country.

Luoyang

The smog-bound, grubby city of Luoyang gains an honorary place as a Silk Road city, largely because of its occasional status as the capital of China. Luoyang is particularly famous for 'peony jade' (*mudanyu*), a black rock speckled with flower-like white granules. This is sold both carved or in simple, unfashioned lumps and is the most distinctive souvenir of the city. Making a bid for being the most expensive entry ticket in China, outcharging even the Great Wall and the Terracotta Army, the **Longmen Grottoes** (Y120) are set into the cliff-sides at the Dragon Gate (*longmen*) river gorge. Like the 'Thousand Buddha Caves' to be found in several sites further to the West on the Silk Road, Longmen features hundreds of devotional images carved into the rock itself, usually hewn with the financial backing of numerous imperial sponsors from the Wei, Sui and Tang dynasties. For Paul Pelliot, who reached the site in March 1908, it was: 'a site of the first order, interesting and picturesque, and of cardinal importance for archaeology.'

The highlight of any visit is the great **Vairocana Buddha**, commissioned by Empress Wu and popularly believed to have been given her face by a grateful sculptor. But don't miss the *smallest* images, some no larger than a finger, carved cheekily into the modern signposts along the path. Seemingly in the belief that anyone who has paid the entrance fee must be loaded, hawkers within the site are uncharacteristically unwilling to haggle. To get the full value of your ticket, remember to cross over the bridge to the far side (it is often invisible in the smog), where there are also a couple of temples and the tomb of the Tang Dynasty poet Bai Juyi. The imposing museum by the entrance is currently (2013) empty – a disappointing discovery if you've just paid £12 to get in.

Luoyang's heyday was in the distant pre-imperial past, of which no impressive structures are still extant. The riverside park on the north bank of the River Luo includes several anonymous piles of rubble – all that remains of the glorious palaces of the ancient dynasties of Shang, Zhou and the semi-legendary Xia. Better evidence can be found in the city museum, which has a hoard of ancient bronzes. For those seeking some to take home, try the underground antique market beneath the charioteer statue in the centre of town. The newly opened **Great Ming Pagoda** (*da ming tang*) is named for Empress Wu's legendary Tang-era tower, and the first shot fired in what is likely to be an ongoing fight for attention with Xi'an. Empress Wu moved the capital to Luoyang during the Tang Dynasty, and the Luoyang tourist board seems faintly annoyed that Xi'an gets all the attention.

For Buddhists, martial artists and lovers of kung fu films, Luoyang's greatest attractions are outside the city, and can be visited in a single day trip. The **White Horse Temple** (Y50 – *baima-si*) is billed as 'the first Buddhist temple in China' – an oddly controversial claim which seemingly disregards numerous temples further to the west, in the regions that the Chinese government is very keen to call 'Chinese' now. Regardless, in the realm of the Han peoples, the White Horse is the grandfather of all other temples, named for the steed on which Kumarajiva brought the first Buddhist holy scrolls to China all the way from India.

An hour further outside of town, after a perilous climb on a winding mountain road, is the world-famous **Shaolin Temple** (Y100 – *shaolin-si*), the birthplace not only of Zen Buddhism, but also of one of China's best-known martial arts. An English-language tour costs an extra Y300, but is well worth it. There is a hotel on-site for those who wish to dawdle. Restaurants are in short supply in the temple complex itself, but turn right outside the entrance and walk past the gas station to find a nest of cheap hotels and cafés in a secluded dale.

Ruoqiang (Charkilik)

Once a remote settlement on the southern Silk Road, now

connected directly to the north by the Tarim Highway, Ruoqiang can serve as a base for visiting several of the region's most famous desert sites. **Washixia**, for example, (Aurel Stein's 'Vash Shari') was a Chinese town from the Tang Dynasty period.

Do not be deceived by the desert and the area's legendary day-long sandstorms. Centuries ago, this was a very different place, watered by streams cascading northwards from the Astintag Mountains. During the Dark Ages, the whole area was richer, greener and more habitable, and likely to have been more like the pastures near Urumqi on the Tianshan slopes. Sudden climate change spoiled the region, shutting off the water supply from numerous rivers that now exist solely as seasonal phantoms of snowmelt. Although inhabited for thousands of years by Tocharian tribesmen, the land was already failing by the Han Dynasty. As one observer reported:

> The land is sandy and salt, and there are few cultivated fields. The state hopes to... look to neighbouring states for field-crops. It produces jade and there is an abundance of rushes, tamarisk, the balsam poplar, and white grass. In company with their flocks and herds the inhabitants go in search of water and pasture, and there are asses, horses and large number of camels.

Several oasis towns, some still to be found, were abandoned and left for the sands which soon swallowed them up.

The ancient city of **Miran** (Y10) is 75 kilometres away across the sands – the low entry cost charged to Chinese disguises a number of additional fees, not least the car and driver that will need to be hired to get you there. Once a riverside oasis near a strategic mountain pass into Tibet, it was abandoned by its river, and then by its people, sometime in the middle ages. By then, it was a *Tibetan* outpost, but it had formerly been a Buddhist site with strong connections to

India, with what appears to have been many migrants from Gandhara around AD 200. Some even had connections to faraway Europe, with temple artwork signed by a Buddhist called 'Tita' – thought to be, if not a Roman called Titus far from home, then a close descendant of someone who was.

Loulan (Y10) is perhaps more famous, ever since its rediscovery by Sven Hedin at the turn of the 20th century. The town that gave its name to the entire region before the Han Dynasty conquests and mass-renamings, Loulan remains an evocative word for the Chinese. It was assigned to the Beauty of Loulan, most famous of the Tarim Mummies (now in the Urumqi museum), and also to a brand of Turfan wine. From here all the way to Dunhuang, there are beacon towers and ruins that point to what was once a thriving part of the Silk Road, but abandoned in the middle ages.

Once a large salt lake the size of Jamaica, teeming with reeds along its shore, **Lop Nur** has declined over the centuries, particularly as irrigation projects elsewhere divert water that once fed it. It became known as the Wandering Lake to foreign explorers, largely because inadequate maps and unreliable, seasonal water sources, coupled with the desert's habit of blocking or re-opening channels with drifting sand, meant that people kept 'discovering' it in different places. It remains off-limits, not the least because parts of it were used for 40 years as a site for testing Chinese atomic weapons. Following a test moratorium in 1996, it has lain abandoned, although there is talk of repurposing one of the test sites, Malan, for tourism. However, it's not all that clear where Malan is – it doesn't show up on Chinese maps, although a Malan *mountain* is on the Xinjiang-Qinghai border several hundred kilometres away. Until the Chinese actually put it on the map, you can't go there.

Shihezi

Xinjiang's second-largest city after Urumqi grew up around a bunch of 20th-century farms and fields, and hence has little from *ancient* history to recommend it. It is, however, the site of the **Xinjiang Military Museum**, which is regarded as *the* prime site for 'red' tourists in the region, not only for matters martial, but also because so many of the aforementioned farmers were resettled veterans from the Revolution and civil war. The city also boasts a **memorial column to the statesman Zhou Enlai**, a choice that surprisingly seems to please all parties. The Nationalist soldiers appreciate being settled in Shihezi instead of being put on trial for being enemies of Communism; the Communists respect Zhou for his leadership and his attempts to intercede on Xinjiang's behalf during the Cultural Revolution. The Xinjiang locals greatly appreciate his 1957 speech that warned against both local unrest and 'Han chauvinism'. In Zhou Enlai, the town has an icon that looks towards a harmonious future. There is also the **Shihezi Nanshan Scenic Area** (Y15), a park that guarantees mountain meadows and views of old-fashioned yurts and herds of horses.

Tashkurgan Tajik Autonomous County

The city of Tashkurgan (Tajik: 'stone fort'; Chinese: *tashiku'ergan*) is believed to have been the 'stone tower' mentioned by Ptolemy in his *Geographia* as marking the westernmost boundary of the land of the Seres (China). Thus, for the ancient Greeks, and presumably the Bactrian descendants of Alexander's men, it was the place where China truly began. A fort located on the same site was described by Tripitaka during his journey to the west, and Aurel Stein arrived 1,000 years later to pronounce both places to be one and the same. He pointed out that Tashkurgan not only lay at a fork in the road which led to either Kashgar or Khotan, but also westwards through the two most passable routes through the Pamir Mountains.

Its inhabitants are mainly ethnic Tajiks, and today it is a

small town where the customs authority for Pakistani border crossings has its offices. For anyone planning to travel on to Pakistan, it is recommended to stay the night here, not only to ensure you have the correct paperwork, but also to take advantage of the maximum amount of daylight for the hairpin turns and sudden drops of the 'Valley of Blood' (*khunjerab*) that slides down into Pakistan. There is not just the pass, but the 81 kilometre border zone to cross before you reach the next outpost of civilisation – the Pakistani town of Sost. It will also give you time to check out the town's two best-known sites.

The mud-brick **Prince's Fort** (Y30) is an imposing, iconic crag-top castle, although little remains inside its impressive walls. It is, however, not the exact stone tower of antiquity, despite Stein's hopes, as it is only 600 years old. Nor should it be confused with the **Princess Castle** (Y15) – this is easier than you might think, as English spelling and apostrophes are not the locals' strong point. But the Princess Castle is the alleged site of one of the region's fairy stories. First set down in the Tang Dynasty, the story goes that a Chinese virgin, locked up in a tower on her way to marry a Persian prince, became inexplicably pregnant. Her execution was postponed after it transpired that she had been visited each night by a 'shining man' – the offspring of this divine union went on to become a powerful king, although nobody is all that clear as to who, and some versions claim that the *virgin* was Persian.

The small museum includes a trio of mummies rescued from a nearby valley before it was flooded by a hydro-electric power plant.

Turfan (Turpan)

For any aficionado of the Silk Road, Turfan's greatest glory is the miraculous *karez* system that nourishes it with cool mountain water through underground tunnels. The city's **Karez Museum** (Y30) is a must-see, but the **Turfan City**

Museum (Y30) has much to recommend it, not the least skeletons of Turfan's oldest residents – dinosaurs.

The city's most iconic man-made sight is that of the **Emin Minaret** (*emin-ta*), a blunt conical tower attached to a 1,000-seater mosque, and the tallest of its kind in China, completed in 1778. Inside the tower, there are no floors, merely a staircase winding around a central column to the apex platform. It is no longer possible to climb to the top, but the view from the pokey windows is limited anyway. When Beijing's museum of ethnic minorities was searching for architecture representative of Xinjiang, it plumped for the Emin Minaret and its hypnotic patterns of crosses and squares, a replica of which can now be seen poking over the park's wall not far from Beijing's modern Bird's Nest Olympic Stadium.

Despite such a high recognition factor, the tower's initial purpose of commemorating Emin Khoja seems to have been thwarted by general disinterest and equivocation – tourist guides are often sheepishly reticent as to who the celebrated Emin was, and why he was commemorated in the first place. The Chinese-language stele outside announces that the tower proclaims gratitude to the Chinese emperor, while the Uyghur inscription simply praises God. This reflects the chequered background of Emin Khoja himself, feted by his own people as a devout man who had made the *hajj* pilgrimage to Mecca, and among the Chinese as a local ally who proved invaluable in the suppression of resistance among the Muslims.

Among Mandarin speakers, it is sometimes referred to as the 'tower of the prince Su[leiman]' (*su-gong ta*) named for the Emin's son, but pointedly giving him the imperial title conferred upon him by Emperor Qianlong. In generations both before and after the construction of the tower, the name Khoja was associated with a dangerous resistance movement in west Xinjiang, but it is Suleiman and his father's devotion to the Emperor that endures in monumental form. The other Khojas, some of whom proclaimed *jihad* against the

Chinese, are not publicly celebrated. There is a statue of Emin Khoja here, carved in such an angular style that he looks like a robot, raising a scroll to the heavens in gratitude – this is a symbol of his acceptance of Chinese suzerainty.

Wine-lovers can also visit the lush **Turfan Vineyards**, otherwise known as Grape Valley (Y60), a few miles outside of town, and the ancient ruins of **Jiaohe** (Y30), which lack a city wall because they were built on an island in a stream. Further afield, there is the **Gaochang** (Qocho) old town, often mentioned in books and guides with the name Kara-khoja or Qara-khoja, recorded by Marco Polo as *Carachoço*. It was built in the 1st century BC, but rose to prominence when the Uyghurs became the de facto rulers of much of Xinjiang, as the influence of the Tang Dynasty waned in the 9th century. Not far from Gaochang, the **Astana Cemetery underground museum** (Y20 – *asitana gumuqun*) is another prime location, as it is the source of many vital documents from the heyday of the Silk Road, many of which were thrown away as scrap paper and then refashioned as paper grave goods. These have since been painstakingly deconstructed and reassembled, and some are on display along with other exotica, such as Byzantine coins previously placed on the eyes of the dead. Many bodies were found with banners representing the archaic Chinese deities Fuxi and Nüwa, a brother and sister who survived a mythological great flood by hiding in the Kunlun Mountains, and returned after the apocalypse to repopulate China with their children. These primal beings, credited with inventing many fundamental elements of life, such as agriculture and fishing, are celebrated in a fantastic modern statue at the Astana site, which faithfully recreates their sinuous, serpentine lower halves. According to myth, the Chinese are descended from these snake people.

The sight of the infamous **Flaming Mountains**, shimmering in the desert haze, is unchanged since the days of Tripitaka, although he did not have the opportunity to get there in a coach, and was not charged Y20 admission. It is, however, an impressive site, with an attendant museum and scattered statues recalling iconic moments from the famous novel *Journey to the West* in which a fictional Tripitaka was accompanied by the famous Monkey King. Some bright spark at the tourist board has realised that no still image will be able to capture the shimmering fire of the mountains themselves, and has provided tourists with something more photogenic – a giant thermometer, sure to be showing an eye-popping temperature. A trip out to the celebrated cliff can also incorporate a visit to the **Bezeklik Thousand Buddha Caves** (Y20). The more geographically-minded can also visit the lowest body of water in China, **Aiding Lake**, 154 metres below sea level – a depth surpassed only by Israel's Dead Sea, or so claim the local signs. Actually, these days, Aiding Lake is often not there at all, and is more like a marsh, and quibblers may wish to raise the possibility that both the Sea of Galilee (in Israel) and Lake Assal (in Djibouti) are technically lower.

Urumqi (Wulumuqi)

Despite being in the middle of Xinjiang, the provincial capital Urumqi is often a traveller's first stop, operating as a hub for flights from Beijing, and also as a point from which to strike out north to the grasslands of the Ili Kazakh region, or south into the desert. Locals, particularly those with a brother-in-law who owns a silk stall, are utterly convinced that the top tourist attraction in town is the **International Grand Bazaar** in the south of the city's Tianshan district. This is no mere market, but a vast modern shopping complex using traditional Islamic motifs, with space for 3,000 trading stalls, a 1,000-seater theatre, a mosque, supermarket, restaurants and cafés, public squares and five office blocks. Vibrant and hectic during the day, and alive with light at night, it gains its 'international' title from modern successors to the travellers of the Silk Road – ethnic minorities from all over China, as well as neighbouring 'Stans, India and Nepal.

Anyone with a desire to *live* the Silk Road owes it to themselves to drop in and wander the crowded, bustling alleyways, but keep your wallet close and your haggling face on. Silks, brassware, statuettes, and all manner of tourist tat can be found here, but it is also not far from the *minjie* (people's street), a grungier street market selling everyday articles for the locals, and likely to be an equally rich treasure trove of sights and sounds.

As a larger city, Urumqi also has something to offer the kids, including the **Tianshan Wildlife Park** (Y30), the **Shuishang fairground** (Y30) and the **Children's Park** (*ertong gongyuan* – Y40). For older visitors, museums include the **Museum of the Silk Road**, which tells you everything you might expect to hear after reading this book, but also the **Museum of the Uyghur Autonomous Region** (Y25), packed with artefacts from the region's rich history. Living history can be found at the Qing-era **Shaanxi Temple**, and the **Nanda Temple,** which dates from the early Republican era. The **Hantenggeli Mosque** dates from 1864, but has been lovingly restored. All these religious buildings charge a nominal Y10 entrance fee.

For the Chinese, the most iconic sight in Urumqi is actually a short drive *outside* of town, at the **Dabancheng Power Station**, right in the path of the strong winds that stream through the gap in the Tianshan Mountains between north and south Xinjiang. Here, dozens of elegant wind turbines spin on the plain – in Chinese reportage on the region, it's as obligatory and archetypal a sight as are Big Ben, the Eiffel Tower or the Empire State building for their respective hometowns. From the future to the past – the **Ulanbay Ancient City** (Y30) presents sand-worn ruins. A trip to Dabancheng can also take in the Tang Dynasty trading post at Baishui, and the Wang Luobin memorial and museum, dedicated to the Beijing-born composer who spent 50 years in north-west China, and whose 700 songs have heavily influenced the shape of popular music from the region ever since. In 1994, he was made the honorary mayor of Dabancheng. You will not fail to hear half a dozen of his songs during your time in Xinjiang, whether you want to or not.

Further afield, a two or three-hour drive will bring you to the Yihao Glacier, a suitably icy respite from the warm desert below. Sixty kilometres outside Urumqi is the **Tianshan International Ski Resort** (Y30), the largest in Xinjiang. In between such extremes, and watered by the inevitable snowmelt, are the unexpectedly viridian vistas of the region's pastures and meadows, providing practically Alpine views of chrysanthemum meadows, lakes and evergreen forests on the slopes of Nanshan and Xibai. It is also not far to the **Heart of Asia** (Y5), a towering tripod that makes a giant 'A' supporting a steel globe, from which hangs a pendulum pointing straight down at... you, standing on a spot on the ground that is supposedly the geographical centre of the entire continent.

Yarkand (Shache, Yarkan)

Owing to the lay of the land and the twists of the terrain, Yarkand is actually 'closer' to the Karakoram mountain pass than Khotan, which is only nearer as the crow flies. The trade route south made Yarkand a bigger regional centre than Kashgar until the late 20th century, when Central Asia began to supersede South Asia as a market. When the Jesuit traveller Benedict de Goes came through in 1603, he noted that '*Hiarchan*, the capital of the kingdom of *Cascar* is a mart of much note, both for the great concourse of merchants, and for the variety of wares.' Caravans of traders from Afghanistan had their terminus here, where merchants would then wait up to a year to join a new caravan heading eastwards to China proper.

The old town, through coincidental neglect, is hence more 'authentic', but will charge visitors an authentic Y25 to come in and look around. The **Golden Graves** (Y10 – *shache wang ling*) are a series of tombs for the local Uyghur rulers, dating from the death of the first, Said Khan in 1533, to the final few who ceded power to the Republic.

The **Mausoleum of Amannisa Khan Nafisi** (Y10) is a beautiful Indian-influenced dome above a graceful colonnade, celebrating the brief life of a woman known to the Chinese as Amannisa Han. Amannisa (1526–60) was a forester's daughter in the Yarkand hills, whose ability as a musician so charmed the local king that he paid her bride price on the spot. Packed off to Yarkand, where she received a decidedly icy welcome from the ruler's senior wife, she busied herself setting down a complete set of melodies and variations, the Twelve Muqams, said to form the musical canon of classical Xinjiang. At the time, her royal husband took a lot of the credit for it, and after her death in childbirth at the age of 34, little more was heard of her. But in 2005, her 12-part musical programme was decreed by UNESCO to be part of the Intangible Legacy of Humanity. The beautiful shrine is an attempt of sorts to make the legacy a bit more tangible, but if you seek her true monument, listen out in every marketplace and bazaar, or turn on the radio.

Yining (Qulja, Kulja)

The capital of the Ili Kazakh Autonomous region has a town museum on the airport road, favouring silk relics, gold and silver and touring exhibitions from elsewhere. The town itself retains many relics of its Russian and Kazakh connections, including tulip gardens, a Stalin Street, and scattered examples of Russian architecture. Eluosi, ethnic Russians, are a recognised minority among the Chinese and still evident in an Orthodox church here.

Yining's Uyghur name *Kulja* ('gold-roofed temple') refers to the site of the same name just outside town, which looks much more impressive on maps than it is in reality. A monastery of legendary, lavish beauty, it was destroyed by the Zunghars during the 18th century wars. Today there is a low earth terrace marking the site, where the Chinese later built a fort, and a few scattered Buddhist statues with a distinctive Tibetan style. Not far away is Huocheng, site of the **Mausoleum of Tughluq Temur** (d.1363), who converted to Islam and took his entire Mongol entourage with him.

The Chinese hero Lin Zexu (1785–1850) stood up to the British in Canton and kicked off the Opium Wars. Scapegoated after the British victory, he was shunted off into internal exile, and spent five years in Ili, where he is commemorated by Yining's **Lin Zexu Memorial Pavilion**, which pointedly lionises him as 'People's Hero Lin Zexu' (*minzu yingxiong lin zexu*). Never cowed, Lin initiated some influential irrigation projects, and filed reports from Ili about the religious and cultural heritage of the Muslims and Kazakhs, and remains the most famous resident of the town. There is also a statue of him in Urumqi, where he presumably once ate lunch.

Thirty kilometres outside the city, the **Huiyang Old Town** (Y15) preserves the old 1883 bell and drum towers from a fortress and trading post originally established in 1763, in the aftermath of the Zunghar wars. The fortress was abandoned when the river changed course and flooded large parts of it. As with several other sites in Xinjiang, some people will tell you this was once 'the little Beijing', although the term seems to have been universally employed at a local level by yokels who had never seen a town before.

Xi'an (formerly Chang'an)

Xi'an's past as the capital of China left it steeped in history – the tourist can stay there for weeks and still not see everything. It is, without a doubt, the most historically diverting city in China, even more so than Beijing, which has only been the capital for a paltry 400 years.

The motorway from the airport cuts through the ruins of the Han Dynasty city, and past the man-made hills of

Han-era imperial tombs; on the city's outskirts is the huge **Da Ming Gong Park**, on the site of the palace of the rulers of the Tang Dynasty.

The statue ***The Start of the Silk Road,*** (*sichou zhi lu qidian qundiao*) occupies a traffic island in the city's western quarter. It is difficult to park legally nearby, so if you get a taxi there and ask the driver to wait, do not be surprised if he puts on an Oscar-winning performance as a man trying to fix his engine while you look around. You may find yourself accompanied by adventurous local kids clambering on the rough-hewn stone, and the occasional bemused oldster having a nap in the mini-park. The **Tang Western Market**, once the terminus for camel trains from the desert, is now an olde-worlde themed shopping mall, dominated by a striking pagoda-like tower, but with its own **Silk Road Museum** on site (Y60), built over the dig site of the original marketplace, which is visible through the glass floor.

The better-informed taxi drivers and the city centre coach tours usually have several ready-made day-trips planned, stretching in one of the compass directions. Apart from the inevitable **Terracotta Army**, there are also the **Huaqing hot springs**, the **tomb of Yang Guifei**, and numerous imperial tombs. The most impressive is China's only mausoleum to contain two previously reigning sovereigns, the **mountain tomb of Empress Wu** and her second husband Emperor Gaozong. The tomb itself remains unopened, but its impressive approaching Spirit Way remains largely intact, flanked by statues of Silk Road exotica, such as ostriches, and dominated by the breast-shaped Nipple Hills (*naitou-shan*) said to have reminded Gaozong of his wife's best attributes. Nearby, two minor Tang tombs are open to visitors, who can descend into the chilly stone depths. Day trips to the west usually terminate at the Famen-si, a richly appointed temple that purportedly holds one of Buddha's finger bones.

For the religiously minded, multiple faiths are represented in a trip out to **Louguantai** (Y50), the multi-level terraced temple where Lao Zi legendarily composed the Daoist classic, the *Dao De Jing* ('*Book of the Path and the Power*'). Close by is the **temple complex to Cai Shen**, the God of Money, not inaccurately glossed as 'Mammon' in the road signs, whose vast size makes it abundantly clear who is king in the modern Chinese pantheon. Several smaller shrines are also in the neighbourhood, most notably the **Daqin Pagoda**, thought to have been the first Christian monastery in China.

Further Reading and References

Guidebooks

As well as the relevant sections in guidebooks that cover all of China, now mercifully available in Kindle editions for ease of portability, several authors have tackled the multinational spread of territories encompassed by the Silk Road. Paul Wilson's *The Silk Roads: A Route & Planning Guide* (Trailblazer, 2010) tries to cram in eight countries and fifty-five city guides. The acclaimed *Silk Road* (Insight Guides, 2012) by Andrew Forbes et al tries for an even more impressive thirteen countries.

Sticking to the Chinese region that is the focus of this book, the best English guide remains Judy Bonavia's *The Silk Road: Xi'an to Kashgar* (Odyssey, 2008), the most recent edition of this twenty-year-old classic now ably revised by Christoph Baumer, himself a prolific author on the region.

The book you hold has also drawn on several Chinese-language guides for the region, most notably *Xinjiang Gonglue How* (China Travel & Tourism Press, 2013), edited by Wang Ying. The 'How' series of books covers many Chinese regions, major cities and several foreign destinations, and offers many insights to sites within China that elude outsiders. In many parts of Xinjiang, of course, the Han Chinese are themselves 'outsiders', and that adds an interesting perspective to much Mandarin reportage on ethnic minority heritage.

Publishers and authors

While modern technology brings many books to your door, or onto your e-reader, at the touch of a button, such instant access is less easy for Chinese publishers. As a result, the English-language sections of Chinese bookstores or museums can be a veritable treasure trove of books unavailable elsewhere, such as He Jianguo and Zhang Yanying's innovative work of applied archaeology, *Hair Fashions of Tang Dynasty Women* (Hair & Beauty, 1987). The Library of Chinese Classics series from Hunan People's Publishing House is another common sight in China but is rare abroad, and comprises cheap bilingual editions of dozens of ancient books, including obscurities such as *The Admonitions of the Yan Clan*, and *A Record of Buddhist Monasteries in Luoyang.*

For similar reasons, your best chance to get a permanent, reviewable record of your museum trips will be in the museum's own bookshop, where English language catalogues are often available for sale. I mention this because many modern readers simply assume that any books they see on their travels will be easy to source by mail-order once they are home. Where China is concerned, this is often not the case; buy it when you see it.

General accounts

Valerie Hansen's *The Silk Road: A New History* is the best modern account of the subject, and distils the author's editorship of the prohibitively expensive *Silk Road Key Papers* (Brill, 2012) into an affordable book. Similarly, Susan Whitfield, one of the editors of *Dunhuang and Turfan: Contents and Conservation of Ancient Documents from Central Asia* (British Library, 1996), put her experiences to more populist use by writing the readable, semi-fictionalised *Life Along the Silk Road* (University of California, 1999). Xinru Liu's *The Silk Road in World History* (Oxford University Press, 2010) concentrates specifically on the hundreds of tiny cultural influences exerted by the Silk Road on European fashion, health and diet. Focusing on the cultures of the Tarim Basin, rather than trade, James Millward's *Eurasian Crossroads: A History of Xinjiang* (Hurst & Co., 2007) begins in prehistory but is weighted towards the last two centuries. It is often confusing, but that is by no means Millward's fault – it is far and away the best book on modern Xinjiang history. As he notes himself, the author in Xinjiang is often left with the impossible choice of faithfully recounting a multilingual, multi-ethnic vortex of chaos, or simplifying for clarity, in the full knowledge that entire tribes or languages might fall by the wayside.

For a specifically Central Asian slant on local history, Victor Mair and Prods Oktor Skjærvø edit a vast and truly detailed entry on 'Chinese Turkestan' in the *Encyclopaedia Iranica*, featuring contributions from many major figures in the field, extensive bibliographies and specifically Islamic considerations of its history and culture.

Places and encounters

Many modern authors have been inspired to retrace the pioneers' steps, finding in their work a ready-made outline for a new travel book. Colin Thubron, arguably the greatest living travel writer, travelled from Xi'an to Antioch in *Shadow of the Silk Road* (Vintage, 2006), writing one of the best books about the subject along the way. His earlier *The Lost Heart of Asia* (Heinemann, 1994) gives a similarly erudite, compassionate treatment of Turkmenistan, Tajikistan, Uzbekistan and Kyrgyzstan in the first heady days of their independence from Soviet Russia. The impact of modernity on the Silk Road has been so swift that he often seems to be writing about another world. So, too, does William Dalrymple in his acclaimed *In Xanadu* (Vintage, 1990), retracing the steps of Marco Polo a generation ago.

John Hare's *The Lost Camels of Tartary: A Quest into*

Forbidden China (Abacus, 1998) is an account of four expeditions into Xinjiang in the 1990s, in search of the dwindling population of Bactrian camels in the wild. For prospective travellers who want to be put off ever leaving the house again, Nick Holdstock's *The Tree That Bleeds: A Uighur Town on the Edge* (Luath Press, 2011) is a witty account of daily life in Yining (Kulja, Qulja) in the Ili Kazakh Autonomous Prefecture, where he seems to have had an entertainingly awful time.

Christopher Aslan Alexander's *A Carpet Ride to Khiva: Seven Years on the Silk Road* (Icon, 2009), presents a rich and detailed account of the setting up of a carpet workshop in Uzbekistan, with much local colour, reportage and trivia about one of Central Asia's most iconic exports, many details of which similarly apply to carpet manufacture in Xinjiang.

Arts and crafts

Nina Hyde's article, 'The Queen of Textiles' (*National Geographic,* January 1984) remains a thorough and globe-trotting account of the silk business from egg to customer. The strange story of Wang Luobin, and the academic hyper-criticalities that attempt to drag pop into politics, is covered by Rachel Harris in her article 'Wang Luobin: Folk Song King of the Northwest or Song Thief?' (*Modern China*, Issue 31, 2005).

The best introduction to Chinese food and drink in historical terms, encompassing the vast changes to ingredients and recipes over the centuries, and the powerful culinary influence of the Silk Road, can be found in Endymion Wilkinson's bulky *Chinese History: A New Manual* (Harvard, 2012), which has extensive bibliographies, not only for the section on 'Food and Drink', but for every other conceivable area of Chinese studies.

The *Journal of the Turfan Studies* (sic), subtitled *Essays on the Third International Conference on Turfan Studies, The Origins and Migrations of Eurasian Nomadic Peoples*

(Shanghai Antiquities Press, 2010) contains several English-language articles nestled among its Chinese and Russian accounts, discussing the Christian library of Turfan, speculations on the laws of the pre-Islamic Uyghurs, monuments, statuary and some local legends. It is likely to be a step too far into academia for the general reader, and is listed here more as a source used by the author rather than as a recommendation for the reader.

Similarly, John David Halsted's *Uyghur Folklore and Legends* (Abela Publishing, 2009) appears to reprint out-of-copyright materials without proper citation or annotation, and is often confused, repetitive and rambling. It is mentioned here in particular because the publishers have provocatively decided to slap an 'East Turkestan' flag on the cover, which is sure to cause trouble for you if you carry it around Xinjiang. Don't take it with you.

Early history (from the beginning to Chapter Two)

Several authors have told the story of the Tarim Mummies, often presenting intriguing perspectives on the same groundbreaking expedition to study them. JP Mallory and Victor Mair offer *The Tarim Mummies: Ancient China and the Mystery of the Earliest Peoples From the West* (repr. Thames & Hudson, 2008), from a historical and archaeological viewpoint. Their colleague Elizabeth Wayland Barber puts the same research trip to different use in *The Mummies of Ürümqi: Did Europeans Migrate to China 4,000 Years Ago?* (Macmillan, 1999), which draws on her own expertise in textiles to concentrate on the ancient peoples' clothes and cloths.

Christopher Beckwith's *Empires of the Silk Road: A History of Central Eurasia from the Bronze Age to the Present* (Princeton, 2009) is a powerful, persuasive polemic that relegates Islam, Europe and China to the sidelines of Central Asia. Beckwith rails against bias and racism in reportage of nomads by Greeks, Romans and Chinese and all authors since, turning the concepts of needy nomads, savage horsemen and barbarian invasions on their heads. He also puts the boot into hand-waving post-modern theories and discourses, which doesn't have a lot to do with the Silk Road, but is very funny nonetheless.

The Han Dynasty and after (Chapter Three)

For those who want to know the whole story of the Chinese end of the Silk Road in the Han Dynasty, Mark Edward Lewis's *The Early Chinese Empires: Qin and Han* (Belknap/Harvard, 2007) does the job. John E Hill's *Through the Jade Gate to Rome: A Study of the Silk Routes During the Later Han Dynasty, 1st to 2nd Centuries CE, an Annotated Translation of the Chronicle on the 'Western Regions' in the Hou Hanshu* is a marvellous work of independent scholarship, heavily annotated to a ludicrous degree, such that only 60 of its pages contain the parallel Chinese/English text of the 'Western Regions'. The rest of its 700-page bulk is taken up by annotations and appendices. It's something to leave behind on the trip, but superb for armchair browsing back at home, as is Joseph Yap's massive *Wars with the Xiongnu: A Translation from Zizhi tongjian* (Author House, 2009), which contains 700 years of dynastic chronicles relating to the nomads.

The Tang Dynasty and after (Chapter Four)

The Golden Peaches of Samarkand: A Study of T'ang Exotics (University of California, 1992 repr) by Edward Schafer remains the best book on all the weird and wonderful things that came down the Silk Road to brighten the culture of medieval China. It is one of those ground-breaking works so rich in detail that several subsequent careers have been built by people worming around in its footnotes; reading it is like taking a guided tour through the sights and sounds of Tang-era Chang'an, and it is a justified classic. It can, however, be rather difficult to find, unlike Charles Benn's *China's Golden Age: Everyday Life in the Tang Dynasty* (Oxford, 2002) which is another cornucopia of fascinating facts about the period, although frustratingly, many of the references cited are to 'forthcoming' works by Benn himself, which have so far failed to appear, and hence leave many of his more interesting arguments founded on little but hearsay.

Christopher Beckwith's eye-opening *The Tibetan Empire in Central Asia* (Princeton, 1987) retells the era of the Tang Dynasty from the point of view of the Tibetans, whose vast mountainous realm dominated Xinjiang (in Tibetan, *stod phyogs* or 'the Upper Region') for much of the period. Marginalised or dismissed in Chinese sources as occasional enemies and distant foreigners, the Tibetans come alive in this ground-breaking work. The 1993 paperback edition includes an entertainingly catty afterword, in which Beckwith puts his critics in their place.

The Silk Road Journey With Xuanzang (Westview Press, 2004) by Sally Wriggins walks the reader through Tripitaka's quest to find the sacred scrolls and return them to China. Of course, he is only on the Silk Road for part of his travels, but Wriggins offers a good account of what happened next.

Wu: The Chinese Empress Who Schemed, Seduced and Murdered Her Way to Become a Living God (Sutton, 2007) is a portrait of the infamous woman who ruled first from behind the throne, and then upon it as China's only historical female sovereign. It includes details of what happened to Tripitaka after his famous trip, as well as the politics of China's dealings with the horse-breeders and silk traders of the Western Regions.

The Middle Ages (Chapter Five)

As noted by James Millward in his *Eurasian Crossroads: A*

History of Xinjiang (2007), the desire to tell history as a *story* favours neat, clear divisions on a map. Big empires come with their own narrative force, as we can watch them grow from smaller states, combine or expand to reach imperial maturity, and then decline. The medieval Silk Road is inconveniently scrappy, its rulers often in chaotic contention, its chronicles fragmentary and contradictory. Societies written off in footnotes or one-line summaries might seem today to be dwarfed by the great empires of China or Tibet, but certainly didn't feel that way to their residents. It is perfectly possible to imagine a ruler of the Uyghur kingdom centred on Turfan in the 1100s, looking over his impressive capital and recalling 200 years of development and expansion, but far harder to visualise the entity of that kingdom as subsumed within a northern Chinese dynasty, as it was in 1130, or under the Mongols. The Uyghurs exerted an immense influence on the course of the 'Mongol' empire, but are hidden between the lines of its histories.

Ronald Latham's edition of *The Travels* by Marco Polo (Penguin, 1958) deftly dovetails variant texts to make a readable edition, much reprinted. There are few biographies of Polo himself that do not simply regurgitate *The Travels* in a different order, but my *Marco Polo* offers annotations on his later life, and explanations of some of his odder stories (Haus, 2007). Frances Wood's controversial and provocative *Did Marco Polo Go to China?* (Secker & Warburg, 1995) remains a rewarding read, although many of the questions it poses have been answered by later scholars, such as John Larner in *Marco Polo and the Discovery of the World* (Yale, 1999) and Stephen Haw in *Marco Polo's China* (Routledge, 2006).

The Ming and Qing Dynasties (Chapter Six)

Treatment of the complex conflicts and allegiances of the Khojas is difficult to find outside of Islamic sources, although James Millward does the best he can to summarise it in

Eurasian Crossroads. The *Encyclopaedia Iranica* (Columbia, 1996) has an article by Isenbike Togan, 'Chinese Turkestan v. Under the Khojas', containing a bibliography of the most useful sources.

Peter Perdue's *China Marches West: the Qing Conquest of Central Eurasia* (Belknap/Harvard, 2005) and Hodong Kim's *Holy War in China: The Muslim Rebellion and State in Chinese Central Asia 1864–1877* (Stanford University Press, 2004) ably tackle complex subjects, although in far too much depth for the general reader. Freely available online is the out-of-copyright 1878 biography of Yaqub Beg by Demetrius Boulger, *The Life of Yakoob Beg; Athalik Ghazi and Badaulet, Ameer of Kashgar* – Google it for a downloadable PDF. For a different perspective on the early Qing's movement into the Western Regions, Martha Avery's *The Tea Road: China and Russia meet across the steppe* (China Intercontinental Press, 2003) includes details of the acquisition of Outer Mongolia, now often neglected in discussions of Chinese history because it is no longer part of China.

The twentieth century (Chapter Seven)

There is an embarrassment of riches concerning the spies, spivs, archaeologists and fortune hunters who converged on the Silk Road in the Victorian age, and many of their own works are easily accessible. Whereas Peter Hopkirk complained in the 1980 introduction to his *Foreign Devils on the Silk Road* that out-of-print works were hard to find and expensive, the rise of print-on-demand publishing has dragged many back within reach of the general public in modern editions, such as Aurel Stein's *Sand-Buried Ruins of Khotan, Personal Narrative of a Journey of Archaeological and Geographical Exploration in Chinese Turkestan* (Forgotten Books, 2012), or Sven Hedin's *My Life as an Explorer* (National Geographic, 2003) and *The Silk Road: Ten Thousand Miles Through Central Asia* (Tauris, 2009). The English-language translation of Gustaf

Mannerheim's *Across Asia from West to East in 1906–1908* (Otava, 2008) restores many passages cut from the original Swedish-language version for reasons of national security and space, but also because the uncut manuscripts contain many ungentlemanly complaints about how irritating it was to travel with Paul Pelliot (see below).

George Macartney, the half-Chinese, half-Scottish consul who was the face of the British Empire in Xinjiang from 1890 to 1918, was virtuously and diplomatically reticent about his life, befitting the standards of his time. A century later, this makes him infuriatingly tight-lipped about his adventures to modern readers, although CP Skrine and Pamela Nightingale heroically tease details from his papers in *Macartney at Kashgar: New Light on British, Chinese, and Russian Activities in Sinkiang, 1890–1918* (OUP, 1973). Macartney's wife, Catherina, a teenage bride who had never left Britain before being sent to Kashgar with her new husband, wrote the still hard-to-find but rewarding *An English Lady in Chinese Turkestan* (repr. OUP, 1985), which is particularly entertaining for her accounts of her frustrations with her servants, and her oft-voiced suspicions that anyone in Kashgar, presumably herself included, was some sort of ne'er-do-well with something to hide. Eric Shipton's explorations in *Mountains of Tartary* (Hodder & Stoughton, 1950) are something of a disappointment if one is not a mountaineering nerd, but his wife's detailed memoir of the same period in Kashgar, *The Antique Land* (Hodder, 1950), is substantially less... climby. Those rare editions that preserve her original 1950s dust jacket show the majestic sweep of Shipton's Arch, looking deserving of its Chinese name, 'Heaven's Gate'.

One of the most erudite and well-read travellers to ever visit Xinjiang was Paul Pelliot, who never tired of pointing this out himself. His diaries, thick with native details and linguistic research, as well as several spectacular blow-ups with his sometime travelling companion Gustaf Mannerheim (see above) remain unavailable in English – any quotes from him in this book are my own translations from his *Carnets de Route 1906–1908* (Les Indes Savantes, 2008) or sourced from Philippe Flandrin's biography *Les Sept Vies du mandarin français: Paul Pelliot ou la Passion de l'Orient* (Éditions du Rocher, 2008).

For those who prefer biographers to sift the adventurers' diaries for the best bits, the most concise account is Peter Hopkirk's *Foreign Devils on the Silk Road: The Search for the Lost Treasures of Central Asia* (John Murray, 1980). Michael Keevak's *The Story of a Stele: China's Nestorian Monument and its Reception in the West 1625–1916* (Hong Kong University Press, 2008) frames foreigners' views of China with their accounts of the famous Nestorian Tablet.

Khalid Sheldrake, that wonderful eccentric who briefly considered himself to be the 'King of Islamistan', has his story told by Max Everest-Phillips in 'The Suburban King of Tartary' (*Asian Affairs*, 21(3), 1990). Peter Fleming and Ella Maillart found themselves travelling together from Beijing to Kashmir in 1935, and wrote up their experiences in twin books, his *News From Tartary* (Cape, 1936) and her *Forbidden Journey* (Heinemann, 1937). Jeannette Mirsky's *Sir Aurel Stein: Archaeological Explorer* (University of Chicago Press, new ed. 1998), Annabel Walker's *Aurel Stein: Pioneer of the Silk Road* (John Murray, 1995) and my *Mannerheim: President, Soldier, Spy* (Haus, 2009) also include several chapters pertinent to the Silk Road.

Books about Xinjiang in the later 20th century tend to be (read: cannot avoid being) heavily politicised, and often view life in the region as one of local ethnic communities swamped by a colonial tide of Han Chinese. Such an attitude informs Christian Tyler's *Wild West China: The Taming of Xinjiang* (John Murray, 2003), and Gardner Bovington's *The Uyghurs: Strangers in their Own Land* (Columbia, 2010). Justin Jon Rudelson, in *Oasis Identities: Uyghur Nationalism Along China's Silk Road* (Columbia, 1998) and Blaine Kaltman in *Under the Heel of the Dragon: Islam, Racism, Crime and the*

Uighur in China (Ohio, 2007) offer two sides of the same coin, describing life among the Uyghurs in post-colonial terms, seeing the region as a series of communities with conflicting ideas about modernity and culture, both daring to suggest, in their own way, that disenchantment among the locals has far more to do with prosaic, global issues of education, poverty and opportunity than with specific religious or ethnic conflicts. Both authors have been attacked for such views – authors writing about modern Xinjiang are in a no-win situation, sure to annoy somebody.

Eric Enno Tamm's *The Horse That Leaps Through Clouds: A Tale of Espionage, the Silk Road and the Rise of Modern China* (Douglas & McIntyre, 2010) is a travelogue retracing the steps of Mannerheim a century earlier, but written by an environmentalist with stern criticisms of the region today.

Chronology of Major Events

91	Ban Chao named as Protector of the Western Regions
102	Ban Chao retires and dies shortly after his return to the capital
221	End of Later Han Dynasty
c. 300	Stirrup introduced by steppe nomads Chinese-style sericulture begins to spread west
343	Birth of Kumarajiva (dies 413)
366	First cave carvings in Mogao, Dunhuang
399	Faxian travels to India (returns 416)
581	**Sui Dynasty** restores control of all China
602	Birth of Tripitaka (dies 664)
618	**Tang Dynasty** overthrows Sui Dynasty
629	Tripitaka leaves on his 'journey to the west'
630	Tang Dynasty establishes Anxi protectorate in Xinjiang
645	Tripitaka returns to China with sacred Buddhist scrolls
651	Arab conquest of Persia
751	Battle of Talas – defeat of Chinese by Arabs, end of westward expansion
856	Uyghur fugitives settle in the Turfan Basin – foundation of Kara-Khoja kingdom
907	Fall of Tang Dynasty. Loss of Chinese authority over Xinjiang for several centuries

960 In Kashgar, '200,000 tents of the Turks' convert to Islam
1000 Qarakhanids from Kashgar destroy the Samanids in Persia
1006 Yusuf Qadir Khan from Kashgar seizes and forcibly converts Khotan to Islam
1009 Qarakhanids in Kashgar send envoy to Emperor Song in China
1130 Turfan recognises authority of the **Western Liao**
1206 Temujin proclaimed leader of all Mongols, the Genghis Khan
1211 Idiqut Barchuq of Turfan defects to the Mongols
1216 'Mongols' invade Xinjiang (conquest complete by 1218)
1227 Death of Genghis Khan
1260 Khubilai Khan becomes leader of the Mongols
1271 Marco Polo sets out for China (returns to Europe 1295)
Khubilai Khan proclaims the Mongol **Yuan Dynasty**
1276 Fall of the last Chinese defenders in the south
1368 **Ming Dynasty** overthrows the Yuan Dynasty
1542 Death of the Sufi mystic Ahmad Kasani. His sons split into the rival White and Black Mountain *khojas* who jostle for power in the region until 1857
1644 **Qing Dynasty** overthrows the Ming Dynasty
1678 Zunghars conquer much of Xinjiang in the name of the White Mountain *khojas*
1722 Tibet comes under Chinese suzerainty
c.1750 Qing Dynasty takes Xinjiang from the Zunghars
1771 The Torghuts return from the West
1830 Khoqandi invasion; granted extraterritoriality in 1831
1831 Han settlement in Xinjiang is encouraged by the Qing government
1847 First Khoja raids – continue for next decade
1851 Sino-Russian Treaty of Qulja

1865 First conquests of Yaqub Beg
1870 Battle of Urumqi
1871 Russia invades the Ili region (north of the Tianshan Mountains)
1877 Yaqub Beg defeated at Turfan. End of 'Kashgaria'
Ferdinand von Richthofen first uses the term 'Silk Road'
1881 Treaty of St Petersburg restores most of Ili to China
1884 Creation of Xinjiang *Province*
1890 George Macartney becomes first British consul in Kashgar
1907 Aurel Stein unearths the earliest printed Diamond Sutra in Dunhuang
1912 **Republic of China** overthrows Qing Dynasty
1933 Eastern Turkestan Republic proclaimed in Xinjiang
1934 Soviet troops invade Xinjiang
1944 Second Eastern Turkestan Republic proclaimed in northern Xinjiang
1946 Second Eastern Turkestan Republic rebranded as the administration of the Republic's 'Xinjiang Province'
1949 Proclamation of the **People's Republic of China** in Beijing
Second ETR cedes control to PRC – the 'Peaceful Liberation'
1952 Demobilised Nationalist soldiers settled in Xinjiang
1955 Xinjiang Province is renamed the Xinjiang Uyghur Autonomous Region
1957 Zhou Enlai warns against 'local nationalism' and 'Han chauvinism'
1964 First atomic bomb test at Lop Nur
1974 Shihezi agricultural colony gains official city status
1990 Chinese and Kazakhstan railways connect at Alashan Pass
1991 Fall of Soviet Union. China loses large-scale border threat

2001 September 11th attacks on America. Clampdowns on Chinese Islamism

2011 Chongqing, China officially linked to Duisburg, Germany by rail

Index